The Economic Development of Ireland since 1870
Volume II

The Economic Development of Modern Europe since 1870

Series Editor: Charles Feinstein
 Chichele Professor of Economic History
 All Souls College, Oxford

1. The Economic Development of France since 1870 (Volumes I and II)
 François Crouzet

2. The Economic Development of Denmark and Norway since 1870
 Karl Gunnar Persson

3. The Economic Development of Italy since 1870
 Giovanni Federico

4. The Economic Development of Austria since 1870
 Herbert Matis

5. The Economic Development of Ireland since 1870 (Volumes I and II)
 Cormac Ó Gráda

Future titles will include:

The Economic Development of The Netherlands since 1870
Jan Luiten van Zanden

The Economic Development of Belgium since 1870
H. Van Der Wee and J. Blomme

The Economic Development of Germany since 1870
W. Fischer

The Economic Development of the United Kingdom since 1870
C. Feinstein

The Economic Development of Sweden since 1870
L. Jonung and R. Ohlsson

The Economic Development of Spain since 1870
P. Martín-Aceña and J. Simpson

The Economic Development of the European Community
R.T. Griffiths

The Economic Development
of Ireland since 1870
Volume II

Edited by

Cormac Ó Gráda

Associate Professor
Department of Economics
University College Dublin

An Elgar Reference Collection

Published by
Edward Elgar Publishing Limited
Gower House
Croft Road
Aldershot
Hants GU11 3HR
England

Edward Elgar Publishing Company
Old Post Road
Brookfield
Vermont 05036
USA

British Library Cataloguing in Publication Data
Economic Development of Ireland Since
1870. – (Economic Development of Modern
Europe Since 1870; Vol.5)
    I. Ó Gráda, Cormac   II. Series
    330.9415

Library of Congress Cataloguing in Publication Data
The Economic development of Ireland since 1870 / edited by Cormac Ó
    Gráda.
        p. cm. — (The Economic development of modern Europe since
    1870 ; 5) (An Elgar reference collection)
        1. Ireland—Economic conditions. I. Ó Gráda, Cormac.
    II. Series. III. Series: An Elgar reference collection.
    HC260.5.E278   1994
    330.9415—dc20   93–50630
                                                                          CIP

ISBN 1 85278 671 X (2 volume set)

Printed in Great Britain at the University Press, Cambridge

Contents

Acknowledgements

The editor and publishers wish to thank the following who have kindly given permission for the use of copyright material.

Academic Press Ltd. and the Cambridge Political Economy Society Ltd. for article: Eoin O'Malley (1985), 'The Problem of Late Industrialisation and the Experience of the Republic of Ireland', *Cambridge Journal of Economics*, **9** (2), June, 141–54.

Basil Blackwell Ltd. for article: Antoin E. Murphy (1978), 'Money in an Economy Without Banks: The Case of Ireland', *Manchester School of Economic and Social Studies*, **XLVI**, 41–50.

Cambridge University Press for excerpt: Brendan M. Walsh (1984), 'Ireland's Membership of the European Monetary System: Expectations, Out-Turn and Prospects', in P.J. Drudy and Dermot McAleese (eds), *Ireland and the European Community*, Irish Studies 3, 173–90.

College Press Ltd. and Brendan M. Walsh for excerpt: Brendan M. Walsh (1985), 'Marriage in Ireland in the Twentieth Century', in Art Cosgrove (ed.), *Marriage in Ireland*, 132–50.

Crane Bag for excerpt: Peter Neary (1984), 'The Failure of Economic Nationalism', in M.P. Hederman and R. Kearney (eds), *Ireland: Dependence and Independence*, 68–77.

Glendale Publishing Ltd. and John Bradley for excerpt: John Bradley (1990), 'The Legacy of Economic Development: The Irish Economy 1960–1987', in John F. McCarthy (ed.), *Planning Ireland's Future: The Legacy of T.K. Whitaker*, 128–50.

Institute of Public Administration for articles and excerpt: T.K. Whitaker (1973), 'From Protection to Free Trade: The Irish Experience', *Administration*, **21** (4), Winter, 405–23; Joseph Lee (1982), 'Society and Culture', in Frank Litton (ed.), *Unequal Achievement: The Irish Experience 1957–1982*, 1–18; Dermot McAleese (1987), 'European Integration and the Irish Economy', *Administration*, **35** (2), 152–71.

Leicester University Press (a division of Pinter Publishers Ltd., London) for excerpt: Philip Ollerenshaw (1991), 'Textiles and Regional Economic Decline: Northern Ireland 1914–70', in Colin Holmes and Alan Booth (eds), *Economy and Society: European Industrialisation and its Social Consequences*, 58–83.

Oxford University Press for excerpt and article: K.S. Isles and N. Cuthbert (1955), 'Ulster's Economic Structure', in Thomas Wilson (ed.), *Ulster Under Home Rule*, Chapter 5, 91–114; Dermot McAleese (1977), 'Do Tariffs Matter? Industrial Specialization and Trade in a Small Economy', *Oxford Economic Papers*, **29** (1), March, 117–27.

Statistical and Social Inquiry Society of Ireland for article: John W. O'Hagan (1979/80), 'An Analysis of the Growth of the Public Sector in Ireland, 1953–77', *Journal of the Statistical and Social Inquiry Society of Ireland*, **XXIV**, Part II, 69–98.

Studies for article: R.C. Geary (1951), 'Irish Economic Development Since the Treaty', *Studies*, **XL**, 399–418.

Every effort has been made to trace all the copyright holders but if any have been inadvertently overlooked the publishers will be pleased to make the necessary arrangement at the first opportunity.

In addition the publishers wish to thank the Library of the London School of Economics and Political Science and the Marshall Library of Economics, Cambridge University for their assistance in obtaining these articles.

1958 to the Present

[1]

IRISH ECONOMIC DEVELOPMENT

SINCE THE TREATY*

BY R. C. GEARY, D.SC.

WE HAVE few natural resources in Ireland, except an equable climate and fairly fertile grasslands. Before the industrial drive of the last quarter century started, there were a few large industries such as brewing, bacon-curing, creameries, biscuit-making and woollens and worsteds, most of them based on native materials but few of them with a high labour content. Our main assets for industrial development are plentiful supplies of labour and capital, though these have exhibited such an astonishing centrifugal tendency that the number of Irish-born adults living outside Ireland is half as many again as the number of Irish-born adults living in Ireland, because of emigration, and Irish capital invested abroad per head of population (about £150 in 1947[1]) is probably larger than for any other country in the world.

During the period of Grattan's Parliament, recourse was had to the policy of protection under which certain industries prospered up to the Act of Union in 1800. After that date a milder system of protection prevailed for some time, but later the Irish fiscal system was merged in the British system of Free Trade. As a result, industry, except in Ulster, was almost wiped out of existence, and agriculture languished. England's vital economic interests proved the undoing of the South. For our present point of view it is important to note that in the century of political agitation which culminated in national independence in 1921, great emphasis had to be placed on this conflict between British and Irish economic interests, and the claim for self-government was based largely on the country's right to economic development in general and to development in industry in particular. The Famine of 1846-47, relatively one of the greatest disasters which afflicted any people during the past two hundred years,

---

* Lecture delivered to the Summer School, University College, Dublin, on 14th August, 1951.

[1] Derived from "Ireland's External Assets" by T. K. Whitaker, Statistical and Social Inquiry Society of Ireland, April 1949.

was seen as a natural consequence of poverty resulting from lack of industry and too great pressure of population on the land and, while political analysis tends towards over-simplification, there is probably little wrong with this conclusion. The mass exodus following the Famine has implanted in the minds of the Irish people the conviction that emigration is an unqualified evil, and almost every nationalist in the hundred years before 1921 believed that the main object of self-government was the development of native industry and the intensification of agriculture, both of which would increase the national wealth (or, as we would say these days, the national income) and diminish, if not stop, emigration.

Emigration

We are only now beginning to realize the extent to which emigration has affected and continues to affect the whole social and economic fabric of the country and this is why I propose dealing with this aspect of my subject at some little length. Its implications go far beyond the magnitude of emigration and the fact that emigration is the sole reason of the failure of the population to increase. Of no country in the world is it more true to say that the political and economic boundaries do not coincide, though this is true in varying degree of all countries. The Irish have always been a great migratory people. In the seventy years before the great Famine of 1846-47, 1¾ million people left the country.[2] Between 1841 and the present day the population of all Ireland has fallen from 8¼ million to 4¼ million, though it has remained fairly constant at the latter figure for nearly half a century. During the past hundred years net emigration from all Ireland amounted to almost 5 million, of which approximately 4 million were from the Twenty-six Counties. From the latter area net emigration in the past quarter century reached nearly half a million. In the ten years following the Famine, emigration reached the dimensions of a national exodus, and has continued down to our own day at a rate which, while tending to diminish, is still very large. Ireland has a normal birth rate and a normal death rate. The natural increase (or the excess of births over deaths) is substantial, but it is skimmed off regularly by emigration so that there has been no significant change in population during the past half century, apart from a relatively small decline attributable directly or indirectly to migration resulting from the change in political status in 1921. It is extremely significant that, despite marked

[2] F. H. Connell: "The Population of Ireland 1750–1845", p. 27.

changes in the intercensal natural increase, the latter always closely coincided with net emigration since 1926. Is emigration inevitable in the sense that a large proportion of those born here are pre-destined to emigrate, that they owe their existence to the fact of emigration? If the recent trend is any indication, the prospect of an appreciable increase in population in the next thirty years, despite economic development at home, is remote.

Since the beginning of the century Ireland is the only country in the world in which the population has declined; while the population of Europe (excluding U.S.S.R.) increased by 36 per cent since 1900, the population of Ireland (Twenty-six Counties) *decreased* by 7 per cent. The contrast is even more striking over the longer period : since 1841 the population of most European countries has doubled while the population of Ireland has halved. As already remarked, the adult population born in Ireland but living outside is more than half the adult population living in Ireland, a fantastically high proportion which makes Ireland unique amongst the nations. Based on the experience of the decade 1936-46, the latest intercensal period for which the calculation can be made, it may be stated that of every hundred males born in Ireland who survive to the age of 60, only 63 are living in Ireland at that age ; the remaining 37 are living abroad. During the last five years the rate of net emigration (or the excess of emigration over immigration) was equivalent to 8 per thousand population per annum, which is very close to the death rate in some European countries. In 1950, it has been officially estimated that net emigration amounted to 41,000,[3] equivalent to nearly 14 per thousand population. Up to the world Economic Depression of 1929–30, emigration from Ireland was directed principally to the U.S.A.; large numbers also went to Great Britain and the British Dominions and Colonies. After 1930, however, it was directed principally towards Great Britain though, since the War, there has been a revival of overseas migration : in fact during the period 1946-51 about one-fifth of the total was directed overseas.

A feature of Irish emigration has always been that it contained a high proportion of women. During the five years period 1946-51 women exceeded men in numbers in the migration stream by nearly 40 per cent. Principally as a result of the high proportion of women amongst emigrants (and to a lesser extent because the mortality of women in Ireland in relation to that of men is less favourable than in other countries), the Irish population contains the lowest number of women in Europe and nearly the lowest in the world. It is a melancholy fact that Irish women show such a marked propensity to emigrate. Poor marriage prospects in Ireland are one cause of this but they are not the sole cause. On the

[3] Irish Trade Journal and Statistical Bulletin, June 1951, p. 84. This estimate must be regarded as subject to a statistical error, in excess or in defect, of 5,500.

other hand the intention to emigrate obviously militates against a high
marriage rate within Ireland. Other reasons which have been suggested
for the low marriage rate are the prevalence of large families which imposes
family responsibilities on the elder members. In rural Ireland the system
of farm tenure is not conducive to a high marriage rate since one of the
farmer's sons is in a position to marry only when he inherits the farm.
It is not the practice in Ireland to divide farms, which in general are small.
As shown in the Census Reports, marriage rates are also low by comparison
with, say, Great Britain in comparable non-agricultural occupations.

The fact that emigration is now directed for by far the greater part
to Great Britain means that there is less of a sundering of family ties
than in previous periods when emigration was directed principally to the
United States. In the past, very few returned of those who went and
those who returned did so after a sojourn of many years abroad. Ireland
is different in this respect from other emigrant countries, Italy, for example.
We are not only the greatest emigrant country in relation to the size of
the home population but we are also the most assimilable from the viewpoint of the countries of immigration. In the case of emigration to Great
Britain, however, very large numbers now return on holidays and a considerable proportion of those who go come back after a year or two. In
1950 while 73,000 went to take up jobs in Great Britain, no fewer than
36,000 returned for more or less permanent residence in Ireland.[4]

It is a gross over-simplification to suggest that emigration is due
solely, or even principally, to lack of economic development in Ireland.
During the past five years when, as already observed, emigration was
at a high level, the country was never so prosperous. On account of the
high prices of agricultural products and the reduction in the agricultural
population, the standard of living in agriculture was never so high as it
has been during the past five years. This recent period of relative agricultural prosperity has been accompanied by the largest migration from
farms ever experienced during any period of five years in the past half-
century. In a stable population the numbers at work in industry have
more than doubled during the past quarter of a century ; the rate of
unemployment is half what it was before the war ; industrial earnings
per head are in real terms 8 per cent higher than prewar ; the wage rate
(but not necessarily the rate of earnings) in Dublin is 10 per cent higher
in purchasing power than in the principal British cities for a group of
important comparable occupations ; housing and social services generally
are at a high level having regard to the national income ; and still the
people go.

---

[4] See preceding footnote. These figures are also subject to statistical errors of estima-
tion.

The view is held by some authorities in Ireland, and it is supported by an impressive weight of evidence, that emigration, even down to our own day, has resulted largely from the attractive power of great populations of Irish emigrants in Great Britain and in the United States of America. On the other hand, during the decades after the Famine, at some periods later and always perhaps from some parts of the country, economic conditions within the country forced large numbers of the people to leave. In simple terms the issue (which is of fundamental importance in the formulation of policy) is whether emigration is " a pull or a push," and a major difficulty in the controversy is the definition of these terms. What is beyond question is that emigration has introduced a distortion, or what I have termed above a centrifugal tendency, into the Irish economy, a distortion which has militated against normal economic cohesion (in which we are " parts one of another "). It is difficult even to find words to describe the condition, still less to prove the thesis or to suggest a cure. The popular view is that each emigrant represents a loss to the State, represented approximately by the cost of his or her upbringing, a view which is more acceptable during these days of manpower shortage and full employment than at other times. To other people this view seems to import into demography, in which it has no place, an idea which is inadmissible even in economics. It would be quite another matter if it could be proved, as commonly alleged on political platforms and widely believed, that " the best are going ".

Government Policy since 1922

In connection with the interpretation of the statistics presented later, it may be useful to indicate very briefly the main outlines of Government economic policy during the period of self-government which began in 1922. Before doing so, however, it is essential to observe that Sinn Fein propaganda before the Treaty of 1921 had a strongly protectionist bias. The most frequently quoted dictum was Jonathan Swift's : " Burn everything English except coal ", a principle which, however, would secure no popular support now, especially if we could get English coal at English prices. Before the first world war, there was a crusade for the use of Irish manufactures. Arthur Griffith propounded the doctrine that protection was necessary for industrial revival and expansion. It is scarcely an exaggeration to say that except for businessmen, directly interested in the distribution of imported goods, and certain sections of the agricultural community, popular sentiment in Ireland has always been protectionist : there is no political cleavage on the issue.

Nevertheless, the first Irish Government made a cautious start in its fiscal policy. Its first move, in June 1923, was to set up a Fiscal Inquiry Committee with the following terms of reference :—

" To investigate and report—

(a) as to the effect of the existing fiscal system, and of any measures regulating or restricting imports or exports, on industry and agriculture in the Saorstát, and

(b) as to the effect of any changes therein intended to foster the development of industry and agriculture,

with due regard to the interests of the general community and to the economic relations of the Saorstát with other countries."

In its interim report the Committee recommended that the British Safeguarding of Industries Act, 1921, which was designed to protect certain industries in the United Kingdom from the effect of depreciation of foreign currency and importation of goods at prices below cost of production, should be repealed. The Committee in its report emphasized that " the extreme difficulty which will be experienced in any attempt to ascertain the precise facts relating to the existing conditions of Irish industries, as well as the difficulty of arriving at a definite conclusion as to the standard to be applied in ascertaining the needs of industry for assistance, suggest the necessity for extreme caution in the adoption of any policy that would produce far-reaching changes in the existing system upon which industry is conducted." One wonders if the Committee would have reported differently if it had the " precise facts " now available regularly from the Census of Industrial Production. The report gave a depressing picture of Irish industry at the time : industrial production was low and many plants were idle. It will be remembered that industrial production had then reached the lowest point of the post-1920 depression.

The Committee concluded that the volume of industry asking for protection was small. The malting, biscuit and jute industries were opposed to the application of protection and the Committee assumed that the brewing and distilling industry and industries connected with agriculture such as bacon-curing and butter-making did not desire protection as they absented themselves from the inquiry. It will be noted that all the industries mentioned were dependent largely on export trade rather than on the home market. Amongst the industries which pressed for protection were grain milling, confectionery, woollen piece goods, clothing, fellmongery, tanning, boots and shoes, cycle and agricultural machinery, manufacturers of galvanized hollow-ware, furniture makers, wood-workers, brush makers, paper manufacturers and printers, fertilisers, glass bottles, pottery etc. Generally it can be said that the firms making application were, with a few exceptions, small and struggling to preserve their existence from strong competition from imported goods. The Committee emphasized the disabilities under which Irish industries suffered, lack of native raw materials and coal, excessive transport charges, lack of a reserve of skilled labour, high level of wages and lack of capital for promotion of Irish enterprise, lack of efficient and experienced management and marketing organizations which left much to be desired. Most serious of all, perhaps, there was evidence of strong prejudice on the part of the Irish public against at least certain classes of Irish products. The position was summarised in the report as follows :—

" Irish industry in a weakened and depressed condition was exposed to a competition so fierce as to dislocate the industrial life even of long-established and well-organised industries in the most highly-developed industrial community in the world. The fierce struggle to hold or to develop markets would, in any case, have found Irish industry a poor competitor ; but in the circumstances the struggle has been exceptionally and unnaturally severe."

It should be remembered that, as stated by the President of the Executive Council, " it is facts and not policy which the Committee is intended to determine." In his Budget speech in 1924, the Minister for Finance stated that " the Government takes up no doctrinaire attitude on the question of free trade and protection. It regards the matter as one of expediency which may be variously decided in different circumstances." In this Budget protective duties were imposed in an experimental way on five classes of goods : boots and shoes, soap and candles, sugar confectionery, cocoa preparations, table-waters, glass bottles for beer, wine and spirits. In the Finance Act of 1925 three further categories of experimental duties were instituted : personal clothing, blankets and rugs, furniture. In 1926 an experimental duty was imposed on oatmeal.

The Tariff Commission Act of 1926 inaugurated the regime of selectivity. The Act laid down the basis on which reports should be drawn up and this basis was entirely economic in character, relating strictly to the merits of each application, having regard in particular to the effect on other industries of the imposition of protective duties. The Commission dealt with applications from fifteen industries during the period 1926 to 1933. Of these fifteen applications, recommendations in favour of protective duties were made in twelve cases. Adverse recommendations were made in respect of flour, fish barrels and coach building. After 1932 the Tariff Commission fell into disuse and only one case was dealt with in 1934. In 1934 the Tariff Commission Act was formally repealed.

In 1927 a duty was imposed on margarine. In 1929 a duty was imposed on certain classes of woollen piece goods and on down quilts. In the Finance Act of 1929 the duty on clothing was increased. In 1931 duties were imposed on butter, harness leather and harness, and on oats.

In November 1931 the Customs Duties (Provisional Imposition) Bill was introduced authorising the imposition or variation of custom duty by the Executive Council where such imposition or variation appeared to be necessary to prevent an expected dumping of goods or other threatened industrial injury, and further to authorise the reference to the Tariff Commission of questions relating to such duties. This Act represented an important step forward towards a protective policy as it enabled the Executive Council first to impose a duty and later to submit to the Tariff Commission the question of whether the duty should be continued, varied or terminated.

After the General Election of 1932 the Fianna Fáil Party came into power, pledged to a policy of protection with the stated object of relieving unemployment and developing the resources of the country. In the Government's first Finance Act in May, 1932, its definite policy of protection was expressed by the imposition of duties on a wide range of goods. The outbreak of the Economic War led to the passing of the Emergency Imposition of Duties Act, 1932. The first Order under the Act had the effect of imposing a penal duty on certain classes of goods coming from Great Britain, namely 5s. per ton on coal, 20 per cent on cement, electrical goods and apparatus and iron and steel goods, and of imposing certain additional duties on sugar and sugar preparations. Broadly speaking, the attitude of the Government was that any firm or group of firms or of individuals, prepared to establish a new industry or to extend an existing industry, could make application for the grant of duties necessary to give ample protection and so create conditions in which external competition was, to a large extent, eliminated. In 1934 a Control of Imports Bill was introduced which gave power for the quantitative regulation of imports by the introduction of a quota system. A wide range of goods were subject to quota orders, including tyres and tubes for motor-cars and motor cycles and bicycles, boots and shoes, sugar, rubber-proofed piece goods and garments ; motor-cars, chassis, bodies and shells, coal, silk and art silk, hose and half-hose, certain woollen piece goods, super-phosphates, soap, candles, raw onions, perambulators, pumps, cement, bulbs, marble chippings. Furthermore, under the Agricultural Production (Sales) Act, 1933 and the Agricultural Production (Regulation of Imports) Act, the importation of certain goods was prohibited except under licence and on which no duty is imposed. These goods include wheat, wheaten flour and meal, certain wheat products, maize and maize products, oats, hay, straw and a wide range of feeding stuffs, fish, live pigs and raw onions.

Based on the value of imports in 1924 of goods which were dutiable at any time during the period 1924-1938 (except goods bearing revenue duties) W. J. L. Ryan has computed that the tariff level on an *ad valorem* basis was 9 per cent in 1931 and 35 per cent in 1938.[5] The aggregate value of imports which were dutiable in 1931 was about one-half of the value of imports which were dutiable in 1938.[6]

General Population Aspects

The first Population Census, the first Census of Industrial Production and the first estimates of agricultural output during the period of self-government were taken in 1926, nearly five years after the Treaty, and this year is accordingly a convenient point of departure for a study of the remarkable economic changes which have occurred during the last thirty years as revealed by statistics. The total population has remained stable during this period in which the marriage rate in Ireland was the lowest in the world. The fertility of marriages, is, however, one of the highest in the world with the result that the birth rate is about average by international standards. Between 1926 and 1951 the proportion of the population living in towns with over 1,500 population has increased from 33 per cent to 41 per cent, the town population as defined increasing by 23 per cent and the rural population decreasing by 12 per cent. The rate of urban increase and rural decline has been proceeding at an accelerated rate during the past five years : in fact the rate of change per cent per annum was nearly twice as great as during the previous decade 1936-1946. One important effect of this change has been that the marriage rate at 5.4 per 1,000 population per annum is perceptibly higher than before the war, though it is lower than in the years 1942-46, when it was nearly 6. Entirely as a result of the increased number of marriages—the fertility rate has declined—the birth rate is now significantly higher than before the war (19.4 in 1938 and 21.0 in 1950). In Ireland a quarter of the population never marry, a proportion which is far higher than for any other country. In fact one exhausts superlatives in describing Ireland demographically. The international norm is the exception in Ireland where, as I have already said, the population halved in the past hundred years while the population of most countries doubled.

Table I shows the numbers at work in main industrial groups as returned at the Censuses of 1926, 1936 and 1946 with somewhat hazardous anticipations of the figures which will be available in due course for the Census of 1951. It seems essential to give the statistics for 1951 since, as the table shows, the changes which have occurred during the past five years are more striking than in any of the other two intercensal periods.

[5] " Measurement of Tariff Levels for Ireland for 1931, 1936, 1938." Statistical and Social Inquiry Society of Ireland, December, 1948.

[6] To this point, the paper derives largely from "Industrial Development in Ireland : A Statistical Review " by the lecturer (Manchester Statistical Society, 1949), which, as regards the account of industrial policy since the Treaty, was based closely on the late R. C. Ferguson's article on " Industrial Policy and Organisation " in " Public Administration in Ireland."

TABLE I

NUMBERS AT WORK

NOTE : The statistics for 1926, 1936 and 1946 are based on the Censuses of Population. The figures for 1951 are to be regarded as rough approximations based on incomplete data from many sources.

	PERSONS			
	1926	1936	1946	1951
	Numbers in Thousands			
Agriculture	646.5	609.2	571.5	500
Other Production	164.1	205.6	211.7	268
TOTAL PRODUCTION ...	810.6	814.8	783.2	768
Transport and Communication ...	38.9	38.4	43.1	47
Commerce and Finance ...	114.1	127.1	128.1	144
Public Administration and Defence	76.3	77.7	89.4	93
Professions	38.9	43.9	50.7	55
Personal Service	127.5	122.2	112.8	104
Other Industries	9.2	9.8	17.5	} 21
Industry not stated	4.7	1.6	2.9	
TOTAL ...	1,220.3	1,235.4	1,227.7	1,232
	Percentage Distribution			
Agriculture	53.0	49.3	46.6	40.6
Other Production	13.4	16.6	17.2	21.8
TOTAL PRODUCTION ...	66.4	66.0	63.8	62.4
Transport and Communication ...	3.2	3.1	3.5	3.8
Commerce and Finance ...	9.4	10.3	10.4	11.7
Public Administration and Defence	6.2	6.3	7.3	7.6
Professions	3.2	3.6	4.1	4.5
Personal Service	10.4	9.9	9.2	8.4
Other Industries	0.8	0.8	1.4	} 1.7
Industry not stated	0.4	0.1	0.3	
	100.—	100.—	100.—	100.—

There has been little change over the whole period in the population at work. The numbers in productive employment have declined since 1936 and the numbers in other employments increased, a tendency which has been observed in other countries and which is consistent with an increasing national income, giving employment to exotic personnel like statisticians who might be regarded as parasitic in a more simple social organization. The most remarkable feature of the table is undoubtedly the showing that since 1946 the number in agriculture declined by about 70,000 or by 13 per cent while the number in Other Production increased by about the same number, but by 27 per cent. The proportion of the working population in agriculture has declined from 53 per cent to 41 per cent in the quarter century and in a short period of five years by no less than 6 per cent. Other Production has increased from the very low proportion of 13 per cent to nearly 22 per cent. The latter percentage is still low by Western European standards and there is reasonable scope for development up to about one-third of the working population. All the indications are, however, that the numbers in agriculture will decline further, a tendency which the proposed considerable investment in agriculture will, if anything, intensify. Quantum output per head of Irish agriculture is low compared with the most advanced agricultural communities even in Europe and the decline in numbers may continue until the best European productivity is reached. Certainly in the Irish system of pasture husbandry increased agricultural productivity is more likely to come about by decline in numbers at work than by increased output, though we must fervently hope for the latter. The prevailing egalitarian tendency as between country and town and the proclivity of farmers' children to migrate will accentuate the decline in numbers. By 1946 a highly interesting stage had been reached in that the number of men " relatives assisting farmers " at 165,000 is considerably less than the number of men farmers which was 210,000, and since 1946 there has been a substantial decline in the number of male farmers' relatives. Where is the next generation of farmers to come from unless amalgamation of farms occurs on a large scale? In this connection it may be observed that during the past twenty years the number of small holdings (size 1-15 acres) in the country has decreased from 104,000 to 89,000.

Figures to be discussed later will show that the total *volume* of agricultural output changed little during the past twenty-five years though, solely on account of the favourable trend in prices in relation to living costs, the *real* income of the average agriculturist increased by about 70 per cent since 1938 when, however, the average income in cash and kind was very low. As Table I shows clearly the decline in numbers in agriculture has assumed the dimensions of an exodus and is continuing. The decline is principally amongst sons and daughters of farmers assisting in farm work : in 1946 only one-fifth of the agricultural labour force were paid

employees. Apparently farmers' children, with the development of transport and communications in the widest sense of these terms, are no longer
content with the social status, social amenities, poor marital prospects for
women, and meagre income in cash and kind which has heretofore been
theirs ; they are bettering themselves from the economic point of view ;
but from the viewpoint of happiness, contentment and health ? Who
knows ?

The most disappointing feature of the economic development of Ireland
since the Treaty is the failure of agriculture to develop and the mass
migration of the people from the lands of their fathers to Dublin and to
cities in Great Britain and the United States which, by repute, are more
familiar to them than Dublin and other Irish cities, so ingrained is the
tradition of emigration. Except for the scale of the rural exodus and the
fact that it is directed outside the country, the same tale could be told
of many other countries. It is easy for the townsman to be censorious
about the shortcomings of agriculture, easy but superficial, and we towns-
folk will all do well to remember a certain saying about a mote and a
beam in this connection. In a great paper[7] the late Thomas Barrington
has shown that the Irish farmer over the long period is an Economic
Man in his ruthless response to economic stimuli. From the 1860's to
the present day the real income of the average agriculturist has more than
trebled as a result of a 25 per cent increase in the output of farms, the
halving of the rural population, and, since World War II, by the favourable
trend in agricultural prices relative to retail prices. Over the shorter term,
no member of the community is more sensitive to price trends than the
farmer. He possibly tends in the short term to think too much in terms
of a fixed income so that if, in response to differential price trends, he
develops one product, output of other products declines. It is difficult
to prove the thesis that in agriculture as a whole there is an inverse relationship between prices and volume of output but there is some evidence of
it, though prices fluctuate prodigiously and volume is very steady. Still
it is pertinent to observe that during the period 1934-1938 the index of
gross agricultural volume output was 104 when the ratio of agricultural
prices to retail prices was 76, whereas in 1950 when the volume was 96,
the price ratio was 141. In every country during the greater part of the
past century depression was the normal condition of agriculture. It is
a devastating fact that only during times of war, hot and cold, does agriculture flourish in the income sense. All this has bit deep into the consciousness
of the farmer. Before he commits himself to intensive development,
the farmer will be merely human if he asks himself what is going to happen
to agricultural prices if the international situation eases. The answer is,
of course, that, despite every kind of international and national bolstering,

---

[7] " A Review of Irish Agricultural Prices " Statistical and Social inquiry Society of
Ireland, May 1926.

prices must fall. It might appear that in such an eventuality the farmer must have recourse to increased volume. My personal opinion is that this view is correct on the whole despite the fact that, as Barrington showed in the case of Ireland, and has also been found in other countries in the past, the bounty of nature and the quantitative reward of his efforts can be a calamity for the agriculturist in inducing a fall in prices proportionately greater than the increase in volume. The economist would put it that the demand for agricultural products is inelastic. At the present time this is probably much less true than in the past, as far as Ireland is concerned, or than is likely to be the case in future because there is an elastic demand for the principal products of Irish agriculture, notably meat, dairy products and eggs.

As Table IV shows later, in recent years gross volume of agriculture has never reached the 1938 level though the shortfall has not been large. This may be accidental, yet it is not improbable that the substantial fall in manpower is now adversely affecting production. This is less a truism than it might appear, as before the war there was a surplus of labour on farms and mechanisation has increased since then. This is a serious consideration which will no doubt be examined by experts.

While farmers, like all of us, want to increase their income, in Ireland incentive appears to be lacking to increase incomes beyond a certain more or less fixed point. It is all to the good that since the war the farmer for the first time since 1920 has achieved a substantial cash income. It is also well that farmers are now partly responsible for the great increase in motor cars in use from 49,000 in 1938 to 85,000 in 1950. When the farmers have had time to savour the sweets of income, the incentive to increase it may also develop, though time will be required to eradicate the bitter experience of the past.

Believe it or not, but the statistician is constantly in the position of reminding the world that it is not by statistics that man in society lives. The life of the farmer is not idyllic but it has many compensations in the satisfaction of possession of land, in health, in security, in being free from direct taxation, in adequacy of food, in low rents and in other respects which add up to a reasonable standard of happiness. It was an American who said that " money does not buy happiness " but, a member of his nation, he added " it buys a damn good substitute ". A friend of mine, an agricultural expert who went for a visit to a great country whose agricultural development is an example for the world to emulate, said that he would never want his fellow-countrymen to start their work at 4 a.m. and sink exhausted on their beds at 9 p.m. And finally I am reminded of a story told me by a Senator from the west of Ireland who was in a position to supply lobster pots to a friend of his who, as is frequently the case in the west, eked out a frugal living on the land by sea fishing. Some time afterwards, being in the neighbourhood, he called on his friend. The Senator found him sitting in front of his neat white-washed cottage, smoking, on a glorious summer day, a light Atlantic breeze blowing, at peace with all men. " Why aren't you out fishing, Michael ? " he said. " Well, Sir," said his friend, " I caught enough lobsters on Monday to do me for the week." Who is going to say that Michael was not behaving in a rational manner ? Why should he work if he was happy ?

National Income and Related Topics

The national economy can best be described by a set of financial accounts which show for the nation as a whole the kind of information which accountants prepare for individual business concerns. These accounts show in particular the national income classified according to main sources (agriculture, industry etc.), national expenditure, savings and capital formation. Table II shows the estimated national income in each of the last seven years and for the years 1926 and 1938 at values current in the years specified and in real terms, i.e. what the values would be if the prices ruling were the same all through, actually those of 1938. It will be seen that in the twelve years 1926 and 1938 the national income in real terms increased by 15 per cent and in the subsequent period also of twelve years by 24 per cent. Actually the latest substantial increase has been confined to the five years period 1945-1950 ; during the war years the real national income declined somewhat. It will be borne in mind that throughout the whole period covered by the table the total population was practically constant, so that the figures also reflect the trend in the average income per person. It will also be recalled that during the quarter century 1926-1950 a great change over from agriculture to non-agricultural employment occurred : since the average income per person in agriculture is lower than the average in non-agriculture, this population transfer must of itself be conducive to an increase in national income. Incidentally it may be pointed out that the discrepancy between the average earnings in agriculture and non-agricultural employments is now much less marked than before the war when agricultural earnings were at a low level. As already indicated, this improvement in the position has been brought about by the great rise in agricultural prices compared even with agricultural living costs, coupled with the decline by one-sixth of the agricultural working population.

TABLE II

NATIONAL INCOME AT CURRENT AND AT FIXED (1938) PRICES

Year	National Income at Current Prices	Price Index (1) (Base 1938 as 100)	Real National Income	
			At 1938 Prices	Index (1938 as 100)
	£m.		£m.	
1926 (2)	147	107	137	87
1938	158.2	100	158.2	100
1944	253.8	170	149.3	94.4
1945	277.1	170	163.0	103.0
1946	289.8	168	172.5	109.0
1947	318.1	177	179.7	113.6
1948	334.1	183	182.6	115.4
1949	352.1	183	192.4	121.6
1950 (3)	363	185	196	124

(1) Retail prices of goods and services.

(2) The 1926 Figures are based on estimates prepared by Professor G. A. Duncan F.T.C.D. (given in a paper read before the Statistical and Social Inquiry Society of Ireland on 26th October, 1939, and in Appendix No. 7 of the Commission of Inquiry into Banking, Currency and Credit) modified in certain respects to bring the concepts involved into conformity with those adopted in later years for the official figures.

(3) Provisional.

TABLE III

NATIONAL INCOME CLASSIFIED BY SECTOR OF OUTPUT

Year	Agriculture and Fishing	Public Administration & Defence	Industry	Distribution and Transport	Other services	Income from Abroad	Total
			£ million				
1938	38.2	11.6		96.4		12.0	158.2
1944	85.8	21.2	40.4	41.6	43.5	21.3	253.8
1945	93.7	23.4	44.1	49.7	45.0	21.2	277.1
1946	91.1	21.5	51.9	57.7	46.0	21.6	289.8
1947	95.2	22.4	62.6	64.2	50.5	23.2	318.1
1948	97.8	24.2	70.8	65.7	53.6	22.0	334.1
1949	101.7	24.7	78.6	69.9	54.6	22.6	352.1
1950 (1)	104	25	86	70	55	23	363

(1) Provisional.

Table III shows that, at the present time, agriculture with 41 per cent of the working population has 29 per cent of the total income, as compared with 24 per cent in 1938. The proportion was about one-third in 1926 when, however, agriculturists formed 53 per cent of the working population. Since 1938 the rise in agricultural income was greater than for any of the other main sectors, but it is important always to bear in mind that the increase was from a very low level. It is only since the war that the agricultural community has become an important market. At the depth of the so-called Economic War, in 1934-35, when the national income was about £140 million, the Irish agricultural community had only £10½ million per annum to spend on household necessities from their agricultural income in cash ; the corresponding sum was £20 million in 1938 but has increased latterly to £70 million per annum. In the increase in agricultural spending power lies the main hope of arresting or retarding the further decline in the rural population by creating employment in transport and distribution etc. (as well as in industry) in the smaller towns and villages.

The volume of consumption of consumers' goods and services increased by 18 per cent in 1949 compared with 1938 : the increase has been continuous and substantial from year to year since 1944. While the relative rise in consumption in quantum terms was much greater in the case of the agricultural than of the non-agricultural population, there can be no doubt that the standard of living of the latter also rose significantly. Percentage increases in quantum terms between 1938 and 1949 were 12 for food, 15 for drink and tobacco, 11 for clothing, 48 for " other goods " and 30 for services, while quantum consumption of fuel and light decreased. It is significant of a rising standard of living that the percentage increases were greatest for " other goods " and services.

The underlying concept of savings and capital formation is that savings plus depreciation plus foreign disinvestment = gross domestic investment = imported capital goods ready for use plus home produced capital plus increase in stocks and work in progress. Between 1938 and 1949 savings increased from £12 million to £30 million or from 7½ per cent to 8½ per cent of the national income. The percentage for 1949 is rather low by international standards. Ireland has been making substantial drafts in her external holdings during the past few years to supplement her savings, for the purpose of investment. The decline in external assets amounted to £30 million in 1947, to £20 million in 1948, to £10 million in 1949, but has risen again to £30 million in 1950. During the second quarter of the present year the decline in external assets was proceeding at an annual rate of at least £60 million, evidence of a full-blooded inflationary situation. While there was a substantial increase in gross domestic investment in 1950 compared with 1949, there are indications that there was a fairly substantial decline in personal savings as well as an increase in personal consumption between 1949 and 1950. During the past twelve months dissaving has occurred i.e. a withdrawal of past savings, some for capital formation proper but the greater part for consumption and stockpiling.

As regards gross domestic capital formation, in 1949 it totalled £48 million and was fairly equally divided between the categories (1) imported capital goods ready for use, (2) building of private dwellings, schools, etc., and (3) other home-produced capital. It will always be borne in mind that these figures are gross, i.e. they include replacements at current cost as well as new capital formation ; they do not include repairs and maintenance. Between 1938 and 1949 gross capital formation (excluding changes in stocks) increased from £14 million to £47 million ; allowing for price changes, the increase in volume of gross capital formation was about 46 per cent. It is for industrial experts to say if this degree of gross capital formation including productive and unproductive (or perhaps a more correct term would be not directly productive) capital is adequate, especially having regard to the fact that during the past four years it was necessary to make substantial drafts on external assets to attain it. Are we saving enough ? *Personal* savings as a percentage of personal income decreased from 5.1 per cent in 1938 to 4.7 per cent in 1949 : during the war years and up to 1946, personal savings were at a considerably higher level but they had largely the character of forced savings since consumption goods were in such short supply : these were the years when we were rapidly increasing our assets abroad. It may, however, be agreed that personal savings at 4–5 per cent of income are too low. As already stated, in 1950-51 there was a substantial dissaving.

TABLE IV

INDEX NUMBERS OF VOLUME OF PRODUCTION AND
PERSONNEL IN AGRICULTURE AND INDUSTRY

(Base 1938 as 100)

| Year | AGRICULTURE | | INDUSTRY | | | |
| | Gross Volume | Male Personnel (June 1) | All Industry (C.I.P.) (1) | | Manufacturing Industry (C.I.P.) | |
			Volume	Personnel	Volume	Personnel
1926 (2)	95.5	111.2 (3)	61.8	61.7	65.7	57.9
1931 (2)	(4)	104.7	68.5	66.5	70.3	62.7
1938 (2)	100	100	100	100	100	100
1946	97.4	96.7	102.1	100.8	111.8	110.2
1947	91.9	94.5	113.3	110.4	120.5	117.8
1948	92.9	93.0	128.6	119.0	132.0	123.2
1949	99.7	89.7	146.1	124.2	149.7	129.5
1950 (5)	96.0	87.5	159.2	132.4	166.4	130.3

(1) Including building, public utilities, and other industries of the service type as well as manufacturing industry proper, as included in the Census of Industrial Production (C.I.P.).
(2) Agricultural year ending during year following.
(3) 1927.
(4) Not available.
(5) Provisional as regards industry.

Table IV may be regarded as an appendix to Table III in showing the trend in the volume of agricultural and industrial production and in parallel employment in these two great divisions of the economy. The table does not call for special comment. It shows the static character of agricultural output and again the sharp decline in agricultural personnel, the great increase in industrial production from its low level in 1926 and the lesser, though substantial, increase in industrial employment during recent years. The available statistics for the present year indicate some decline in the volume of agricultural production, a further substantial decline in agricultural manpower and also a perceptible retardation in the rate of increase in industrial production and employment. This retardation is possibly due in part to the high prices and scarcity of imported materials on which Irish industry is largely based.

A very satisfactory feature of the recent industrial trend has been the unbroken increase in productivity, i.e. output per man hour. Taking 1936 as 100, productivity in manufacturing industries was 99 in 1946, 106 in 1947, 111 in 1948, 121 in 1949 and (approximately) 129 in 1950. During the war years the figure was as low as 84, due largely to shortage and poor quality of materials and to the policy of keeping people in jobs. The recent figures are a tribute to the increasing efficiency and better training of employees, as well as to managerial organization, increased mechanization and, no doubt, to increased availability of more suitable materials. In this connection it is also pertinent to observe that the maintenance of the pre-war level of agricultural output from a considerably reduced labour force—the number of men in agriculture declined by 12½ per cent between 1938 and 1950—means that agricultural productivity increased by about 10 per cent since prewar. Admittedly the employment situation was fundamentally different pre-war in agriculture and industry, in that in agriculture the low output per person engaged was due to the endemic under-employment of relatives assisting farmers who constituted a large part of the labour force.

Balance of International Payments

The Irish Balance of International Payments is characterized by a very considerable import excess (£17 million in 1938, £87 million in 1950, and, as already observed, a further increase in 1951), financed by a substantial balance on invisible current account (the principal items of which in 1950 were net income from visitors £24 million, emigrants' remittances £10 million, net income from investments £9 million) as well as by large drawings on external assets, and by extern transfers to this country, on the capital side. As already remarked Irish external assets are largely the result of forced savings during the two wars when imports were at a low level while exports, mostly of agricultural products, were more or less maintained.

Unemployment

It is another paradox in the Irish economic situation that, during the inter-war period, Ireland had many of the signs of over-population and at the same time our density of population is low. During that period, for instance, our rural income per head was very low, and the general emigration rate and the unemployment rate were high by Western European standards. In 1950 the percentage unemployed averaged 7.5, less than half the rate of 15.6 per cent in 1939, and comparing with 9.0 per cent in 1949. Substantial declines occurred in all industrial groups, most important in the case of building in view of the large number in this industrial group, from the high average of 26.2 in 1939 to 9.6 per cent in 1950, concomitant with the high level of building activity during recent years.

Concluding Remarks

In this paper I have had time only to treat the generalities of the economic trend since the Treaty. I have scarcely dealt with, for example, individual industries, particular areas of the country etc., in which regard I must be content to refer you to the special statistical reports which display the relevant statistics in considerable detail. You may find the Selected Bibliography useful in this connection.

Over the past quarter century the economic and social trend may be summarized as follows :—

(a) Greater political stability than in almost any other country in the world, which is not to praise us unduly.

(b) Stability of the population which may not be unrelated to (a) by cause or by effect.

(c) At a time when the level of national material prosperity was never so satisfactory, emigration continues at a high level without a decline in the total population because emigration is merely a skimming-off of the high natural increase. The marriage rate remains the lowest in the world though it was high by Irish standards during the years 1942-1946 at 5.9 per thousand population per annum, but has since receded. Fertility of marriage is still high, though it also is declining. The net reproduction rate gives no cause for concern at its present level of 1.4.

(d) Development of subsidized housing and other social services to a fair relation, if not to the limit, of what our resources permit.

(e) Increase in the national income in real terms by 24 per cent since 1938 and by over 40 per cent since 1926.

2 D

(f) Increase in industrial output by 150 per cent since 1926 though from a low level so that the proportion of the working population in industry is now about one-fifth, as compared with one-third for countries in Europe with balanced economies : there is accordingly great scope for further development, by this test.

(g) Stagnation in agriculture, though with an increase of 70 per cent in agricultural real income per head since 1938, due to increase in prices of agricultural produce with a slight fall in total volume of output and a decline in the agricultural working population which in the last five years has assumed the dimensions of an exodus and is continuing.

(h) A marked inflationary tendency during the past twelve months, characterized by a considerable rise in prices, increases in wages and salaries, a marked propensity to consume instead of to save on the part of the general public, and a steep increase in the import excess.

R. C. Geary

[2]

FROM PROTECTION TO FREE TRADE — THE IRISH EXPERIENCE*

by T. K. WHITAKER

May I begin by congratulating the University of Exeter, and, in particular, its Professor of Social Administration, Dr Robert Leaper, as well as the Irish universities and Institute of Public Administration for arranging to honour an outstanding Irish statesman of our time by establishing a commemorative series of lectures to be given alternately in Exeter and in Dublin. To be asked to give the first Seán Lemass Memorial Lecture is a special privilege which I gratefully acknowledge. I regard it as a great honour. It is also a personal pleasure to be for the first time in Exeter.

The influence which Seán Lemass exerted on Ireland's economic and social development and political evolution extended over many years and bore fruit in different ways. Its effects can be traced not only domestically, in such domains as industry, energy, transport, social and administrative organisation but also in the Republic of Ireland's political and economic relations with Northern Ireland, Great Britain, the European Economic Community and the world at large. The monuments to his achievements include national air and shipping fleets as well as a large number of manufacturing and service industries and promotional bodies. There is inspiration here for many memorial lectures. Out of this richness of record I have time tonight to take only one theme. I hope it will be of interest to trace the movement of a man's thought and action across a policy spectrum, from high protectionism to free trade. I was fortunate, as Secretary of the Department of Finance from 1956 to 1969, to have been close to Seán Lemass during his final period as Minister for Industry and Commerce (1957 to 1959) and his tenure of office as Taoiseach (1959 to 1966). I can, therefore, draw on my own experience in dealing with the latter part of the transition towards free trade in contemplation of EEC membership.[1]

How Seán Lemass applied his talents as a member for thirty-three years of an Irish government can be fully understood only by reference to his family background and the motivation and experience of his youth. He was born in Dublin in 1899 and went to O'Connell School (Christian Brothers) where he was an exhibition winner. He grew up during a period of intense nationalist activity. His grandfather had been a Parnellite member of Dublin Corporation. He himself took an early interest in politics

---

*Text of Seán Lemass Memorial Lecture delivered at the University of Exeter, 17 January 1974.

1. I am indebted to Adrian Masterson, M.Sc. (Econ), an economist on the staff of the Central Bank, for substantial help in preparing this lecture.

and joined the Volunteers at fifteen. He took part in the 1916 Rising and the subsequent War of Independence before being interned in 1920. Like many another active person condemned to physical inactivity, he gave his mind as free a range as possible. As an ardent nationalist, he read Arthur Griffith's writings and came under the influence of his economic views. Arthur Griffith was himself a disciple of the German apostle of protection, Friedrich List, and adopted his National System of Political Economy as a headline for much of his own propaganda. Indeed, he wished to see List's book in the hands of every Irishman. Griffith's teachings are summed up in *The Resurrection of Hungary* in which he reproduced the arguments (with acknowledgements to List) which he had advanced in 1905 in favour of a Sinn Féin policy of developing Ireland's "manufacturing arm" with the aid of tariff protection, particularly for infant industries. Griffith emphasised the interdependence of agriculture and industry and the concern of Sinn Féin "to give Ireland back her manufacturing arm, not to make fortunes for dishonest manufacturers" who had no need of protection. Griffith's views had a profound influence on Lemass; they can indeed be said to have laid the basis of his life's work.

When the Irish Free State was founded in 1922, Lemass was still in jail. Shortly after his release in 1923 he was elected to the Dáil but did not take his seat. He subsequently helped form a new political party, Fianna Fáil. As one of the secretaries of the party, he spent the next few years moving around the country organising branches and preparing for the next election. In this capacity his administrative abilities first became apparent.

Offering a policy which included the imposition of a wide range of protective tariffs, the new party gained a strong minority position in the general election of 1927. They took their seats and Lemass gradually assumed the role of opposition spokesman on economic affairs. In this capacity he pressed for increased tariffs on imports. It may seem strange that he should have to castigate the tardiness of the then government in following the Sinn Féin principles of Arthur Griffith. But one of the leading spokesmen of that government, Kevin O'Higgins, Minister for Home Affairs, had earlier moved to a critical stance:

> The propagandist writings of any one man cannot be accepted simply as revealed truth, requiring no further investigation, something that must be accepted for ever as beyond question, beyond doubt, beyond the need of examination.[2]

It is true that a few moderate tariffs were introduced during the 'twenties but they were certainly not designed in scope or degree to promote the ideal of self-sufficiency.[3] Perhaps this reluctance to embrace an outright

---

2. *Parliamentary Debates*, Dáil Éireann. Vol. 16, Col. 1884, 30 June 1926.
3. For a summary of pre-1932 protective attitudes and actions, see Professor James Meenan's *The Irish Economy Since 1922*, pp. 137-141.

FROM PROTECTION TO FREE TRADE—THE IRISH EXPERIENCE 407

protectionist policy can be explained by the first Irish government's desire to establish the standing of the state in the eyes of the world by observing a rather strict orthodoxy in this as well as in other economic and financial matters. Free trade was the accepted commercial philosophy of the day. Moreover, agriculture was by far the stronger arm of the economy and the government leant towards this side of the Sinn Féin policy balance. It was hoped that the benefits of agricultural prosperity would percolate to other sectors of the economy, leading in time to an expansion of home industries. A Tariff Commission was set up to consider tariffs on certain imports but it moved slowly and cautiously.

In 1928 Lemass made a speech in the Dáil which clearly defined his views on the policy which should be pursued:

> We believe that Ireland can be made a self-contained unit, providing all the necessities of living in adequate quantities for the people residing in the island at the moment and probably for a much larger number . . . .

> Until we get a definite national policy decided on in favour of industrial and agricultural protection and an executive in office prepared to enforce that policy, it is useless to hope for results.[4]

In 1932 Fianna Fáil were voted into power and Seán Lemass became Minister for Industry and Commerce. Thus the stage was set for a vigorous policy of protection and industrialisation. The drive towards protection was reinforced by a dispute with Great Britain — the so-called "Economic War" — which stimulated recourse to tariffs and quotas as retaliatory devices. Internationally, also, the trend of events was running against free trade and in favour of resort to national protectionism.

The "Economic War" centred on the refusal of the new government to pay certain land purchase annuities to the British government: the details need not concern us here. What is relevant is that the British government decided to recoup its losses by imposing duties of 20 per cent. *ad valorem* on Irish cattle and on the other main Irish agricultural exports to the United Kingdom. These duties were later increased in severity. These were not the only restrictions placed on Irish exports. It was decided to exclude Ireland from the preferential tariff agreements which were negotiated amongst members of the Commonwealth at the Ottawa Conference in 1932. It was hardly surprising, therefore, that the new government should have pursued its policy of self-sufficiency with more political zest than economic calculation. In 1936 the so-called "Coal-

---

4. *Parliamentary Debates*, Dáil Éireann, Vol. 22, Cols. 213/4, 22 February 1928.

Cattle Pact" marked the first step towards resolving the difficulties between the two countries, and in 1938 an agreement was signed which in
effect brought the "Economic War" to an end. This agreement, although
partly revised in 1948, formed the basis of trade between the two countries
until the Anglo-Irish Free Trade Area Agreement in 1965. It provided for
review by the Irish Prices Commission of existing protective duties and
other import restrictions, for the holding of this review *first* "upon the
classes of goods for which the Government of the United Kingdom request
early consideration" and for full right of audience before the Commission for UK producers and manufactures. The advent of World War II,
however, effectively prevented any reduction in tariffs; in fact, it height-
ened the degree of Ireland's isolation and self-reliance.

The protectionist policy of the nineteen thirties received valuable
support from a famous economist — John Maynard Keynes. Keynes,
while mentioning the dangers of economic nationalism, spoke out in favour
of a move towards greater self-sufficiency, declaring to his audience at the
first Finlay Lecture in University College, Dublin, on April 19, 1933 :[5]

> I sympathise, therefore, with those who would minimise
> rather than with those who would maximise, economic entangle-
> ment between nations. Ideas, knowledge, science, hospitality,
> travel — these are the things which should of their nature be
> international. But let goods be homespun whenever it is reason-
> able and conveniently possible and, above all, let finance be pri-
> marily national.

and again

> . . . . if I were an Irishman I should find much to attract me in
> the economic outlook of your present government towards self-
> sufficiency.

Neither Friedrich List nor Arthur Griffith could have put it more forcefully. Unlike them, Keynes spoke when all was in place — the time, the
opportunity, the mood and the man. It is understandable that less attention was paid to the "fundamental question" which Keynes also posed in
his lecture, whether "Ireland is a large enough unit geographically, with
sufficiently diversified natural resources, for more than a very modest
measure of national self-sufficiency to be feasible without a disastrous
reduction in a standard of life which is already none too high". The
answer Keynes himself suggested to this question is interesting, in view
of Seán Lemass's signature much later (1965) of the Anglo-Irish Free
Trade Area Agreement:

> I believe, I should answer that it would be an act of high
> wisdom on the part of the Irish to enter into an economic
> arrangement with England which would, within appropriate

---

5. Reproduced in *Studies* of June 1933 under the title 'National Self-Sufficiency'.

FROM PROTECTION TO FREE TRADE—THE IRISH EXPERIENCE 409

limits, retain for Ireland her traditional British markets against mutual advantages for British producers within the wide field which for long to come will not interfere with Ireland's own developments. I should see nothing in this the slightest degree derogatory to her political and cultural autonomy. I should look on it merely as an act of commonsense for the preservation of the standard of life of the Irish, at a level which would alone make possible the country's new political and cultural life.

In those early years of the 'thirties, the world at large was in the grip of the Great Depression; the prices of primary products had plummeted, the demand for goods had fallen catastrophically, unemployment was severe and widespread. In 1931 the new government in England announced its intention of imposing a tariff — the first general British tariff since the eighteen fifties — and of protecting British agriculture. The practical and theoretical considerations supporting free trade were thus undermined and no inhibition lay in the way of a policy of protection aimed at securing self-sufficiency. On the contrary, the sharpness of the British reaction to the withholding of the land annuities caused protection proper to be enveloped in a heated atmosphere of retaliation which was hostile to any careful adjustment of aid to need. On several occasions in the 1932-38 period the desirability of a more scientific basis for the tariffs was suggested to Lemass by the Secretary of his Department, only to receive an Augustinian reply: the advice was appropriate but premature. Lemass did not, however, object to the provisions in the 1938 Anglo-Irish Trade Agreement for tariff reviews.

One of the first acts of the new government in 1932 was to introduce the Control of Manufactures Act which was aimed at restricting, to a minority position, foreign ownership and board membership of Irish manufacturing companies. The intention was to lay the foundation of a domestic industrial base:

> We are endeavouring to undertake and promote rapid industrial development in this country. We are in the process of imposing a system of protective tariffs designed to ensure the production in this country in much greater volume of goods which were produced here heretofore and some classes of goods which were not produced in this country before this.[6]

With the same purpose in mind, the government, realising the undeveloped state of the industrial capital market and the absence of financial facilities for new industries, set up the Industrial Credit Company in 1933 to remedy these deficiencies.

---

6. *Parliamentary Debates*, Dáil Éireann, Vol. 42, Cols. 1234/5, 14 June 1932.

The Control of Manufactures Bill was vehemently attacked by the opposition in one of the longest debates of the new Dáil. A wide variety of arguments, legal, political, administrative and economic, were adduced against it. One deputy, J. J. Byrne, in the course of a speech, put some rhetorical questions which may be read as indicating the general state of mind as well as the position of industry at that time:

> Will capital be attracted or repelled if this Bill passes? Is there any attraction for the investment of Irish capital if the Bill becomes law? Do not men who possess capital realise the short-comings from which Irish industrialists suffer? Do they not realise that they have not the experience of their competitors either in technical processes of manufacture or in large scale pro-duction? Do they not realise that when people invest capital they do not ask 'is this an Irish or a foreign firm' but rather 'what are they going to receive on any money they invest'?[7]

The truth lay between this pessimism and the optimism reflected in the expectation of a "rapid industrial development" which would be foreign-dominated unless legislative provision were made otherwise.

A few figures will give an idea of the zeal with which what Professor Meenan has called "the last surviving example of a predominantly free-trading state" was transformed into one of the most highly protected in the world. At the end of 1931, the list of tariffs covered 68 articles includ-ing 9 revenue tariffs. In the Finance Act of May 1932, the new Fianna Fáil government imposed *ad valorem* duties ranging from 15 per cent. to 75 per cent. on 38 classes of goods with specific duties on 6 other classes. Following the Emergency Imposition of Duties Act, which provided for the imposition of retaliatory duties, the next major round of tariffs was introduced in October 1932 with *ad valorem* duties ranging from 15 per cent. to 75 per cent. on a further 29 classes of goods (including component parts for motor vehicles, ropes and yarns, and coffin plates) and specific duties on 7 commodities (including food items and machinery). In 1933 *ad valorem* duties ranging from 22½ per cent. to 75 per cent. were imposed on 22 classes of goods (including heavy electrical equipment, mattresses, leather goods and candles, to name but a few) and specific duties on 15 classes. In 1934, 45 further commodities were made subject to import duties; in 1935 *ad valorem* duties ranging from 20 per cent. to 100 per cent. were imposed on 29 classes and specific duties on 17 goods; in 1936, 44 new duties were imposed; in 1937, 31 new duties were imposed and in 1938 14 new duties were added.[8] Tariffs on intermediate products piled up

---

7. *Parliamentary Debates*, Dáil Éireann, Vol. 42, Col. 1270, 14 June 1932.
8. Figures derived from various Finance Acts. See also Professor James Meenan, *The Irish Economy Since 1922*, pp. 142-3.

FROM PROTECTION TO FREE TRADE—THE IRISH EXPERIENCE   411

to create a pyramid of protection for some final products. There was not much time for tea-breaks in the Department of Industry and Commerce in those years!

Estimates of the tariff levels obtaining in 1931, 1936 and 1938 have been made by Professor Louden Ryan of Trinity College, Dublin, and they show how the intensity of protection mounted.[9] The calculations are based on a representative list of commodities bearing either a specific duty or an *ad valorem* duty, and altogether some 161 commodities subject to tariff protection, but not to revenue duties, were considered. The resulting tariff level indices, by comparison with a *nil* rate for 1924, were as follows: 1931 9 per cent.; 1936 45 per cent.; 1938 35 per cent. The year 1931 was chosen to measure the level of protection reached under the selective policy of the previous government. The year 1936 marked the high-water mark of tariff protection by the Fianna Fáil government, Seán Lemass being Minister for Industry and Commerce. The year 1938 saw the signing of the Anglo-Irish Trade Agreement, completing the settlement of the Anglo-Irish dispute initiated by the Coal-Cattle Pact of 1936; some tariffs had been reduced or abolished in the intervening period. The calculations are based on figures which represent the 'potential' height of the tariff wall and do not allow for abatement of the tariffs in special circumstances. On the other hand, the protective effect of quota restrictions is not measured by the index. Professor Ryan estimated that the prevailing U.K. tariff level in 1937 was about 65 per cent. of the corresponding Irish tariff level. The table in which this estimate appears also contains estimates of the relative tariff levels of other countries at that time; with figures of 152 for Germany (relative to Ireland's 100), 70 for Switzerland, 55 for the United States and 53 for Japan, the table is striking evidence of the international incidence of protection before World War II.

The percentage duty applicable to particular categories of imports into Ireland was high, and where the basic value was low had often to be underpinned by a minimum specific duty. As a category, fuels were subject to an *ad valorem* rate of approximately 250 per cent., foods to 72½-82 per cent., textile products to 35½-37½ per cent., but such was the prevalence of protection in those pre-war years that even these rates had, individually, near counterparts in some European countries or in North America. *The Economist* calculated in 1938 that 1,947 articles were subject to restriction or control in the Irish Free State. These restrictions were administered with thoroughness, and few exemptions were granted. Licences to import goods duty-free were given only if the prospective importer could show that no reasonable substitute was available from home producers. On the other hand, it is only fair to the recipients of such unscientifically gener-

---

9. Paper read on 3 December 1948 to the Statistical and Social Inquiry Society of Ireland entitled 'Measurement of Tariff Levels for Ireland, For 1931, 1936, 1938'.

ous protection to say that most of them did not take full advantage of the high tariffs in fixing their domestic prices; many regarded the full tariff as a safeguard against dumping, and relied in practice on a lower degree of price differential, more closely related to productivity and cost differences.

Reviewing the progress made towards self-sufficiency in the cramped circumstances of those pre-war years, one cannot record spectacular success but nevertheless there was progress, and this was seen to be worthwhile in the scarcity conditions of war and post-war years. Rather indiscriminate particulars of "the number of new industries and extensions of existing industries" were published periodically, but the best indication of the extent to which industrialisation had proceeded before World War II is afforded by the following summary:

	1926	1931	1938
Value of *total* net industrial output	£23m.	£26m.	£35m.
Index of volume of total industrial production, 1929=100	92	102	149
Numbers employed in industry	102,515	110,589	166,513

Source: *Irish Statistical Bulletin, March* 1973,
        Statistical Abstract 1955.

It was many years later — after the scarcities had disappeared and the supporting structure of education, power, communications and finance had been strengthened — that significant progress was realised. When Lemass retired to the back benches towards the end of 1966, the volume of industrial production (1929=100) had reached 452 — though figures such as these are best interpreted as rough indications only — the numbers employed in industry were over 260,000 and industrial exports amounted to £128 million, as against a mere £5 million in 1938. Indeed a few years later, in 1969, industrial exports exceeded agricultural exports for the first time. This growth in output was accompanied by another encouraging development — an increase in the size of firms, a trend likely to continue during the coming years.

But this is to take a glimpse forward from those pre-war days when industry — much of it small in scale — was almost entirely confined, by cost considerations, to a protected and stagnant home market, the agricultural arm having been weakened by the prolonged dispute with Britain. It has been estimated that, whereas in 1931 the average income per head in Ireland was 61 per cent. of that in Britain, by 1939 the corresponding figure was 49 per cent.

FROM PROTECTION TO FREE TRADE—THE IRISH EXPERIENCE   413

>   While protection had created a whole complex of vested in-
> terests not necessarily compatible with present efficiency or
> future prosperity, emigration, by removing some of the pres-
> sures for change, contributed its share to what seemed the immu-
> table inertia of Irish economic life.[10]

When the war came, Lemass was given charge of the newly-created
Department of Supplies where his dynamic energy, his decisiveness (and
eagerness to decide) and his organisational capacity received full scope.[11]
The scarcity of essential supplies made protection irrelevant and protective duties were suspended for all practical purposes in 1942. Only as
supplies became fully available in the post-war years were they gradually
put into effect again.

With the insight into the industrial situation afforded by his experience as Minister for Supplies, it was natural that Seán Lemass, on his
return to Industry and Commerce, should reassess the merits of the policy
of hurried and indiscriminate protection pursued in the pre-war years.
He was too intelligent a man not to learn from experience and too patri-
otic to neglect any lessons relevant to the long-term development of the
Irish economy. This pragmatic nationalism was his outstanding characteristic and it showed up constantly in his approach to economic as well
as to political problems.

One sign of it was the increasing concern he displayed about the cost
and price effects of high protection and the complacency and inefficiency
it induced. The Prices Acts of 1932 and 1937 had not been very effective:
the legislation was directed against profiteering rather than high costs of
production, and the possibility of restraining prices by reducing tariffs
and allowing more foreign competition was not, in effect, entertained.
Speaking on the second stage of the Control of Prices Bill, 1937, Lemass
had said :

>   In relation to most industries I have tried to promote a
> reasonable amount of competition, but I think it is wrong to
> assume that competition is always an unmixed blessing. . . . .
> Competition may be all right on paper and in textbooks but in
> actual practice it is often the cause of many social evils.[12]

But the obvious deficiencies of enterprise, management and technique in
many protected industries, and the deeper realisation of the enormity of

---

10. This is the rather harsh judgment of Professor F. S. L. Lyons in *Ireland Since
    the Famine*, pp. 611-612.

11. For most of his time in ministerial office, in Industry and Commerce and Supplies,
    Seán Lemass had the good fortune to be assisted, and at times creatively inspired,
    by a Permanent Secretary of outstanding quality, John Leydon.

12. *Parliamentary Debates*, Dáil Éireann, Vol. 69, Col. 264, 7 October 1937.

the task of industrialisation gained by his wartime experience, convinced Lemass that more effective measures were needed to set the economy on the path of competitive efficiency and growth. So in 1947 he introduced an Industrial Efficiency and Prices Bill. This was a watershed in his thinking. He proposed to establish a Commission which should exercise

> . . . . a continued supervision over the efficiency of industries engaged in the production of protected commodities and shall endeavour to improve the efficiency of such undertakings by giving expert advice and assistance and by consultation with the representatives of the industries concerned.
>
> *(Industrial Efficiency and Prices Bill, 1947—Explanatory Memorandum).*

The chairman of the Commission, acting with the minister's consent, could undertake a special enquiry into the efficiency of an industry. If the Commission decided that this was below a reasonable standard, measuring efficiency by reference to such matters as the quality and cost of the products by comparison with similar products in other countries, the arrangements for purchasing of materials and the economic use of capital and labour, the minister was to have the power to give a direction to the manufacturers to make such changes as were necessary to promote greater efficiency in the industry.

Furthermore, the government was empowered to set the maximum profit which a firm could make and if the firm made any excess profit then the minister could claim that excess.

The Bill was not solely concerned with punitive measures; there were also provisions for helping industries to develop. One such provision was the establishment of development councils for industries, which would be mainly concerned with

> . . . promoting by voluntary efforts the efficiency of industries which the council represents. The functions of a development council were to include the promotion of scientific research and of enquiries into the methods of production and the management and use of labour. A development council was also to be concerned with the extension of facilities for technical training of workers and the promotion of improved standards and design and standardisation of products and of market research.
>
> *(Explanatory Memorandum).*

A development council to encourage cooperation between firms in the supply of materials and equipment and the coordination of production, marketing and distribution was also envisaged. The Bill also proposed to re-establish the Prices Commission and to extend its investigatory scope to include services as well as commodities.

FROM PROTECTION TO FREE TRADE—THE IRISH EXPERIENCE   415

This mixture of carrot and stick, for those infant industries loath to grow up, never got a chance to prove itself. The coalition government which took office in 1948 did not proceed with the legislation and it is now chiefly of interest as an indication of Lemass's concern at the time — a concern which extended also to the fragmented state of trade union organisation — and as a precursor of the more comprehensive measures of industrial survey, tripartite consultative and advisory machinery, grants for modernisation and adaptation, and even unilateral reduction of protection which he put into effect in the early nineteen sixties after applying for membership for Ireland in the EEC.

The Fianna Fáil government were out of office from 1948 to 1951 and again from 1954 to 1957. The final phase of transition from protection to free trade coincided with Lemass's own final period in government, from 1957 to 1966, for the seven last years of which he was Taoiseach (Prime Minister). This period was preceded by a dark night of the soul, shared by the principal politicians both in and out of office and by concerned citizens and public servants. For the first half of the nineteen fifties economic progress had been brought almost to a standstill by balance-of-payments and other difficulties. The years 1955 and 1956 had plumbed the depths of hopelessness. One of the recurring series of balance-of-payments crises had been overcome — indeed, the basis laid for a surplus on current account in 1957 — but at the cost of high unemployment and emigration. The mood of despondency was palpable. My own impression of the state of the nation at that time is set out in the following passage:[13]

A sense of anxiety is, indeed, justified. But it can too easily degenerate into feelings of frustration and despair. After 35 years of native government people are asking whether we can achieve an acceptable degree of economic progress. The common talk amongst parents in the towns, as in rural Ireland, is of their children having to emigrate as soon as their education is completed in order to be sure of a reasonable livelihood. To the children themselves and to many already in employment the jobs available at home look unattractive by comparison with those obtainable in such variety and so readily elsewhere. All this seems to be setting up a vicious circle — of increasing emigration, resulting in a smaller domestic market depleted of initiative and skill, and a reduced incentive, whether for Irishmen or foreigners, to undertake and organise the productive enterprises which alone can provide increased employment opportunities and higher living standards. There is, therefore, a real need at present to buttress confidence in the country's future and to stimulate the interest and enthusiasm of the young in particular.

13. *Economic Development*, 1958, page 5.

A general resurgence of will may be helped by setting up targets of national endeavour which appear to be reasonably attainable and mutually consistent.

Lemass himself had reacted to Ireland's evident failure in the post-war world of reconstruction and development by presenting, when in opposition, a simple 'Keynesian' prescription of increased public investment to generate 100,000 new jobs and provide full employment in five years. His ideas were expounded in a supplement to *The Irish Press* and subsequently to party members in Clery's Ballroom in early 1956. Other studies of the deficiencies of the Irish economy were also undertaken around this time. These included a paper on Capital Formation, Saving and Economic Progress, which I read to the Statistical and Social Inquiry Society of Ireland in May 1956, and reports of the Capital Investment Advisory Committee, which had been established in 1955. These various products of the dark night of soul-searching at least agreed on the need to devote more resources on an orderly basis to productive investment. Finally, over the winter and spring of 1957-58, a comprehensive survey of the economy, extending to its potentialities as well as its deficiencies, and containing a systematic set of proposals for action, was prepared in the Department of Finance. This was presented to the government in May 1958, and was published under the title *Economic Development* in November of that year, simultaneously with the First Programme for Economic Expansion which was acknowledged to be based largely upon it.

Lemass, as Tánaiste (Deputy Prime Minister) and Minister for Industry and Commerce, chaired the cabinet committee which put this First Programme into final shape. Here again his pragmatic nationalism was in evidence, for the Programme indicated a distinct and courageous change of emphasis in the traditional policy of his party. The aim of self-sufficiency, involving, for instance, protected or subsidised home production of wheat and sugar beet, had been pursued in agriculture as well as in industry; now the importance of the 85 per cent. of Ireland's agricultural land which was under grass was expressly recognised.

> Grass is the raw material of our principal export trade, beef and cattle, of milk production and of sheep and lamb production. While the outlook for milk products in export markets is uncertain, there is fortunately little doubt that there will be a continuing demand for meat. We are singularly well situated to take advantage of this prospect . . . .[14]

Not only, to oversimplify a little, did the new Programme put grass before grain but, on the industrial side, it put export-oriented expansion, even if foreign-owned, before dependence on protected domestic enterprise. The new policy was stated straightforwardly as follows:[15]

---

14. *Programme for Economic Expansion*, November 1958, (Pr. 4796), p. 12.
15. ibid. pp. 37-8.

FROM PROTECTION TO FREE TRADE—THE IRISH EXPERIENCE   417

It would be unrealistic, in the light of the probable emergence of a Free Trade Area, to rely on a policy of protection similar to that applied over the past 25 years or so. Assuming that a Free Trade Area is set up in Western Europe and that Ireland joins the Area, the Government will, of course, still be prepared, in suitable cases, to grant protection to worth-while new industries up to the limits permissible under the rules of the Free Trade Area, but it must be expected that in future the criterion to be applied in determining what is 'worth-while' will be very much stricter than hitherto. Bearing in mind that the only scope for substantial expansion lies in the production of goods for sale on export markets, it is clear that there can be no place for weak or inefficient industries. Even where only the home market is involved, it must be accepted that such industries place a burden on the economy generally and render other industries less able to meet foreign competition. Hence it must now be recognised that protection can no longer be relied upon as an automatic weapon of defence and it will be the policy in future in the case of new industries to confine the grant of tariff protection to cases in which it is clear that the industry will, after a short initial period, be able to survive without protection. The rules of the Free Trade Area will require a gradual and systematic reduction in existing tariffs.

The industrial Free Trade Area then envisaged never came into being. It was viewed as an alternative to a wider Common Market, and Britain would have preferred it because it had no agricultural implications. It was, however, effectively killed by French opposition. The Six held fast to their Common Market and the outer Seven (Britain, the Scandinavian countries, Austria, and Portugal) formed the European Free Trade Association. Ireland had been pressing hard in the original Free Trade Area negotiations for a transitional period of some twenty-five years for the gradual elimination of industrial protection, in this respect claiming the same derogations as Greece and Turkey. When the break-down occurred and Europe split into sixes and sevens, Ireland was isolated. Much thought was devoted during the period, 1959 to 1961, at Lemass's insistence as Taoiseach, to ways of overcoming this isolation. In particular, the possibility of special bilateral trade arrangements with Britain and the question of joining EFTA were studied. The Secretaries of the four main economic Departments — Finance, Industry and Commerce, Agriculture, and External Affairs—met frequently as a committee reporting on these matters to a cabinet committee chaired by Mr Lemass. The correspondence which passed between the four Secretaries — particularly Finance and Industry and Commerce — was intended also for the eyes of the Taoiseach and other Ministers on the cabinet committee and may be presumed to have had some influence on policy.

This was, in fact, a 'crunch' period in the move to free trade. Despite recognition of its probable inevitability, free trade, naturally enough, was not universally welcome and the original impetus towards it ran the risk of running into the sands of frustrated isolation. The Department of Industry and Commerce was concerned about the sensitivity of Irish industry to external competition, to shifts in demand, and, worse still, to dumping. There was apprehension about the risks of industrial set-back and unemployment inherent in even a gradual commitment to dispense with protection. In the Department's view, even if protection was intended only for infant industries, most Irish industries, if one excluded the war years and their aftermath, were still in their 'teens'. While the risks involved in premature withdrawal of protection were acknowledged, the following were the chief points on the other side of the argument:

(1) Protected manufacture for a home market of present population and purchasing power and already well exploited offered little prospect of *increased* employment.

(2) In an increasingly competitive world, in which real wages would be rising, continued high protection could not guarantee the maintenance of existing employment in Ireland at *acceptable* real wages.

(3) If employment opportunities were to be created for the fresh thousands seeking work every year — indeed even if existing employment were to be safeguarded — industry must quickly become more efficient so that its products could be sold on an increasing scale in export markets.

(4) The rapid and general increase in industrial efficiency required by national progress could most effectively and advantageously be secured by accepting an external commitment to reduce tariffs, accompanied by appropriate internal incentives and aids towards industrial adaptation and modernisation.

Lemass had been convinced since 1958 of the inevitability of free trade and his frequent contacts with European economic ministers at the OEEC had helped towards his gradual Europeanisation. His mind is revealed in a statement made by him when concluding the adjournment debate on government policy on 11 December 1959:

The world trend, however, is towards freer trade and we must not blink our eyes to it. The Common Market is already making gestures towards a world agreement. Whatever may be the outcome of negotiations with Britain or the EFTA or anyone else, we must face up to the fact of our having to reduce

FROM PROTECTION TO FREE TRADE—THE IRISH EXPERIENCE 419

our protective measures at some time and not too far ahead at that. Indeed there is a case for doing it in our own interests apart from external arrangements. Everybody concerned, whether in management or as workers in industry must face up to the prospect and prepare for it.[16]

A pamphlet published about that time by the Federation of Irish Industries recognised the imminent necessity for progressive reduction of protection leading eventually to free trade, and claimed that Irish industry was sufficiently strong and adaptable to meet the situation successfully.

This more open view of Ireland's future trading relations was reflected in the decision in 1960 to join GATT, and was confirmed beyond all doubt in the decision to apply for membership of the European Economic Community in 1961. This application had to be put aside in 1963, when de Gaulle exercised his veto on British membership. Ireland saw more problems than advantages in trying to pursue the goal of independent membership, which was probably unrealisable in any event. So again there was a setback and the search had to be renewed for an alternative interim trading framework offering some benefits in return for the only thing Ireland had to offer — a progressive lowering of tariffs. In the end, after two brave unilateral and across-the-board 10 per cent. tariff cuts in 1963 and 1964, intended not only as notices of serious intent to Britain and the EEC but also as spurs to internal reorganisation and adaptation, the interim framework was found. In the new world of free trade areas and common markets, it naturally conformed to accepted patterns; it took the form of a free trade area with Britain with some elements, on the agricultural side, of a common market character. The Free Trade Area Agreement, signed by Lemass in December 1965, provided for the immediate removal of the remaining British tariffs on Irish manufactures (mainly on synthetic textiles) together with concessions and assurances for the Irish meat trade in return for the progressive removal over ten years of all Irish protection against British manufactures. This Agreement held the field until it was subsumed into the transitional arrangements for the entry of both countries into the European Economic Community on 1 January 1973.

I have run ahead to complete the obituary of protection, or at least to register its fatal decline, and have given less than proper attention to important complementary policies which eased it out of the Irish economic system without as much upset or redundancy as some originally feared. In a recent publication[17], it has been estimated that the number of potential (not actual) jobs lost as a result of the expansion of imports

16. *Parliamentary Debates*, Dáil Éireann, Vol. 178, No. 9, Col. 1574, 11 December 1959.
17. McAleese and Martin, 'Irish Manufactured Imports from the UK in the 'Sixties: The Effects of AIFTA', Economic and Social Research Institute, Paper No. 70, May 1973.

attributable to AIFTA and other competitive factors was no more than 2,000 in 1969-70. Moreover, economic progress has continued, though somewhat erratically : over the period 1966 to 1973 the real increase in GNP has been over 35 per cent.

One of the first moves towards achieving a more efficient, outward-looking industrial sector was the Industrial Development (Encouragement of External Investment) Act passed in 1958. This removed the restrictions on foreign ownership of capital in Ireland embodied in the Control of Manufactures Act and reinforced the steps already taken by the previous government, through the Industrial Development Authority, to attract foreign industry from a wider range of countries.

The title is eloquent testimony to the change in policy engendered by the frustrating experience of continued emigration and lukewarm external interest in exploitation of Irish resources. During the debate on the Bill, Mr Lemass said :

> I believe this Bill will be effective in what it sets out to achieve. What does it hope to achieve? Its object is to attract external capital into new industries and into industries with export possibilities and in that way to put more people into employment. It is not to put existing factories out of business but to ensure that the capital which can be attracted will be channelled into the activities which we want to promote.[18]

In industry, the main objective of the First Programme was to encourage private enterprise — "the private sector will be the principal source of new productive projects" — while, at the same time, switching public capital resources to productive purposes. Foreign capital was to be actively attracted by means of more liberal capital grants, export tax concessions and other incentives. The Finance Acts of 1959 and 1960 extended the tax concessions of profits and investment originally introduced in 1956. The Industrial Credit Company was given greater resources for making loans to industry. By making existing as well as new industry eligible for the benefits of the Industrial Grants Acts, it was hoped to develop the entire industrial sector.

It would be unfair to give the impression that Lemass was the only politician who had reconsidered traditional policies in the light of experience. The export tax incentives introduced by the coalition government in 1956 were available for all, whether native or foreign, and Mr Gerard Sweetman, Minister for Finance in that government, declared :

> The real need at the present time is for a substantial increase in the volume and efficiency of our national production.[19]

---

18. *Parliamentary Debates,* Dáil Éireann, Vol. 166, No. 9, Col. 1131, 27 March 1958.
19. *Parliamentary Debates,* Dáil Éireann, Vol. 159, Col. 1603, 25 July 1956.

FROM PROTECTION TO FREE TRADE—THE IRISH EXPERIENCE 421

Speaking in 1957, Deputy Norton (leader of the Labour Party) declared:

It is not very important what the Minister does at the moment with regard to the Control of Manufactures Act. Speaking for my own Party I should like to say that we recognise it is out of date, that it has lost its early significance, that there is a change in the whole industrial and economic situation and that in contemplation of these circumstances the Act should be modified, if not in fact abolished altogether. Except for the purpose of the directional powers it gives the Minister it has little or no value in the present circumstances.[20]

Much of the basic organisation for the industrial expansion of the nineteen sixties was laid during the nineteen fifties — including the establishment of the Industrial Development Authority (1950), Córas Tráchtála (the export promotion body) in 1952, and Foras Tionscail (the grant-giving authority), also in 1952. The first export tax reliefs followed in 1956.

Shortly before Lemass succeeded de Valera as Taoiseach in 1959, he asserted that "the historic task of this generation is to ensure the economic foundation of independence". If there was failure to achieve economic goals, this would set the political gains to nought. Furthermore, the growth in the economy was to be achieved by means of an outward-looking, competitive approach. There was to be no more hiding behind stultifying trade barriers: the industrial forest must be cleared of dead-wood and new growth created.

Expert foresters were sent in to survey and report. A Committee on Industrial Organisation was established, the members being drawn from trade union and employers' organisations as well as the public service, and teams with economic and technical backgrounds conducted surveys for this Committee of the main industries as a basis for recommendations on the measures to be adopted to prepare them for intensive competition. The Department of Agriculture similarly reviewed the agricultural processing industries and the Industrial Reorganisation Branch of the Department of Industry and Commerce a further twenty-four industries. The general finding, as one might expect, was that most firms needed to invest in new machinery and to rationalise the whole productive process, from raw material buying to marketing. Measures of cooperation and integration were needed. Special Adaptation Councils were recommended for most industries. The government decided to make available, for a finite period, special grants, loans and tax incentives to encourage firms to modernise and adapt to more competitive trading conditions.

---

20. *Parliamentary Debates*, Dáil Éireann, Vol. 163, Cols. 481/2, 2 July 1957.

Undoubtedly, the confidence and responsiveness of industry during all this adjustment phase were greatly increased by the success — far beyond the initial modest expectations — of the First Programme for Economic Expansion. To find the economy growing year by year at a rate of 4 per cent., with no trouble on the balance-of-payments front and prices rising only moderately, was a psychological tonic for the whole community. Even later, under the more specifically ambitious Second Programme, when expectations ran ahead of resources, the balance-of-payments deficit never quite regained its former frightening and inhibiting power, partly because the financing of the deficit by capital inflows, autonomous or arranged, became easier; indeed, these inflows tended to raise the external reserves and not just offset their depletion.

Relations between the state and both sides of industry, indeed between the 'social partners' themselves, were also improved by the active interest in industrial welfare manifested by all the surveys, the financial aids offered, the tax reliefs granted, the concern to safeguard and promote employment and improve training facilities, and the participation in the shaping of policy through the National Industrial Economic Council. This Council was set up in 1963 to advise the government on the principles which should guide the development of the economy; its membership included representatives of industry and the trade union movement, university professors of economics and other distinguished persons outside the public sector, as well as a few public servants. As its chairman, my judgment on the Council cannot claim objectivity. It seems to me that its chief value lay in its being a forum for continual analysis of economic and social problems and for enlightening discussion. *Ex parte* and committed views were softened under exposure to fact and argument. The best work of the Council was done in studying the conditions on which full employment might in time be attained — "the arithmetic of a full employment policy" as it was called — and in outlining the principles of a prices and incomes policy. The Council's examination of the Second Programme and, annually, of the economic prospect also helped towards more widespread understanding of critical issues.

I have no doubt that this intermeshing of cooperative study and action played a significant part in preparing Ireland, psychologically and technically, for the approach of free trade. The disposition to face it — indeed, the general recognition that only if Irish manufactures could attract an increasing *export* demand was there any hope of escape from unemployment, under-employment and emigration — was not impaired by the failure to get into the EEC at this time, nor by the 15 per cent. levy on manufactured imports which Britain imposed in 1964, nor by the re-emergence of domestic inflationary problems in 1965. The impetus carried through to the signing of the Anglo-Irish Free Trade Area Agreement at the end of that year.

In retrospect, one can scarcely doubt the economic advantage to Ireland of the time gained through the reluctance of France (at least) to see Great Britain in the EEC, of the surveys and adaptation measures taken in the nineteen sixties, and of the experience provided by the tariff reductions of 1963 and 1964 and under the AIFTA.

Seán Lemass did not live to see Ireland formally enter the European Economic Community; he died in 1971, having retired altogether from politics the year before. One can, however, safely assert that this pragmatic nationalist, who had erected the high tariff wall in the nineteen thirties to shelter Ireland's infant industry, would have been happy to see it razed to the ground in return for the benefits to Ireland of membership of the Community. He would have been gratified that many of the 'infants' were strong enough to make their way against Continental as well as British competition. No doubt he would still have misgivings. But I suspect these would relate more to Ireland's relatively high current rate of price and cost inflation, rather than to the dismantling of protection. He had always, like many others, been apprehensive about the effects of removal of the lowest 10 per cent. or so of the protective shield. I remember assuring him that the pound sterling was almost certain to be devalued again in advance of Britain's entry to the EEC and that this, whatever its disadvantages, would at least afford both countries some 'residual' protection against the stronger Continental members. On top of the formal devaluation of 1967, the floating of sterling since mid-1972 has had this effect. Ireland's main problem is to hold its competitive position in relation to Britain. It has been estimated that, as late as 1966, the tariffs and export incentives were the equivalent of a 19 per cent. devaluation of the Irish currency in relation to sterling; that is, their removal on a unilateral basis without reciprocal concessions by Ireland's trading partners would require a devaluation of this magnitude to restore equilibrium in the balance of payments.[21] Given that the tariff instrument has been set aside, that export aids may not endure for ever, and that the EEC is committed to move towards a monetary union in which exchange parities will be irrevocable, Seán Lemass would undoubtedly endorse all the emphasis which Ireland has placed on the need for effective Community policies, financed by adequate regional, social and investment funds, to mitigate the economic imbalance between the member countries. These matters are now the concern of other statesmen. We can salute Seán Lemass for having so effectively pursued policies which have taken Ireland from the embattled and impoverished protectionism of the nineteen thirties into the more exposed but also better-off nineteen seventies.

---

21. Dermot McAleese, *'Effective Tariffs and the Structure of Industrial Protection in Ireland'*, Economic and Social Research Institute, Paper No. 62, Dublin, June 1971.

[3]

Excerpt from Mark Patrick Hederman and Richard Kearney (eds), *Ireland: Dependence and Independence*, 68–77.

The Failure of Economic Nationalism

Peter Neary*

"We are suffering just now from a bad attack of economic pessimism."

These are the opening words of a lecture by one of the greatest economists of the century, John Maynard Keynes, entitled "Economic Possibilities for our Grandchildren." It was delivered in 1930, at the lowest point of the British Great Depression. Yet Keynes's words seem to catch the mood of 1984 just as accurately as they caught that of 1930, in spite of the enormous economic progress since then. Is our current economic pessimism justified? What lessons for economic policy can be learned from our past experience? And what measures could be taken to improve the economic possibilities for ourselves and for our grandchildren?

In trying to answer these questions this evening, I want to relate my discussion to the general theme of these lectures: the ways in which *political* independence for the twenty-six counties since 1922 has interacted with continuing *dependence* on foreign events and ideas. I want to suggest that, especially in the economic sphere, a failure to recognise this dependence — what I will call "economic nationalism" — has been responsible for many of our mistakes of economic policy — mistakes that could have been avoided.

Economic nationalism can take many forms, but in Ireland the first which comes to mind is summed up by the phrase "Sinn Fein." At least when first used by Arthur Griffith in the 1900s, this phrase stood to a considerable extent for a basic economic principle: that self-sufficiency was the route to economic development. Griffith argued that Ireland's economic decline in the 19th century was caused by the Union with Britain; that the opening of Irish markets to British firms had wiped out whole sectors of Irish industry and prevented the establishment of others; and that the only route to industrial development was to impose tariffs on imports and so encourage the growth of Irish firms protected from foreign competition.

Nowadays, many economists and historians would disagree with this simplified view of history. But it was readily accepted by Griffith's followers; economic nationalism became a central part of the policies of the Sinn Fein movement; and, though neglected by the Cumann na nGaedheal governments of the 1920s, it was wholeheartedly adopted by the Fianna Fail governments from 1932 onwards, led by Eamon de Valera. High tariffs were imposed on a wide range of imported goods; foreign control of Irish firms was penalised; and strenuous efforts were made to encourage self-sufficiency in all branches of industrial and agricultural production.

In trying to judge the success of these measures, we have to keep in mind the circumstances of the time. For one thing, the 1930s was the period of the Economic War with Britain. De Valera's refusal to pay land annuities to Britain led to a cold war between the two countries, during which each imposed barriers on imports from the other. Hence, any favourable effects of protection had to coexist with the collapse of our export markets. In any case, for de Valera himself, economic issues were only one aspect of the continuing struggle for complete independence from Britain; for him, economic nationalism was an instrument of political nationalism, not an end in itself. In addition, the 1930s was a decade of world-wide depression. Faced with mass unemployment, more and more countries abandoned the principles of free trade, trying to protect their own industries and to dump their surplus produce on foreign markets. So, a similar response might well have been forced on us in any case, whether we wanted it or not. Certainly, it would have been unavoidable during the Second World War, when the disruption of world trade forced us back on our own resources for everything from textiles to tobacco.

We should recognise therefore, that economic nationalism in the 1930s and 1940s was largely inspired by political considerations and might have been unavoidable in any case. This said, the question must be asked: how successful was this strategy in encouraging economic development? From some points of view, the policy was extremely successful. For example, industrial employment grew by over 7,000 jobs a year for much of the decade — an achievement not equalled even in the prosperous 1960s and 1970s. But this growth did not really represent an industrial revolution. Rather, it was a once-off adjustment as local firms expanded or established to fill the gaps resulting from the increased cost of imports. The firms involved were relatively small in scale; they were almost completely oriented towards the home market; and they were to show little potential for further growth in future years. Moreover, the emergence of these firms did not mean a genuine increase in self-sufficiency. On the contrary, the value of imports (other than food) actually rose during the 1930s. Then, as now, a substantial proportion of our imports consisted of raw materials or semi-processed goods. The expansion of domestic industry raised our dependence on these rather than lowering it.

Overall, therefore, the policy of economic nationalism, inspired by Griffith and implemented by de Valera, must be judged a failure. This became painfully clear in the 1950s. The special circumstances of the preceding decades — world depression and world war — no longer applied, and the rest of Europe began to grow at extremely rapid rates. But Ireland failed to share in this prosperity. Industrial output stagnated; the flight from the land accelerated; and emigration grew to frightening levels, not seen since the worst years of famine and land war in the 19th century. Between 1951 and 1961 almost half a million people left the country. Many of those who remained behind began to wonder aloud whether an independent Ireland could ever be a viable economic unit.

Indeed, a new feature in the 1950s, which has continued up to the present day, was the much greater attention given to the nation's economic performance in public debates. Partly this was because of a greater awareness of what was being achieved in other countries. It was impossible to ignore, for example, how Northern Ireland was benefiting from the introduction of the Welfare State. This was surely the ultimate failure of economic nationalism: not only did it erect barriers between the economies of North and South, but it failed to prevent an increasing divergence of living standards between the two parts of the island. It thus threatened to undermine one of the fundamental bases of political nationalism itself.

Another reason for the increasing attention given to economic performance was a gradual shift in attitudes as the age of de Valera gave way to the age of Lemass. A new generation was growing up which took political independence for granted; and the form which that independence should take ceased to be controversial with the declaration of the Republic in 1949. Newspaper editorials and political speeches might still refer to the need to end Partition and to revive the Irish language; but more and more attention was focussed on the need for material prosperity. It is hardly an exaggeration to say that, for better or worse, in the 1950s, political nationalism was replaced by materialism as the dominant theme of political debates.

By these new higher standards, therefore, economic nationalism was increasingly seen to have failed. The high tariffs erected in the 1930s insulated our industry from foreign competition and discouraged it from seeking export markets; while our continuing restrictions on foreign ownership cut us off from the increasingly mobile flows of international investment. In the 1950s, a consensus emerged that these policies had failed; and, in a remarkably short period of time, a complete reversal of economic policy took place. The whole structure of economic self-sufficiency which had been erected in the 1930s was dismantled and a new set of much more outward-looking policies instituted instead. The requirement of minimum levels of Irish ownership in all new firms was abolished; a range of tax and grant inducements was introduced, supplementing our many natural advantages as a location for foreign investment; and domestic industry was exposed first to the threat of foreign competition and then to its gradually dawning reality with the signing of the Anglo-Irish Free Trade Area Agreement in 1965 and our accession to the European Economic Community in 1973.

Of course, these new outward-looking policies were not the only reason for the dramatic improvement in economic performance which took place around 1958. Our export markets, especially in Britain, improved around this time; and some bad mistakes of budgetary policy which were made in the 1950s were not repeated. But it seems undeniable that it was the reorientation of our policies towards international trade and international investment which really made the difference.

And what a difference! The figures speak for themselves. For example, the 1966 Census was the first since the Great Famine to show an appreciable rise in population; emigration in the 1960s and 1970s fell to a trickle; and the annual rate of growth of national income, which had been low or negative in the 1950s, averaged around 4% throughout the 1960s and 1970s. Behind these figures was the reality of continuing growth in incomes for many as well as a long-overdue extension of the social welfare system. Of course, not everything in the garden was rosy: economic development failed to solve some old problems (such as unemployment and the flight from the land); and it contributed to some new ones (such as pollution and inner-city decline). But it was clear that the country had turned a corner. The old despondency of the 1950s disappeared as Ireland participated fully in the worldwide economic boom of the 1960s and early 1970s.

Economic nationalism in the sense of a policy of self-suffiency clearly failed therefore; but the failure was recognised and appropriate changes in policy were made. So far this sounds like a story with a happy ending. However, the very success of the new economic policies became associated with a different but equally dangerous form of economic nationalism; a tendency to exaggerate our ability to control our own destiny. In particular, we tended to give a lot of the credit for the improvement in the economy to a new development: the arrival of economic planning. Economic planning may be said to have started in Ireland in 1958, with the publication of the First Programme for Economic Expansion. This document was a landmark in Irish economic history: for the first time the government set out a comprehensive statement of its policies and objectives, not just for one year ahead but for the following five years. The Programme was also a landmark in that it explicitly admitted that self-sufficiency had failed and it called for a change in policy. It stressed the need for agriculture and industry to modernise, so that they could compete on world markets. And it looked forward to the arrival of free trade as an opportunity for Ireland to participate in worldwide economic growth.

In all these respects the First Programme was a hugh improvement on anything which had gone before. The changes in economic policy which preceded and followed it were rightly given credit for the turn-around in our economic fortunes. It is hardly an exaggeration to say that, but for them, many of us would not now be here. But success on this scale calls for a repeat performance. The First Programme was followed by a Second and a Third, between them covering the years from 1963 to 1972; and similar (though more modest) documents were issued by the Coalition government of 1973 and the

Fianna Fail government of 1977. As each of these documents followed the other, the tendency to see them as directly influencing our economic development increased. They were given credit for our successes while the response to our failures tended to be another plan or programme, rather than a rethink of the whole strategy of economic planning. All of this was in spite of a curious fact which tended to be ignored by everyone apart from a few academic economists: the fact was, that as actual forecasts of the economy's development, the programmes and plans were extremely poor. They were not even very accurate as a summary of the government's own policies.[1]

These points can be made about all the programmes and plans, including the First Programme for Economic Expansion. For example, it suggested that an annual growth rate of 2% might be achievable from 1958 onwards. In fact the Programme proved to be far too cautious: the actual growth rate was closer to 4% a year. The First Programme also emphasised the growth potential of agriculture, yet it was industry which proved to be the dynamic sector (especially new, export-oriented industry). The Programme called for a shift away from social investment (like schools and hospitals) towards what it called "productive" investment; yet this did not really take place. And it called for a reduction in the level of taxation which then and since has also failed to materialise. Many other examples can be given of the gaps between plan and reality in the cases of the other programmes. The Second Programme, for example, set growth targets for the years 1963 to 1970 which were very close to the average performance of the economy over that period; but in fact the good years during that period came after 1967, the year when the Second Programme was officially abandoned.

The conclusion I draw from all this is that the Programmes were not really the cause of the economic progress which occured in the 1960s and early 1970s. They accompanied it and charted its course. And the First Programme in particular ushered in the new outward-looking policies towards foreign trade and investment. But it was these policies, rather than the programmes themselves, which caused the Irish economy to take off.

Did it matter if we gave ourselves a little more credit than we deserved for our own growth? To a large extent it did not matter; nicely-produced documents full of noble aspirations and sound advice did no harm so long as we pursued appropriate policies and so long as the rest of the world continued to grow. But always behind our approach to planning there lurked dangers: the danger that we would neglect the external constraints facing our small open economy; the danger that we would not be flexible enough to respond to changes in these constraints; and the danger that we would build up expectations of continued growth which could not be realised.

All these dangers became real with the coming to power of the 1977 Fianna Fail government. Critics of that government's policies sometimes forget that all of them had been adopted by previous governments. Reliance on foreign borrowing; the use of government spending to raise employment without great attention to the efficiency of that spending; and the attempt to build up confidence and optimism in the private sector; these had all been characteristics of earlier governments' policies. What was new about the approach in 1977 was that all these elements were brought together and carried further than they had ever been. That Government's statement of objectives — the White Paper "National Development 1977-1980" — did not read very differently from earlier plans and white papers. But it took the rhetoric of planning seriously. Where earlier plans had talked about achieving full employment, this one meant what it said.

It was a brave strategy but a risky one. It gambled on continued growth in the rest of the world; and it gambled on Irish workers being willing to accept lower wage increases than our competitor countries, so that we could increase our share of growing world trade. Regrettably, both bets lost. In particular, the second oil crisis of 1979 plunged the Western World into the worst recession since before the Second World War. Our exports faltered but imports, fuelled by foreign borrowing, continued to grow. From the beginning, the dangers of these policies were pointed out by economists. But for a long time, their warnings fell on deaf ears. It is easy to understand why: for, whether justified or not by the underlying trend of production, the economy was booming. I remember some years ago, a friend of mine asking me: "Why are all you economists so pessimistic? Everywhere you look people are prosperous: they are buying new cars, buying new houses, taking foreign holidays and so on." I had to point out that it was precisely that apparent prosperity, or rather, that boom in consumption, which was the problem. For, whether the individuals involved could afford it or not, the country as a whole could not; and as a result we were building up foreign debt at an unsustainable rate.

Today, that lesson has been learned. Politicians of all parties agree on the need to bring the public finances back to order. To take just one example, the 1982 Fianna Fail economic plan ("The Way Forward") showed a much greater awareness than previous plans of our vulnerability to what is going on in the rest of the world. Indeed, we may have overreacted, as Government and Opposition vie with each other in their zeal to cut the current budget deficit — rather like rival pilots of a ship who devote all their energies to controlling the flow of smoke from the funnel. Though Keynesian economics is out of fashion nowadays, we should not forget one of its important messages: that the level of the Budget Deficit will vary with the level of economic activity.[2] Slowing down the engine will reduce the flow of smoke but does nothing to ensure that the ship is moving in the right direction. In fact, whether the deficit is reduced to zero in four or eight years is not of enormous importance in itself. What matters is that public spending (whether it is of the current or capital variety) be required to pass stringent tests of economic efficiency and that no politician or public speaker be allowed to call for tax cuts or increases in government spending without specifying how they are to be financed. It is only by these means that we can avoid falling once again into the second trap of economic nationalism which I have discussed.

I have talked so far about economic nationalism at the levels of events and actions. But there is yet another sense of the term I want to point out: economic nationalism at the level of ideas. By this I mean a failure to pay attention to economic ideas which are current abroad; and a failure to take note of and to learn from the economic experiences of other countries. This form of economic nationalism is perhaps the most dangerous, for the problems associated with the other forms are by now well understood. It would, I hope, take a huge change in attitudes or in world conditions before we repeated the mistakes of excluding foreign investment or over-borrowing to try and achieve full employment. But in the realm of ideas there are many lessons which we have still not learned; and whether or not we learn them may have a lot to do with how we progress economically in the years to come. Unfortunately, there is often resistance to the suggestion that economic ideas and principles which have been developed in other countries are relevant here. Many people seem to think that there is something distinctively Irish about the way our economy operates. To some extent, of course, this is true. But the laws of physics do not stop at Holyhead; and, although economics is not an exact science in the same sense as physics, its lessons are just as applicable on this side of the Irish Sea as elsewhere. Moreover, many of its messages are simple common sense: if we want to raise employment, we should not subsidise employers to use more capital or tax them on the labour they employ; if we want to encourage productive investment, we should not tolerate a tax system which subsidises investment in property rather than in industry; and if we want to foster economic growth, we should be wary of using scarce funds to prop up declining firms; and we should think twice before creating yet more government agencies charged with picking winners in an era of extraordinarily rapid technological change.[3] These are some of the many things we can learn from economic ideas current abroad.

A second way in which we need to broaden our horizons is to learn from the economic experience of other countries; in particular, we should look further than the British case, on which our traditions usually lead us to focus exclusively. Equally relevant to us is the experience of other smaller European countries whose economic structures more closely resemble our own. Studying their experience can be revealing and can also be heartening, for it demonstrates that, where making mistakes in economic policy is concerned, we are not alone. Thus Belgium's unemployment and foreign debt record is little better than ours; Sweden has gone to much greater lengths to prop up declining industries and to restrict labour mobility; and Norway, for all its oil wealth, has publicly-supported white elephants which dwarf our Knock airports, electrified railways and NET's. As for overall economic performance, a recent study of this in seven smaller European countries[4] shows that all have attempted to adapt to the crises of the 1970s with some combination of the same basic policy tools which have been advocated here — incomes policy, demand deflation and devaluation. The study concludes that "there appears to be no painless method."

However, in looking at these and other foreign countries there do appear to be two alternative approaches which have coped remarkably well with the recent recession. One, which might be called the Austrian model, relies on centralised wage bargaining and an explicit social contract with a very high degree of good-will between government, business and trade unions. As a result, when the oil price rises and other shocks of the 1970s reduced real national income, real wages were reduced in line. Since many of Austria's competitors did not adopt the same strategy her industries obtained a competitive edge which enabled her to keep unemployment below 4% and to maintain an almost uninterrupted growth in industrial production throughout the 1970s. The alternative model, which we may identify with the strategy pursued in the United States, is a highly decentralised system, very responsive to the pressures of supply and demand. As a result, unemployment rose dramatically in the U.S. after both oil crises, but fell again even more dramatically after a very short period. As my colleague Brendan Walsh has recently pointed out, this was accompanied by an amazingly successful performance with regard to employment.[5] Fifteen million jobs were created between 1973 and 1981: all in a period during which EEC employment stagnated and in a country where there are no public agencies charged with deliberately fostering economic performance.

Now, I am not suggesting for a moment that we should try to impose either the Austrian or the American models in Ireland. But I do think we have much to learn from both. In particular, I would like to note that probably the major characteristic of both these successful models is their adaptability to changing economic circumstances. In this respect, we in Ireland have no choice as to whether our economy is dependent on the ups and downs of world markets; the choice we face is in whether we choose to adapt to the new challenges which confront us; or whether we try to maintain living standards which are (temporarily) no longer affordable. For, if we follow the second course, we may threaten our ability to participate in the coming upturn in the world economy.

To conclude, I have tried to argue this evening that economic nationalism has failed us in a number of different ways. In the area of international trade and investment, the Sinn Fein approach failed to promote economic development. In the area of planning, the "go for growth" of the 1970s failed to recognise the constraints facing a small open economy. Finally, in the realm of ideas, our tendency to look for Irish solutions to Irish problems fails to draw on the economic ideas and experiences of other countries. But I would also argue that there are dangers in overreacting to our mistakes. Certainly, we should not delude ourselves into thinking that we have complete control of our economic fortunes. But we should not go to the other extreme either: to throw up our hands in resignation; and to say that there is no hope for us unless American interest rates come down or EEC farm prices go up or some new crock of gold (like a nice large oil field) is discovered. Of course, whether or not these happen will have a large impact on our future prosperity. But, one way or another, there are a great many positive things which we can do ourselves. In particular, we must do everything in our power to ensure the flexibility of living standards, of economic structure and of ideas and attitudes which a constantly changing economic climate requires of us. This means a willingness to adopt tax reform, a willingness to adopt civil service reform, a willingness to accept that some established industries must inevitably decline in the process of economic growth, and to plan ahead accordingly. Above all, it means an ability to learn from our mistakes without overreacting to them.

The phrase "Sinn Fein" is often translated as "Ourselves Alone", and I have criticised this evening the economic strategy that implies. But perhaps a looser translation — "doing our own thing" — comes closer to describing the balance we require between dependence and independence — between turning our backs on the world economy and thinking we can do nothing until it improves. We owe it to ourselves and to *our* grandchildren to try and strike this balance as we cope with our current economic difficulties.

* Without implicating them in the final product, I would like to thank the following for helpful comments on earlier drafts: P.T. Geary, D. McAleese, M. McCarthy, J. Neary, B. O'Buachalla, C. O'Grada, G. Quinn, F.P. Ruane and B.M. Walsh.

1. For further details, see O. Katsiaouni, "Planning in a Small Economy: The Republic of Ireland", *Journal of the Statistical and Social Inquiry Society of Ireland*, 1977-78, pp.217-256; and J.P. Neary, "Economic Planning in Ireland: The First Twenty-Five Years" (in preparation).

2. The importance of correcting the measured budget deficit for the effects of inflation and unemployment is demonstrated in B.R. Dowling, "Budget Deficits and Fiscal Policy", in B.R. Dowling and J. Durkan (eds.), *Irish Economic Policy: A Review of Major Issues*, Dublin: ESRI, 1978 pp.151-189; and G. Basevi et al., "Macroeconomic Prospects and Policies for the European Community", Centre for European Policy Studies, Economic Paper No. 1, Brussels, 1983.

3. Substantiation of some of the points made here may be found in: Commission on Taxation: First Report — Direct Taxation, Dublin 1982; and F.P. Ruane, "Government Financial and Tax Incentives and Industrial Employment," *Irish Banking Review*, June 1983, pp.20-28.

4. L. Calmfors: "Cost Adjustment in Smaller OECD Countries," *Skandinaviska Enskilda Banken Quarterly Review*, 1982, pp.111-119.

5. B.M. Walsh: "Employment and Competitiveness", Policy Paper No. 7, Centre for Economic Research, University College Dublin, November 1983; forthcoming in: *The World Economy*.

[4]

Excerpt from Thomas Wilson (ed.), *Ulster Under Home Rule*, 91–114.

CHAPTER 5

ULSTER'S ECONOMIC STRUCTURE

By K. S. ISLES and N. CUTHBERT

NORTHERN Ireland is economically so interwoven with Great Britain that, looked at broadly, it is not a separate economy at all but an un-differentiated part of a single economic system embracing the whole of the United Kingdom. This economic unity is closely bound up with political unity. On the one hand, natural conditions promoting economic interdependence with Great Britain form one of the main foundation stones on which political union rests; and, reciprocally, this natural tendency to economic integration has been greatly strengthened by the fact of political union. As a result of political union, and its implied recognition that economic union is desirable, the main policy decisions affecting economic conditions in Northern Ireland are made by the central government and apply indiscriminately to the whole of the United Kingdom; and, likewise, the main economic and financial institutions are common to the whole. Thus Northern Ireland and Great Britain are served by the one monetary and financial system and are both subject to the same monetary policy. Again, though Northern Ireland's fiscal system is not wholly common with that of Great Britain it is very largely so, and even where differences are formally permissible the scope for effective independent action by Northern Ireland is not very great in practice. Then again, social services are in all important respects on the same footing as those in Great Britain; for even though they are formally separate, economic integration is too close in other ways to permit of significant differences. Even more important, between Northern Ireland and Great Britain there is no restriction whatever on the passage of goods or the transfer of capital in either direction; and people are free to move from one to the other without let or hindrance and to live and work wherever they please.[1] Moreover, most of the other economic institutions, such as trade unions, trade associations and wage-fixing machinery, are either unified with those in Great Britain or are run on parallel lines; many of the trade unions, for example, are national bodies with their headquarters in England.

[1] Owing to the existence of heavy unemployment, the government of Northern Ireland has in recent years imposed a system of employment permits in certain occupations with the object of giving preference to local workers. But this restriction does not affect the migration of Northern Ireland workers to Great Britain or their subsequent return.

H

92   ULSTER'S ECONOMIC STRUCTURE

Because of this close integration, industrial growth and economic stability in Northern Ireland are subject to the same general conditions and the same general measures of control as they are in Great Britain. There is therefore a similar trend in economic development. But, as in other regions, production is largely concentrated in the kind of industries most suited to the particular environment; and since the economy of Northern Ireland is therefore not simply a small-scale model of that of Great Britain, important differences can also occur both in the rate of economic development and in the degree of economic stability. Differences do in fact occur mainly because the industries which have become traditionally established in Northern Ireland are very limited in range. It so happens that the pattern of industry suited to the environment is such that some of the general factors retarding growth, and some of those causing instability, tend to bear on Northern Ireland more heavily than they do on the British economy in general. In this respect the province is closely akin to the Development Areas in Great Britain—those areas in which the government gives special encouragement to industrial development because they contain pockets of unemployment. For, like the Development Areas, it is differentiated from the rest of the British economy by having a very specialised industrial structure and unemployment much above the average.

Northern Ireland is set apart from the Development Areas, and is further differentiated economically from Great Britain, by the fact that it is a separate area of subordinate government. It is thus in the unique position of having control over its own domestic affairs. This, however, is not to say that its economic differentiation from Great Britain would inevitably be less marked than it is if this constitutional difference did not exist: the pattern of industry would not necessarily be either more or less varied than it is, nor would the general economic state of the province necessarily be more satisfactory or less satisfactory. For, on the one hand, there is no reason in principle why a central government should feel itself debarred from singling out the problems of any particular area for separate treatment; indeed, the Development Areas have already been singled out in this way. On the other hand, while a provincial government might find the limitation of its powers a serious handicap in dealing effectively with certain provincial needs, a central government might be expected generally to be less well apprised of what the changing provincial needs are. It must therefore not be taken for granted, as something which is self-evident, that domestic autonomy has been a dominating factor in causing Northern Ireland's present economic position to be what it is. Nevertheless, the Government of Northern Ireland certainly

ULSTER'S ECONOMIC STRUCTURE 93

does possess considerable powers of control over the rate and pattern of industrial growth and, as we shall see, it has in fact made a good deal of use of them. Hence, notwithstanding the difficulties, some attempt will be made to see how far the course of economic development has been due to the particular constitution, and how far it has been determined by the basic economic facts.

Provincial self-government has had an important indirect effect by focusing attention on the differences which exist between economic conditions in Northern Ireland, looked at in total, and those in the whole of the United Kingdom. Since the care of industrial development within its own borders is one of the provincial government's chief functions, governmental authorities and the public alike have had it thrust upon their notice that industrial growth in Northern Ireland is hampered by special difficulties, requiring special treatment, apart from those affecting the whole country. Separate statistical data relating to economic conditions in Northern Ireland, and bearing on those special problems, are therefore regularly collected and published. Although these data are disappointingly inadequate for a thorough study of the provincial economy, they do contain information not available for other regions of the United Kingdom. Moreover, apart from the official statistics, which are collected for the province as an entity because it is a separate area of government, certain other economic statistics relating to the whole region can be collected, more readily than for specific regions in Great Britain, because it is separated from them geographically. For these two reasons many of the data required in the study of economic conditions in Northern Ireland can be obtained even by the private investigator.

Economic conditions in Northern Ireland illustrate some of the main difficulties by which industrial development is hampered in the more outlying parts of the United Kingdom generally. It is therefore important that the factors responsible for these conditions should be understood, outside Northern Ireland as well as inside. For regional diversity within the United Kingdom is so pronounced that it may significantly affect the way in which some, at least, of the general economic measures work out on balance in the country as a whole. It is specially liable to distort the effects of measures for controlling the general level of employment. Modern employment theories, and the general policies based upon them, are largely derived from a consideration of the mutual dependence which exists between various aggregate quantities for the whole country. Thus budgetary policy (formulated with an eye to the effects on levels of income, prices and employment for the whole country) takes account of such entities as the total national income, total expenditure on consumption, total savings, total exports, imports and the balance of payments, and the total amount of investment (replacing and increasing the country's stock of capital goods) that would consequently be great enough to sustain a high level of employment without promoting a cumulative rise in prices. It is recognised that in any region or regions with persistently heavy unemployment investment in new industry may need to be given special encouragement. But in considering how much additional investment would be required at any time in order to give some desired fillip to total employment, it is implicitly assumed that the total effect would be the same whichever region received the initial stimulus of the investment. Although this is a natural assumption to make in the absence of greater knowledge than we at present possess about the factors governing employment in individual regions, it is one which obviously needs to be checked as soon as possible through regional studies.

Moreover, in deciding how best to bring about a desired increase in employment in any particular region in which there is heavy unemployment, as there is and always has been in Northern Ireland, it is important to know how employment (and income) in the region would respond to different stimuli. It is important, for example, to know how far employment (and income) would increase altogether if the government succeeded in bringing about an initial increase, of a given size, by inducing business men to establish new undertakings. Through the expenditure of the additional income associated with it, the direct increase in employment, in or for the new undertakings, would induce some secondary increase in employment (and income) in other industries; but compared with the initial increase this indirect increase might be large or small. It is therefore necessary to study the particular region, and its economic relations with other regions, in order to find out what is the normal ratio for it, between the direct effects on employment and income, caused by an increase in investment, and the direct and indirect effects taken together. It may be that, if the people of the region are very thrifty, induced effects are largely prevented through additional saving. Again, it may be (as it seems to be in Northern Ireland) that they are largely spilled over into other regions through the expenditure of much of the initial increase in income on goods imported from outside. If that is so, and if at the same time employment in the rest of the country is running at a very high level, investment in industrial undertakings in the particular region will not only be so much the less effective in raising the level of employment there, but will also aggravate the inflationary tendencies which will consequently exist in the economy as a whole. Likewise, in these conditions, the steps taken to curb general inflation will aggravate unemployment in

ULSTER'S ECONOMIC STRUCTURE

the particular region. There seems no doubt that the monetary and fiscal policies of the early fifties have had effects of this kind on Northern Ireland. The inference is that the central government should supplement its general data for the whole country with regional studies; since, if it did, it might consider it undesirable to apply all general measures to the different regions indiscriminately.

That provincial self-government has not been extended to other parts of the United Kingdom might seem to imply that it has not worked well. Such an inference would be over-hasty. The system was devised for Northern Ireland not for economic reasons but as a political expedient, as part of the arrangements for settling the Irish constitutional question. In Great Britain it appears still to be regarded essentially in that light. At any rate the central government has shown no inclination to regard it as a serious experiment for testing how well this alternative technique for handling the economic problems of a region works in British conditions. Nevertheless, the control of internal economic matters (within its limited constitutional powers) is among the provincial government's most important functions. The question therefore arises whether, in economic matters, this form of government is more effective than control from the centre—and might with advantage be extended to other clearly-defined regions such as Scotland and Wales—or whether it is a handicap and should be abandoned even for Northern Ireland. There is also the important supplementary question whether in the light of experience there appear to be any significant respects in which the powers exercised by the provincial government could with advantage be modified. A full discussion of these questions would be out of place in a general work like the present, especially as it would involve detailed comparisons with other regions whose data would have to be specially collected and analysed; but some of the relevant considerations will be briefly touched upon in Chapter 7.

Since Northern Ireland is merely a sector of the British economy, subject to the same general conditions as the rest of the country, its economic position can best be discussed in relation to that of the United Kingdom in general. In what follows, therefore, the complex of external conditions and internal policies which are common to the whole will be taken for granted, and the discussion will be confined to the special economic problems and policies of Northern Ireland regarded as a region with limited powers of self-government. This means that the object will be to indicate the nature, causes and effects of those features of its economic structure which cause the trend of economic development to diverge somewhat from the common trend. Hence in assessing these

96   ULSTER'S ECONOMIC STRUCTURE

various conditions in the economic life of the province the method will
be to relate them to, and measure them against, their counterparts for
either Great Britain or the United Kingdom as a whole, whichever is the
more relevant in each particular case; for only in this way can their
significance be judged.

The present chapter, on Northern Ireland's economic structure, will
examine the main features of the provincial economy and their mutual
dependence; in Chapter 7, on economic policy, an outline will be given
of the provincial government's powers and the chief policies which it has
pursued; some comments will be made on the effectiveness of these
policies and on the possibilities of making use of other devices which
formally come within its existing powers; and attention will be drawn
to the possible need for enlarging its effective powers by making its
financial relations with the central government more flexible and more
liberal.

(a) *Area and Population.* Northern Ireland has an area of 5,238
square miles. At the time of the 1951 Population Census it had a population of 1,371,000. There was an average population density of 262 per
square mile, compared with 755 per square mile in England and Wales
and 172 in Scotland. Within Northern Ireland itself, however, the population is very unevenly distributed, about 53 per cent of the total living
in urban areas. What is even more striking is that about two-fifths of the
total are in Belfast and the surrounding towns and villages; a fact which
emphasises that this compact region must play a highly important part
in the social and economic life of the province. The age distribution of
the population differs somewhat from that of Great Britain, partly, at
least, because there is a somewhat higher rate of natural increase. Thus,
at the 1951 Census, there was a smaller proportion of the population
than in Great Britain (72·4 per cent compared with 77·5 per cent) who
were over 15 years (i.e. of working age or above it) and a correspondingly
higher proportion under 15. On the other hand, the difference in the
proportion of the population gainfully occupied is small.

According to the Census figures the proportion of the total population gainfully occupied is practically the same as in Great Britain. On
the one hand, the proportion gainfully occupied, taking males and
females separately, is lower than in Great Britain in the main working-
age group, 15-65. But, on the other hand, the proportion is considerably
higher, for both sexes, in the age-group 65 and over; it is also higher
in the age group under 15, since in Northern Ireland the school leaving-
age is still 14.

Northern Ireland is an area from which there is a fairly large migration

ULSTER'S ECONOMIC STRUCTURE   97

of people. Between 1926 and 1951 there was a net emigration of about 10 per cent of the total size of the population at the outset.

TABLE 1

NET LOSS (OR GAIN) BY MIGRATION PER 1,000 OF POPULATION

	Scotland	*United Kingdom*	*Northern Ireland*
1921–31 ..	−80	−15	−82
1931–39 ..	− 7	+11	− 4
1939–49 ..	−21	+ 4	−35

Source: Registrars-General.

Table 1 shows that, over the past three decades taken as a whole, emigration from the United Kingdom has been about balanced by immigration. By contrast, Scotland and Northern Ireland have both lost fairly heavily, the rate of loss in Northern Ireland being rather higher than in Scotland. Between 1926 and 1937 about one-third of the net loss was to European countries, including Great Britain—principally, no doubt, Great Britain. This net emigration to Great Britain (or continental Europe) during the eleven years taken together amounted in total to only about 20,000 people. But from estimates which we have made for the individual years, it appears that the annual net flow, in or out, was in most years quite large in comparison with the net movement during the whole period. The evidence goes to show that there is a fairly large mobile section of the population which moves to and fro between Northern Ireland and Great Britain in response to changing conditions of employment.

(*b*) *The Industrial Structure*. The industrial structure of Northern Ireland has three outstanding features. These are: firstly, the predominance of agriculture, which is by far the biggest single industry whether judged by the number of persons gainfully occupied or by the value of net output; secondly, the almost complete lack of extractive industries apart from agriculture; and, thirdly, the high degree of concentration of industrial workers in a very few industries. These features are shown up, with varying degrees of clarity, by the following table, which gives the industrial distribution of the 470,000 employees insured under the National Insurance Acts at May 1954.

Table 2 greatly underrates the real importance of agriculture since it covers only employees and not family workers. It is estimated that of the 603,000 persons gainfully occupied in Northern Ireland, almost 105,000

ULSTER'S ECONOMIC STRUCTURE

TABLE 2

INDUSTRIAL DISTRIBUTION OF INSURED WORKERS IN
NORTHERN IRELAND AT MAY 1954

Industry	Percentage of all insured workers
Production:	
Agriculture	4·0
Forestry and fishing	0·4
Mining and quarrying	0·9
All production	5·3
Manufacture:	
Building and contracting	8·1
Treatment of non-metalliferous products (other than coal or oil)	0·9
Shipbuilding	3·6
Engineering	5·0
Vehicles	4·0
Linen	9·9
Other textiles	5·5
Clothing	7·6
Food, drink and tobacco	5·3
Manufactures of wood and cork	1·1
Paper and printing	1·2
Other manufacturing industries	1·6
All manufacturing industries	53·8
Services:	
All Service industries	40·8
Unclassified	0·1
Total	100·0

Source: Ministry of Labour.

or about one-sixth, are engaged in agriculture. This compares with about 5 per cent for the United Kingdom as a whole. As regards male labour the contrast is still more striking. At the Northern Ireland Census of 1951, 24 per cent of all gainfully occupied males were engaged in this industry, while the comparative figure for Great Britain, as shown by the Census of the same year, was only 6 per cent. But, as Table 2 shows, agriculture ranks among the most important industries of the province even when judged by the number of insured employees.

The predominant form of agricultural organisation in Northern

ULSTER'S ECONOMIC STRUCTURE   99

Ireland is the small farm worked mainly by the farmer and his family,
and only calling on outside labour at busy seasons of the year. The Census
of the Ministry of Agriculture taken at June 1952, for example, shows
that, of the total of 145,000 persons gainfully occupied in agriculture in
any capacity, paid workers formed less than one-sixth. Of late years the
tendency has been for this proportion to fall. At the same time there has
been a noticeable decrease in the amplitude of the seasonal variations
in employment of insured agricultural workers. For the three years
1937–8 to 1939–40 the average amplitude of these seasonal variations,
away from the employment trend, was about 29 per cent of the average
volume of employment represented by the trend figures. For the years
1942–3 and 1943–4 the average variation was only 11 per cent of the
trend. Although it has risen somewhat since the war it still lies well
below the pre-war average; thus, for the three years 1947–8 to 1949–50,
it was less than 20 per cent.

Small-scale farming is much more typical of agriculture in Northern
Ireland than in Great Britain. In 1952, for example, 78 per cent of farms
in Northern Ireland were under 50 acres in extent, compared with 64 per
cent in Great Britain. At the other end of the scale, only 2·4 per cent of
Northern Ireland farms were over 150 acres, compared with 12·1 per
cent in Great Britain. In fact the contrast is even greater than these
figures suggest. For "rough grazing" is excluded from the figures for
Great Britain but is included in those for Northern Ireland. But even
though the figures for Northern Ireland do contain this bias, the mean
size of holding is only about 36 acres compared with 100 acres in Great
Britain.

There are two other general points of contrast between farming in
Northern Ireland and Great Britain apart from the size of holdings.
Firstly, owing to such factors as the difference in soil fertility, the greater
distance to the main British markets, and the smaller range of climatic
differences, Northern Ireland has a different pattern of production and a
smaller range of products. Because of these physical differences, the
tendency has been towards proportionately more livestock farming
than in Great Britain and proportionately less arable farming. The
second point of contrast is that, by and large, Northern Ireland suffers
from a deficiency, compared with Great Britain, in agricultural equipment. Although this relative deficiency cannot be accurately measured,
it is well authenticated and has been officially stressed, as recently as
1947, in the Report of the Agricultural Inquiry Committee. In that
report it was pointed out that, in many parts of Ulster to-day, farmers
and labourers are working with implements which show little advance on

those used a century ago. This comment refers more particularly to the position on the smaller farms, where the deficiency has been largely due to the farmers' lack of capital. Nevertheless, there has been a considerable increase in mechanisation of late, even on the smaller farms, especially since the beginning of the war. Between 1939 and 1945 the number of tractors increased ninefold, and there has been an increasing tendency for small farmers to make use of up-to-date equipment by getting work done on contract. However, the relative lack of equipment still persists. There is evidence for this in the greater number of persons per acre engaged in farming in Northern Ireland than in Great Britain. A strict comparison is not possible in this respect, both because of the greater proportion of part-time workers on Northern Ireland farms and also because of differences, noted above, in the composition of the total output. But even if only regular male workers are taken into account, the difference is still very marked. In 1951 there were 30·2 regular male workers per thousand acres in Northern Ireland, compared with 21·5 in Great Britain.

The dominance of agriculture in Northern Ireland is shown not only by the large share which it takes of the working population but also by the large proportionate contribution which it makes to the total income. We estimate that in 1951 the total income earned by all persons gainfully occupied on farms was £37·6 million, or 17 per cent of the total private civilian income of the province. In the United Kingdom in the same year the corresponding proportion amounted to about 6 per cent. In view of the much greater dependence of the population on agriculture in Northern Ireland than in the United Kingdom as a whole, both for employment and income, it is not surprising that the provincial government has made special efforts to increase agricultural income. As we shall see in Chapter 7, it has done so by improving both the standard of husbandry and the methods of marketing the produce.

The second important feature of the industrial structure indicated by the distribution of man-power in Table 2 is the small proportion of the total engaged in extractive industries. The reason is that there are no important mineral deposits that can be profitably worked. Although small deposits of coal are to be found here and there, they are all unworkable (except on a very small scale in one or two places) because of severe faulting. The chief products of the mining and quarrying industry are limestone, sand, gravel, road metal and granite. These provide materials for the building and construction industries and for the manufacture of cement and bricks, though not in sufficient quantities to provide for all the needs of the province. The lack of domestic sources of coal and of the

ULSTER'S ECONOMIC STRUCTURE   101

principal minerals required in the basic heavy industries is one of the greatest handicaps to industrial development, It greatly narrows the range of industries which can be profitably carried on in the province—in particular, the range of industries which employ men. At the same time, by raising the cost of power to all industries, it reduces the profitability, and hence the vitality, of those industries which are nevertheless able to take root.

Owing to these effects, the lack of mineral resources is itself one of the main reasons for the third distinctive feature of the industrial structure—namely, the concentration of a large proportion of the workers in a very few industries. Another important reason for this specialisation on a few industries is that the domestic market for many varieties of goods is too small to permit of production on a profitable scale unless part of the output can be exported, either to Great Britain or abroad. Production even for the local market therefore tends to be limited to goods which, being light and valuable in proportion to their bulk, can compete success-fully in Great Britain—that is, to light industries with comparatively low costs of transport. The textile industries form the most important group, accounting for about 30 per cent of the total number of workers engaged in manufacturing. Another unified group consists of engineering, vehicle building and repairing, and shipbuilding. This group provides employment for about another 20 per cent of the total. Thus the two groups, each composed of closely related industries, together employ about half the total workers engaged in manufacture. A feature of the two groups is that from the point of view of employment they are com-plementary rather than competitive. In the textile group almost two-thirds of the workers are women, while in the engineering, vehicle and shipbuilding group there is a preponderance of men.

For purposes of comparison we have roughly classified manufacturing trades into two groups, according to whether they produce instrumental goods or consumption goods. The industrial subdivisions used by the Ministry of Labour are not detailed enough to enable this to be done accurately. But it appears that about one-third of all insured male workers in Northern Ireland are employed in instrumental trades. This figure represents about two-thirds of the total males insured in manufacturing industries, which is a substantially higher proportion than in Great Britain. The industrial distribution of insured women workers, on the other hand, is very different. Slightly more than half of the total (or 90 per cent of those insured in manufacturing) are engaged in consumption-goods industries.

These facts indicate much of the weakness in Northern Ireland's

industrial structure. Since industries producing capital goods are subject to wider variations in employment than consumption industries
and services, depression tends to strike Northern Ireland with unusual
severity, causing heavy unemployment, particularly among men. Moreover, though most of the female workers are employed in consumption-
goods industries, this does not have as great a stabilising effect as might
be expected *à priori*. The reason is that employment in this group is
heavily concentrated on a few industries which do not enjoy as much
stability as most consumption industries, particularly those producing
necessaries for a sheltered home market. For the goods produced are
largely of a luxury or semi-luxury type, and a large proportion of the
output has to be exported. Easily the most outstanding industry in this
group is the linen industry. This industry alone employs about three-
eighths of all the women engaged in manufacture, and if we include in the
linen industry the making up of linen goods, the proportion is still higher.
The industry has experienced the usual fluctuations of employment
associated with textiles; but since linen is one of the more expensive
fabrics, and since Northern Ireland specialises in the finer grades of
linen, the demand is subject to greater variations than is the demand for
textiles in general.

(c) *Dependence on Exports.* An important result of the high degree of
specialisation on a few manufacturing trades is that economic prosperity
is to a very great extent dependent on external trade. For the provincial
markets of the three main industries—agriculture, textiles, and shipbuilding and engineering—and of others making very specialised products, only absorb a small proportion of their total output; and the
surplus has to be sold outside the province, as a means, in effect, of paying
for imports into it. Official estimates are made of the quantities and value
of goods exported annually to all places outside Northern Ireland's
own borders; but because of differences in the way in which these
external-trade statistics and those of the Census of Production are
grouped it is impossible to estimate with any precision, what proportion
of Northern Ireland's own production is thus exported. From an examination of the figures it appears, however, that the goods exported from
Northern Ireland embody between 60 and 70 per cent of the value of the
total net output of goods produced in the province.

Whatever their final destination, most of these exports are sent
initially to Great Britain. Some go there as sales to merchants, others as
consignments on their way to foreign purchasers. Many of those which
are sold in the first instance in Great Britain are eventually exported to
destinations outside the United Kingdom by the export houses which

ULSTER'S ECONOMIC STRUCTURE   103

buy them. But exports of Northern Irish goods to places outside the United Kingdom (exports in the international as distinct from the interregional sense) cannot be ascertained, at any rate not from published statistics. On the one hand, few direct exports to places outside the United Kingdom are recorded in Northern Ireland's own trade statistics. For few foreign-going ships call at Northern Ireland ports—fewer, indeed, than before the war, a fact which has weakened Northern exporters relatively to their competitors in Great Britain. On the other hand, exports passing through Great Britain, even those consigned to foreign countries, cannot be distinguished from goods produced in Great Britain itself, since in the trade statistics of the United Kingdom exports are classified according to port of shipment. Though exports across the land border with Eire are recorded separately, they include re-exports of goods produced in Great Britain. Hence for an indication of the importance of exports abroad it is helpful to supplement the official statistics by private inquiries. According to a small sample inquiry among business men which we made in 1946, exports to foreign countries accounted for about 45 per cent of the total output of linen and for about 40 per cent of that of engineering products.

The great dependence of Northern Ireland's chief industries on markets outside its own borders has important consequences for the stability of both employment and total income. Between exports and employment there is a direct physical relation. So much of the total production is for export that one would expect an increase in the physical volume of exports to be associated, either as cause or effect, with an increase in employment, and a decrease in exports to be associated with a decrease in employment. One would likewise expect exports and unemployment to be correlated inversely. When the three series are compared with each other over a period—we have examined them for the period since 1924—the expected relationships are clearly discernible, notwithstanding the many conflicting forces which tend to obscure them.

The dependence of total money income on the total value of exports (including those to Great Britain) stands out even more clearly. A comparison which we have made of the two series for the period since 1935 shows that, notwithstanding the great change that has occurred in money values in the meantime, the ratio of the value of exports to money income has been remarkably stable both from year to year and over the whole period: total income has generally been a little more than half as great again as the value of exports. It is not surprising that there should be a fairly close relationship between the value of exports and income earned in producing for export. What is noteworthy is that there

104   ULSTER'S ECONOMIC STRUCTURE

has also been a fairly constant ratio between the value of exports and total income, and therefore between the value of exports and income earned in producing and supplying goods and services for the domestic market. In other words, variations in income earned in export production have generally been accompanied by roughly similar proportional variations in income earned in producing for the home market.

Such changes in the volume and value of exports, together with the associated changes in income and thence imports, are the media through which alterations in economic conditions, either in Great Britain or abroad, are transmitted to Northern Ireland; they are the means by which the provincial balance of payments is kept in equilibrium. When a change in external conditions reduces the amount of income earned in the production of goods sold outside the province, the balance of external payments is equilibrated through a reduction in total income sufficient to bring down imports to a level at which they can be paid for by the reduced value of exports. This adverse effect may be partly offset through an increase in industrial efficiency stimulated by the resulting fall in the rate of profit. In so far as it is not, the reduction in income required to effect the necessary reduction in imports may be brought about either through a fall in rates of wages and profits—relatively to those in Great Britain—or through a relative increase in unemployment.

This explains how Northern Ireland's great dependence on external markets (both for getting raw materials and selling finished goods) acted as a major cause of its depressed state during the period between the wars. It explains the operation of one of the principal sets of forces responsible for the greater severity of the depression in Northern Ireland than in Great Britain. The unemployment rate among insured workers in Northern Ireland was substantially greater than the annual average for Great Britain in every single year throughout the interwar period—and, indeed, it has consistently maintained a higher level right down to the present time. In the very first year for which statistics for Northern Ireland were collected separately, 1923, it averaged almost 18 per cent, whereas in Great Britain it was only about 12 per cent. Though the divergence has tended to be rather smaller in years of comparatively light unemployment than in the worst years, it has been quite appreciable even in the best of times. Thus in 1927 the annual unemployment rate was lower than in any other year from 1923 right down to the early years of the war, and yet it only fell to 13 per cent compared with 9 per cent in Great Britain. In 1938, one of Northern Ireland's worst years of unemployment on record, the divergence was much greater, the corresponding percentages being 28 and 13. The average amount by which the

ULSTER'S ECONOMIC STRUCTURE 105

annual average rate for Northern Ireland *exceeded* that for Great Britain during the years 1923–39, taking the simple arithmetic averages of the annual rates, works out at an unemployment percentage of 8·5. During the interwar period the unemployment rate was substantially higher than in any of the Ministry of Labour's administrative regions in Great Britain with the exception of Wales. Since the war it has been substantially higher than in Wales also. Notwithstanding the great reduction in unemployment throughout the whole of the United Kingdom since 1939, the differential rate in Northern Ireland has continued to be fairly high; from 1945 to 1952 it averaged between 5 and 6 per cent. The pre-war figures of unemployment for Northern Ireland—as, indeed, those of other relatively depressed areas—may in some years have been swollen by the inclusion of returning migrants who were last employed in other regions. For, under the reciprocal arrangements relating to unemployment insurance, unemployed workers may draw their insurance benefit at any employment exchange, at which they are registered, anywhere within the United Kingdom. Considerable numbers of workers do, in fact, migrate from Northern Ireland to jobs in Great Britain, and when trade becomes slack many of them return to their homes in Northern Ireland and register as unemployed there.

(*d*) *Transport Costs.* Where there is neither undue harshness of climate nor deficiency of people willing to work and capable of working efficiently, the problem of location of industry tends to resolve itself into a problem of transport. As we have pointed out above, Northern Ireland is highly dependent on its external trade because of the limited size of the home market and the need to import a high proportion of the raw materials used. In comparison with competing firms in Great Britain, producers in Northern Ireland therefore tend to be at a twofold disadvantage. The extra cost of transport on raw materials, over and above the amount paid by competitors in Great Britain, tends to make their costs of production relatively high; while the corresponding extra cost of transporting the finished goods to market tends to make the net price obtained—the price at the factory—relatively low. This narrowing of the gross margin means that, unless the efficiency of industry in Northern Ireland is maintained at a higher level than in Great Britain, less will be available for distribution among the various factors engaged in production.

The full extent of the transport disadvantage is hard to gauge. On some materials that are imported from abroad the difference is slight or non-existent. This is so where the price of the materials includes transport to any British port. In a few instances materials produced in Great

106   ULSTER'S ECONOMIC STRUCTURE

Britain are consigned to manufacturers throughout the United Kingdom at a uniform price, the transport charges being in effect pooled. But in most cases the additional transport cost to Northern Ireland has to be borne by the producers. Coal is a most important example, since in one form or another it enters into the costs of nearly all manufactures. In the linen industry the average cost per ton of the coal actually used in 1935 (still the last year for which these figures for Northern Ireland and Great Britain can be compared) was about 43 per cent higher than the corresponding average in Great Britain; in textile finishing it was 36 per cent higher than the average cost in the same industry in Great Britain; in engineering it was 29 per cent higher; in gas production 14 per cent higher, and in electricity generation 20 per cent higher.[1] The greater the importance of coal in comparison with the value of the net output of the goods concerned—i.e. the value added to the raw materials by the work done on them in Northern Ireland—the more significant are these percentage differences in raising the total costs of the goods. Thus the effect of the additional cost of coal is to restrict industrial development, so far as unsheltered production is concerned, to those industries in which the proportion of coal costs to the value of net output is low. In some industries, it is true, the additional cost amounts to upwards of 10 per cent of the value of net output. But, in general, such large differences in total cost make production in Northern Ireland impossible except in industries which produce wholly for the local market, are thoroughly sheltered from outside competition, and are therefore able to charge higher prices to cover the extra costs. There is no doubt that this factor dictates a very strict limit to the range of unsheltered industries which it is profitable to locate in Northern Ireland. In all the industries which have developed on a fairly large scale—notably linen, engineering and ship-building—the cost of coal forms such a small proportion of total costs that the extra cost of it in Northern Ireland amounts to a fairly insignificant percentage of the value of net output—in none to more than 2 per cent and in some to much less.[2]

Outward transport costs vary greatly according to the class of goods and their packing qualities. In most of the unsheltered industries which have thriven in Northern Ireland, the actual freight charges form only a small percentage of the selling value of the goods—often less than 1 per cent. But there are some industries which have managed to survive even though their outward freight charges exceed those paid by manufac-

[1] Source: Census of Production, United Kingdom, 1935.
[2] It is difficult to compare the transport costs on raw materials other than coal, because the data in the Census of Production (1935) are not sufficiently defined.

ULSTER'S ECONOMIC STRUCTURE   107

turers of the same products in Great Britain by as much as 8 to 10 per cent of the selling price. On the other hand, on some products the total outward transport charge is under 0·5 per cent. In addition to the direct charges, however, the packing of the goods in such a way as to enable them to survive the risks of cross-channel transport is often a sizeable item in itself. For this reason the introduction since the war of a ferry service capable of dealing with loaded road vehicles has meant a considerable saving to many manufacturers. Even so, the handicap due to distance from the main markets in Great Britain is intensified by the handling costs and damage of goods in transit, and there is room for improvement in port facilities.

So far as can be judged, internal transport charges do not differ greatly from those for similar hauls in Great Britain. Both rail and road transport rates are controlled by the Transport Tribunal provided for in the Transport Act (Northern Ireland) 1948. In sharp contrast is the lack of control over the rates and charges for cross-channel shipping services. These are fixed by the Chamber of Shipping, a body which is composed of members of the industry and which effectively prevents competition on the basis of rates.

(e) *Wage Rates.* Where transport costs are higher than for competing industries in Great Britain, the difference is generally taken into account in wage-bargaining, as a reason for a somewhat lower wage than in Great Britain. Though, in general, wages tend to be rather lower than in Great Britain, they are by no means uniformly so. In some industries skilled workers are paid at rates higher than the average rates paid to similar workers in Great Britain, while the wages of unskilled workers are generally lower. In occupations in which wage rates are lower, the differential is greater, as a rule, for women than for men. During the war and early post-war years the percentage margin between wage rates in Northern Ireland and Great Britain tended to become narrower. A wage index which we have calculated for Northern Ireland (on a comparable basis to that of the official index for the United Kingdom) shows a rise between September 1939 and May 1948 of 100 per cent. The rise in the United Kingdom as a whole during the same period was 75 per cent. Since 1948 the two indexes have risen at about the same rate. One reason for the faster rise in the index for Northern Ireland is that agricultural wages, which form a larger proportion of the total than in Great Britain, rose from their very low starting-point in 1939 more rapidly than industrial wages. But another and important reason is that there also occurred a considerable decline in the differential in industrial wage rates themselves.

I

Northern Ireland's future industrial prosperity may well depend on the exercise of wage restraint. In the absence of higher productivity, complete wage equality with Great Britain could, in adverse conditions, ruin the competitive position of many of its industries. The danger here is that trade unions, many of which have their headquarters in Great Britain, may be over-zealous in getting and preserving parity; they may, in doing so, undermine the economy by stifling new investment. It is fairly clear that the reduction which has occurred in the differential in wage rates during the past decade has not been so damaging to employment in Northern Ireland as it might have been if employment in Great Britain had been less buoyant. For many firms in Great Britain, owing to the greater scarcity of labour there, have to pay more of their workers at overtime rates, and have to offer more generous scales of bonus payments (than are paid in Northern Ireland) as a means of retaining their workers; so that the additional labour cost there is probably a good deal greater than the difference in wage rates. But if selling becomes difficult an increase in the wage difference may be the only way of maintaining Northern Ireland's competitive position.

The fundamental reason why rates of wages, particularly those of unskilled workers and women, have tended generally to be lower than in Great Britain is that the supply of labour has been (and still is) more plentiful than in Great Britain in relation to the demand; or, to express the difference the other way round, the demand has been weaker than in Great Britain in relation to the supply. This contrast was even more marked before the war than it is now. On the one hand, because of the natural handicaps already mentioned, industrial employment did not increase as fast as in Great Britain. On the other hand, workers generally were unwilling to migrate to Great Britain, in search of work there, merely because rates of pay in Northern Ireland were lower and unemployment was heavier; some workers did migrate, particularly from among the unemployed, but not enough of them did so to bring down the unemployment rate, and raise wages, to equality with Great Britain.

During the early years of the war, however, when war needs were causing the demand for labour to increase generally throughout the kingdom, employment expanded a good deal faster and farther, proportionately, than in Great Britain, since there was more slack in the form of unemployment to take up. This was the main reason for the tendency for wage rates in Northern Ireland to catch up with those in Great Britain. But there were also contributory causes operating from the side of the workers. In particular, though the regulations governing the wartime direction of labour did not apply officially to Northern

ULSTER'S ECONOMIC STRUCTURE 109

Ireland, the Ministry of Labour co-operated effectively with the Ministry of Labour in Great Britain, and many thousands of workers were placed in jobs in Great Britain through its agency and were given financial assistance in getting to their places of work there. In addition, many workers migrated to jobs in Great Britain on their own account. The resulting decrease in the supply of labour in Northern Ireland, compared with what it would have been otherwise, enabled the trade unions to bargain more effectively for higher wages.

The strengthening of the bargaining power of the workers due to this cause, and the resulting tendency for wage rates to rise faster than in Great Britain, has been reinforced by the agricultural and food policy adopted by the United Kingdom as a means of dealing with the general food shortage.[1] For this policy tended to cause a greater rise in the cost of living in Northern Ireland than in Great Britain. It did so because of the arrangement under which the Ministry of Food, in order to stimulate the production and to control the distribution of rationed foods, bought the main agricultural products at uniform prices throughout the kingdom, accepting delivery in the various agricultural districts, and also, through the medium of distributors, sold at uniform (and lower) prices to consumers. Before the introduction of this system the surplus produced in Northern Ireland above local requirements had to be sold in Great Britain at whatever price it would fetch there. Hence, under competitive conditions, the local price was forced down below the price in the principal markets in Great Britain, by the amount of the direct and indirect costs of transport from the place of production in Northern Ireland. This price differential was, indeed, an important cause of the pre-war disparity in wage rates, since it was generally recognised that workers in Northern Ireland *pro tanto* had the advantage of a lower cost of living. By removing the differential, the system of uniform agricultural prices tended to reduce real wage rates in Northern Ireland compared with those in Great Britain, and by so doing it tended to promote a greater rise than in Great Britain in money wage rates.

(*f*) *Output per worker.* The obstacles which natural conditions have put in the way of industrial development in Northern Ireland show their effects in practically every aspect of the economy. Directly, they take the form of a lack of indigenous raw materials and a remoteness from markets; and indirectly, in consequence, they exert a powerful control over the industrial structure—both the pattern of industry and the technique of production—and also over the rate of industrial growth and the level of incomes. Since they involve for most industries some

[1] *Cf.* below, chapter 7 (*a*).

additional transport costs above those borne by the same industries in Great Britain, they tend to confine industrial growth to a fairly narrow range of light industries requiring a comparatively small investment of capital per worker and a large number of women in proportion to men. Average wages earned per worker are lower than in Great Britain partly for this very reason—that women form a substantially larger proportion of the labour force—but also because rates of pay themselves tend to be rather lower and because the lack of heavy industries means that there are proportionately fewer of the high-wage jobs. No doubt rates of profit on the average are affected in a like manner, but it is impractical to verify this point statistically.

These and other adverse effects of Northern Ireland's natural industrial handicaps show themselves collectively in the difference, between the province and the United Kingdom as a whole, in the average value of net output per person engaged in manufacturing industries. It is therefore instructive to compare net output in Northern Ireland and the United Kingdom, in order to see how great the difference is on the average and how far it is due to a difference in industrial structure and how far to other causes.

The average value of net output per employee, measured over the whole of industry covered by the 1949 Census of Production, was £515 in the United Kingdom and £369 in Northern Ireland. Thus the value of net output per employee in Northern Ireland was only 73 per cent of that for the United Kingdom as a whole. But when a comparison is made of the individual trade-groups the difference is not so great as it appears when output is looked at in total. In only nine trade-groups out of thirty-nine was the figure for Northern Ireland lower than 73 per cent of that for the United Kingdom, and these nine together accounted for about 5 per cent of the total employment covered by the Census. The result looks worse in total than in the individual trade-groups because these groups are very differently weighted (according to their employment) from what they are in the United Kingdom. In Northern Ireland, because of the natural disadvantages already discussed, there is a greater tendency to specialise on industries in which there is no need for enormously heavy and expensive capital equipment and in which, in consequence, the value of net output per head is fairly low.

We can get an idea of how much of the difference in the average net output per head was due to Northern Ireland's different pattern of industry by calculating what its average per head would have been if— net output per head in each separate industry being what it was—the workers had been distributed between the different industries in the same

ULSTER'S ECONOMIC STRUCTURE 111

proportion as in the United Kingdom: that is, by weighting the net output in each of Northern Ireland's industries in accordance with the relative sizes of these industries in the United Kingdom as a whole. We cannot in this way allow for industries not represented in Northern Ireland at all—some of them high-productivity industries—or for Northern Ireland industries which did not possess true counterparts in Great Britain. But taking the 39 trades which can be compared, the effect of the reweighting process is to raise the average value of new output in these trades from 72 per cent of that of the United Kingdom to 77 per cent. This suggests that Northern Ireland's greater concentration on industries with a low value of net output accounts for only a minor part of the difference in the average value of net output over all industry. But the full effect is not shown by these figures. For it appears that Northern Ireland tends to concentrate, more than the United Kingdom as a whole, on low-productivity industries within each trade-group. An adjustment based on a finer subdivision of industries, in the limited number of trade-groups which it is possible to break up for this purpose, shows that some part of the remaining disparity can be explained in this way.[1]

But there are other differences between the province and the kingdom which must also be taken into account. It has already been shown that transport costs both on raw materials and on the finished goods, in excess of those borne by the same trades in Great Britain, have the effect of reducing the value of net output per head. We must also bear in mind that relatively few of Northern Ireland's industries are engaged in the production of goods bearing trade marks which give them a distinct and secure market to themselves. In industries which do produce such goods there are specific selling costs, particularly advertising costs, and—if these accomplish their purpose—also high profits; and the value of net output is inflated on both counts. In Northern Ireland, on the contrary, a very large part of the total output of manufactured goods is sold in highly competitive markets by comparatively small producing units which have no power to charge a price much above production costs.[2] In the linen industry, for example, the many individual producers in Northern Ireland not only compete keenly among themselves, but in addition have to sell their wares in competition both with linen manufactured abroad and with other fabrics. In other industries the position is similar. The goods are sold on the basis of high quality and low price,

[1] *Cf.* Leser, *Journal of the Royal Statistical Society*, Part II, 1950.
[2] An examination of the Report of the Census of Production of 1949 shows that, in thirty-five trade-groups represented in Northern Ireland, the average size of firm

not on that of expensive advertising and monopolistic control. Moreover, in many trades, owing to the lack of coal and minerals, only the less-capitalistic stages of production are carried on in Northern Ireland, and in these the value of net output per head is generally lower than in those which require a large amount of capital per worker. Finally, as noted above, most of the industries which can be carried on profitably in Northern Ireland employ a large proportion of women, who earn low wages compared with men and who consequently depress the average value of net output per worker.

It follows from what has just been said that it would be quite wrong to attribute the disparity between Northern Ireland and the United Kingdom, in average value of net output per worker (often loosely called productivity), to a difference between them in the average efficiency of the workers. If such a difference in efficiency does exist, it is not indicated by these figures, still less measured by them. The best guide to the relative efficiency of labour as such is the opinion of industrialists who have had experience as employers in Great Britain as well as Northern Ireland. We have personally discussed the question with a considerable number of employers of this kind. All those whom we have asked have been unanimous in their answers. Their experience is that, once workers in Northern Ireland have been trained for the specific work which they are to do, they are in every respect as efficient as workers in Great Britain in the main centres of the particular industries concerned, and, in addition, they are generally more adaptable, have more aptitude for improvisation, and show a greater willingness to work.

(g) *Income per Head.* A useful index of the level of economic prosperity in Northern Ireland compared with that in the United Kingdom as a whole is the relative volume of the income flow in the two regions, a flow which, for this purpose, can most conveniently be represented by the average amount of income per head. It must be emphasised, however, that income statistics are principally of use in observing the direction and causes of change, through time, in economic conditions and welfare within the country to which they refer, not in comparing the level of economic welfare in different countries, or even different regions of the same country; they are mainly useful as a guide to domestic policy. Comparisons between the level of income in different countries are notoriously difficult to interpret correctly. If the countries compared are

---

(measured by the number of workers) was in general much smaller than in Great Britain. This was not true, however, of a few of the individual trades, namely, timber, building and contracting, bread and cake baking, linen and hemp, and tailoring and dressmaking.

very different from each other in their industrial structure—and hence in the composition of total production and income—or if for this or other reasons the money prices of the goods which they produce are not brought into very close relation with each other and with those in other countries, the comparative figures of money income per head may give a false impression of the comparative level of real income. This difficulty is encountered even when comparing Northern Ireland with the United Kingdom as a whole. The most awkward complication is due to the much greater relative importance of farming than in Great Britain. For in Northern Ireland, as in every country, agricultural incomes, as measured in money, are lower than industrial incomes; and yet it is not clear that real incomes are lower in anything like the same proportion. Hence, in comparing the figures of total money income in Northern Ireland and the United Kingdom, we must not take them as being strictly accurate; in particular we must bear in mind that, for the reason stated, the figures for Northern Ireland probably underestimate its comparative position. There is a further reason, however, for keeping the comparison broad in the present case; namely, that there are no official estimates of income for Northern Ireland. We have therefore had to make our own estimates, and in doing so have been forced to indulge in even bolder assumptions than generally have to be made in compiling official statistics.

Owing to the type of statistics on which we have had to depend, the last year for which an estimate can at present be made is 1951. In that year total Private Civilian Income, on our estimates, was approximately £250 million.[1] This amounted to 1·85 per cent of the corresponding Private Civilian Income of the United Kingdom, the latter being adjusted to allow for certain items that could not be separately estimated for Northern Ireland. Expressing the total income as an average income per head of the civilian population, the comparative figures were £182 for Northern Ireland and £267 for the United Kingdom; which means that the average for Northern Ireland was only about 68 per cent of that for the United Kingdom. Taking 1938 as the base year, since it was the last full year before the war began, we find that by 1951 income per head in the United Kingdom had risen by about 150 per cent, whereas in Northern Ireland it had risen by over 200 per cent. Hence the two outstanding facts about income per head in Northern Ireland, as shown up by the comparison, are: firstly, that it is appreciably lower than the average for the United Kingdom; and, secondly, that since the beginning of the war

[1] For details and methods of calculation, see article by Norman Cuthbert in *Journal of the Statistical Society of Ireland*, 1951.

it has grown at a somewhat faster rate. These facts are indicative of the extent to which Northern Ireland differs economically from the United Kingdom as a whole, and of the relative changes that have occurred since just before the war.

The relative improvement in income per head in Northern Ireland has been due, in the main, to the very factors which have caused the increase in income per head in the United Kingdom as a whole during the same period—factors which have affected the whole economy but some regions more than others. Owing to the great increase entailed in the demand for goods and services of all kinds throughout the whole economy, the level of employment has risen to the point at which labour has become generally scarce. For this reason the percentage rise in employment, and therefore in income, has tended to be greatest in those regions which, at the outset, had the highest percentage of unemployed workers on whom to draw. Northern Ireland at the outset had more slack of this kind than any other region. In 1938, our base year for the comparison, the annual average unemployment rate was nearly 30 per cent, which was even higher than in 1931. With the great increase in industrial activity during the war, wage rates rose faster and farther (from their somewhat lower starting-point) than in Great Britain, and profits also rose steeply. At the same time, the policy of uniform agricultural prices, by transferring the cost of transport to the Ministry of Food, raised farmers' incomes more than it did those in Great Britain.

But in spite of the relative improvement since 1938, income per head is still considerably lower than the average of the United Kingdom, and there does not appear to be any factor in operation which is likely to raise it to the average in the near future. The industrial handicaps due to the climate, the lack of fuel and other raw materials, and the remoteness of the chief British markets, are hard facts to overcome.

76-95

[1987]

[5]

European Integration and the Irish Economy*

DERMOT McALEESE

Dermot McAleese is Whately professor of political economy at Trinity College, Dublin. This article is based on the 1986 Busteed Memorial Lecture, delivered at University College, Cork in November 1986.

The Single European Act (SEA) aims to achieve a complete internal market by 1992, with full freedom of movement for goods and factors of production and the dismantlement of border controls. To enable this objective to be achieved, the Commission has set out a detailed programme of action in its White Paper, *Completing the Internal Market* (1985). The SEA's provisions for qualified majority voting are designed to ensure that this programme will not be hamstrung by nationalistic wrangling at Council level. In order to widen the basis of support for its proposals, the SEA also provides for a complete reassessment of the structural funds with a view to bringing about closer economic and social cohesion within the Community.

Do trade regimes matter?

An underlying assumption of the entire European integration debate is that trade regimes do make a difference. The Treaties of Rome (1957) were succeeded by an unprecedented burst of growth in intra-Community trade and also in Community GNP. The temptation to argue *post hoc ergo propter hoc* was difficult to resist. All the evidence showed that trade liberalisation would lead to some expansion in trade. It also indicated that sizeable welfare gains would accrue to the Community as a result of this expansion; but it proved very difficult to tie down the precise magnitude of the trade gain and to relate it to the

---

*I am grateful to Kieran Kennedy for helpful comments on an early draft. Thanks are also owed to the audience at University College, Cork, whose observations prompted numerous revisions in the final draft.

European Integration 153

overall growth in the economy. Benefits such as those arising from a more intense competitive environment, a greater exploitation of economies of scale and an improved investment climate, resulting from a larger internal market, are notoriously difficult to quantify — other than to say that they are likely to be appreciable. Rightly or wrongly, on *post hoc ergo propter hoc* and on more scientific grounds, trade liberalisation has received much of the credit for the golden age, 1958–73.

In the case of the present proposals for further liberalisation, influential opinion has asserted that the Community's progress is being held back by its fragmented internal market. *The Economist* (24 November 1984) pronounced with *ex cathedra* certitude:

> The crippling, and widening, technology gap growing between Europe and its main competitors shows that *it is the absence of a continent-wide free market, more than anything else, which is blighting Europe's future.* [writer's italics]

In a similar vein, in a communiqué of 29/30 March 1985, the Council of Europe emphasised the need for action to achieve a single large market, with the aim of 'creating a more favourable environment for stimulating enterprise, competition and trade.' Important industrialist representative groups, such as UNICE (Union of Industries of the EEC), endorse a similar point of view. Indeed, it is very difficult to find any respectable source which argues on first principles against completion of the market.

A number of points may be made about the market unification process envisaged under the SEA. First, given the overwhelming problem of unemployment, it might have been thought that the Community would devote its main efforts to securing some aggregate demand stimulus or to achieving greater labour market flexibility, rather than to pursuing the indirect approach embodied in the market-opening processes of the SEA. The reason why it has not opted for common action on the former targets is presumably because agreement would be more difficult to reach on them. For example, there is no consensus that demand stimulation is either necessary or that it could be achieved by government policy. Likewise, measures to secure

greater labour market flexibility provoke ideological and practical difficulties between member states. Of course, exposing the
markets of the Community to more competition in the long run
necessarily will force more flexibility into their respective labour
markets also.

Secondly, there is considerable opposition in the Community
to the idea of promoting integration through large income distribution between member states. The opposition is most determined in potential donor countries such as West Germany. The
climate of opinion in the Community has turned completely
against the type of federal solution suggested in the MacDougall
Report (1977). Even within Ireland there is ambiguity. As
Matthews (1984) has pointed out, we want the transfers that a
federal Europe would offer, but not the degree of political
integration that would be necessary to make the Community a
federal state. The enlargement of the Community to include
poorer nations such as Greece, Spain and Portugal has reinforced the determination of the better-off members to avoid any
commitments to integration via resource transfers. The entire
emphasis has been on keeping the European market big but
keeping the Commission budget small.

Thirdly, a key element in the new regime proposed by the
SEA is the need for a large internal market to develop high technology industries. This argument is based on economies of scale:
Europe's fragmented markets are contrasted with the internal
market unity of Japan and the United States. Technology
industries have prospered in the two countries on the basis of
their large domestic markets. On these grounds, the main direct
beneficiaries of the internal market will be the more technologically advanced of the twelve member states, with the less
advanced members benefiting indirectly, through 'trickle-
down' effects from a more prosperous Community.

Fourthly, studies of the effects of trade regimes in the Third
World (including newly industrialised countries) show that
trade policies can have powerful effects on an economy for good
or ill. The World Bank view, for example, which is based on
extensive research over two decades, has crystallised into the
firm conclusion that:

There is a convincing body of quantitative evidence from

cross-country studies that developing countries with less dis-
torted policy regimes (particularly those that are less biased
against exports) have fared better in terms of growth performance, coping with external shocks, and employment
creation.[1]

All this suggests that, for poorer countries as for richer, for the
technologically advanced as for the technologically weak, for
those with flexible labour markets and those without, there are
significant advantages to be gained from closer integration between countries on the basis of world trade prices. China, India,
the countries of Eastern Europe and the Mediterranean countries are the latest in a long line of converts to this view. In a
sense, it could be said that the Cold War is over, and has been
won by the Americans!

What European integration meant to Ireland

It is difficult for a present-day audience to realise the full extent
of the pessimism about Ireland's prospects in an integrated
Europe which prevailed only thirty years ago. Fortunately,
Denis Maher's recently published *The Tortuous Path* documents
the fears and misgivings among the officials advising the Irish
government on this matter. Consider, for example, the conclusions of the interim report of 5 February 1957 prepared by
the secretaries of the main government departments in response
to the Organisation for European Economic Cooperation's proposal for a European Free Trade Area. Its three major
conclusions were that:

> as regards a large sector of existing industries, the Department
> of Industry and Commerce can see no prospect of their sur-
> vival even as suppliers of the home market, except with
> *permanent* protection
> the Department of Industry and Commerce can see no pros-
> pect of a significant expansion of industrial exports from
> Ireland to the continental part of the free trade area
> the Department of Agriculture sees little prospect of a signifi-
> cant expansion of agricultural exports from Ireland to the
> continental part of the free trade area. (Maher, 1986, p. 63)

This illustrates an astonishing lack of foresight and also a simple lesson: that the balance between the perceived opportunity and the threat of a more integrated market is very much determined by recent economic performance. The 1957 assessment was flavoured by the dismal experience of the Irish economy in the 1950s. As economic performance began to improve, it yielded to the more upbeat evaluations of the late 1960s and early 1970s.

Three main economic themes underlay the pre-accession negotiations: *market access*, *safeguards* and *transfers*.

Market access applied to both industrial and agricultural goods. In the case of industrial goods, the issue was comparatively simple. Ireland had for a long time enjoyed free access to the British market and membership of the Community offered the prospect of widening that access to continental European markets. No extravagant hopes were held out of a major penetration of these markets being speedily achieved by domestic producers. It was thought possible that overseas manufacturing subsidiaries would use Ireland as an export platform and the scale of response after 1972 proved these expectations correct. A twist to the story was that entry entailed Ireland losing its preferential position in the British market, but very little was heard of this after 1973.

The market access aspects of Irish trade negotiations assumed much greater importance in the case of agricultural goods. First, since World War I, apart from the actual war period itself, the need to obtain market access for Irish agricultural exports was seen as a vital strategic aim of Ireland's trade policy. Experience during the Economic War had shown just how vulnerable Ireland was on this score. Being in a commodity market with little differentiation of brand loyalty, it was easy for Britain to deflect its food purchases from Ireland to other competing sources of supply. In this context, access to the British market on preferential terms was an especially valuable prize. For example, it was written into the 1938 Anglo-Irish Trade Agreement that Britain would maintain duties on some agricultural imports from non-Commonwealth countries and would not alter the terms of Irish preference without consultation.

Would complete free trade in agriculture, with equality of access to each other's markets, for all European producers have been a better option for Ireland? The general tendency has been to believe that it would not have been. For one thing, the fear has long existed, going back to the 1950s during discussions about the free trade area, that national subsidies would continue to prevail, giving an advantage to the richer countries.[2] Superimposed on this was the nagging doubt about where Irish comparative advantage really stood, even if genuinely free trade conditions were present. These doubts have lasted into the 1980s as the current debate over the respective merits of quotas versus the dismantlement of the Common Agricultural Policy (CAP) price supports illustrates.[3]

Although the link with Britain has greatly weakened since 1973, the issue of market access boiled down to access to the British market. Ireland's bid for entry into the European Community in July 1961 was in effect conditional on Britain's application being successful, although naturally this was not stated explicitly. When that condition was not met, Ireland's application was allowed to lapse along with Britain's. British membership was also a key feature in favour of Ireland's entry to the Community in 1973, although by then the relevant argument was that, since Britain was going to join anyway, the *status quo* could not be maintained and that market access could be assured only within a Community context.

While much emphasis was placed on safeguards at the time of the entry negotiations — and earlier in the Anglo-Irish Free Trade Area Agreement (AIFTA) — it is doubtful if these really had much long-term impact. The protocol, the competition rules, the special provisions for motor car assembly, the sugar quota discussions, which continued to the end of the negotiations, had little effect on the broad evolution of Irish trade. Tax relief on export profits has been replaced, as has the motor assembly industry. The sugar quota has never been fully used. There have been few cases of anti-dumping provisions being brought to bear against Community partners and only rare instances of special provisions being introduced to protect Irish producers against extra-EC competition under the Common Commercial Policy, or of Community rules on state aids being interpreted with special liberality on Ireland's behalf.

Transfers were the third main theme in the pre-accession debate. The scale of CAP transfers has already been well documented and in this instance the themes of market access and resource transfers clearly overlap somewhat. According to Sheehy, the combined budgetary and trade benefits from the CAP amounted to £660m. in 1981, a sum well in excess of family farm incomes of £510m. and equivalent to 7 per cent of GNP.[4] The Regional Fund, too, has been a useful source of transfers, but the size of the Fund has increased slowly and it has not developed into the major catalyst of change that its proponents thought it might become (Drudy, 1984). Ireland has done unusually well in its allocations from the European Social Fund. ESF assistance amounted to £93m. in 1983, a five-fold increase in real terms over the 1973 level (Laffan, 1985). To complete the list, between 1979 and 1984 the subsidy element in European Monetary System (EMS) selected loans amounted to £45m. a year.

The huge scale of these transfers by Brussels has had an undoubted impact on Ireland's economy, mostly for the better. Yet there have been critics. Perhaps the strongest disapproval has come from Alan Matthews (1983), who refers to their adverse effects on the nation's psyche and its willingness to confront its problems. Matthews refers approvingly to Professor Lee's 'sponger syndrome' thesis. Living standards, Matthews argues, were built initially on the increasing transfers from the Community during the transition period and subsequently by recourse to foreign borrowing. Matthews's assessment is a refreshing contrast to the rather bland enumeration of budgetary 'benefits' of EC membership which other sources are prone to publicise. But are Matthews and Lee correct? Certainly the sponger syndrome was reinforced, but does this mean that Ireland would have been better off without the transfers? The capital assets of Ireland's farmers and the nation's economic and social infrastructure have also been reinforced. The word 'reinforced' also needs emphasis: the sponger syndrome was strengthened, not created, by Brussels.

Special features of the integration strategy

(i) Has there been convergence?

The first question is whether membership has been associated with greater economic convergence between Ireland and other member states. Contrary to a public impression, Ireland's real

European Integration   159

GDP per capita has tended to converge to the EUR12 average. Measured by standards of purchasing power, Irish GDP per capita was 66.7 per cent of the EUR12 average in 1970 and by 1985 had risen to 70.7 per cent. During the same period, real GDP per capita rose by 34 per cent in EUR12.[5] These figures indicate that Ireland's productive capacities have risen significantly in absolute and relative terms.

Another important area of convergence is inflation. Irish consumer prices rose by 13.8 per cent a year in the period 1970–77, four percentage points above the EUR12 average. By contrast, Ireland's average annual inflation rates in the 1982–86 period at 6.1 per cent had fallen to fractionally below the EUR12 average.

Since 1980, however, this picture must be balanced by the increasing divergence between rich and poor member states in the level of unemployment. The Irish unemployment rate at 18 per cent is over six percentage points above the EUR12 level in 1986, compared with a three percentage point divergence over EUR9 in 1970. Evidence at a regional level within the Community shows a similar trend of widening divergence since the mid-1970s. Whereas the weakest 25 regions of the Community had an average unemployment rate of 8 per cent in 1976, relative to 2.4 per cent for the 25 strongest, the figures for 1985 were respectively 21.1 per cent and 6.6 per cent. Indeed, smaller member states have fared badly in terms of the unemployment rate relative to the larger Community countries (Kennedy, 1985). The huge increase in public sector budget deficits in recent years has also tended to be concentrated in the poorer members of the Community.

Ireland's experience, therefore, provides no justification for simple-minded conclusions about the inevitability of decline in peripheral regions. This statement is clearly not the case as far as GDP per capita is concerned. Moreover, the deterioration of Ireland's relative unemployment and public finance positions, two elements in a divergent direction, owes more to bad domestic economic management than to integrative processes.

(ii) Has protection really gone?

The process of tariff reduction in intra-Community trade has proceeded according to schedule. Protection, however, con-

tinues to apply against imports from extra-Community countries. Irish agriculture, for example, is sheltered from competition by the variable levy system; the clothing/textile/footwear
industries receive protection against LDC (less developed
country) imports. Increasingly these are non-tariff barriers
(NTBs). In 1983, 18.6 per cent of imports into the Community
from industrial countries and 25.4 per cent of imports from
LDCs were subject to NTBs.[6] The post-Tokyo round tariff
average for the Community is 6 per cent on finished and semi-
finished manufactures.

Although significant in an absolute sense, and with respect to
particular sectors, Ireland's level of NTB protection against
LDCs is well below the Community average. Only 13.4 per cent
of our extra-Community imports from industrial countries and
19.6 per cent from developing countries are subject to NTBs. In
the case of textiles, for instance, the NTB coverage ratio (the
proportion of imports to which NTBs apply) is 52 per cent for
the Community average but only 31.7 per cent for Ireland. Steel
and electrical machinery NTBs are also much less pervasive,
and have less impact on Ireland's imports, than in most other
member states (Nogues et al, 1986).

In addition to the continuing protection on extra-
Community trade, a considerable amount of protection is provided to factors of production in industry in the form of industrial incentives. Bond and Guisinger (1985) show, for example,
that investors in Irish industry who receive maximum cash
grants of 60 per cent of their fixed assets, and a corporation profits tax rate of 10 per cent, are benefiting from an effective protection rate of 24 per cent, this on top of the 27 per cent effective
tariff implicit in the Common External Tariff. These authors
also demonstrate systematically how investment incentives can
act as substitutes for tariffs; they are simply alternative means of
protecting domestic industry. Indigenously owned industry
receives further protection via the various incentives prescribed
in recent years for this sector (the 'hands-on' approach). Hence,
for these two reasons — restrictions on imports from extra-EC
sources and industrial incentives — the Irish market cannot be
described as entirely non-protected, and the integration process
has certainly some way to go yet.

(iii) The importance of real exchange rates

The importance of maintaining realistically valued exchange rates has received increasing recognition in recent years. Dornbusch and Helmers (1986) have described choosing the right level of the exchange rate as 'the most critical decision in an open economy'. Balassa (1986), the most persistent advocate of outward-looking policies, has recently made the point that:

> adopting a realistic exchange rate is the *sine qua non* of a policy package for economic growth as it will simultaneously contribute to export expansion and efficient import substitution.

In contrast, adoption of an unrealistic, or overvalued, exchange rate will inhibit exports and will lead to inefficient substitution of imports for domestic import-competing production. Overvaluation can be politically popular in the short run because it artificially raises standards of living. Often an overvalued exchange rate is sustained by foreign borrowing, which can subsequently become very expensive. Paradoxically, in a highly indebted country, an eventual devaluation in excess of that indicated by real exchange rate calculations will be necessary to allow for the servicing of the debt. However, short-term considerations, including concern over the value of the debt and interest payments in domestic currency, will lean in the opposite direction, urging a devaluation less than that required by real exchange rate fundamentals.

Ireland was one of the few countries to implement a far-reaching and comprehensive removal of protection without an accompanying devaluation. Normally a devaluation is needed to soften the impact of import penetration on the balance of payments. The depreciated exchange rates often help previously protected firms to make the transition to a more competitive, export-orientated environment. Ireland did not have to succumb to devaluation for two special reasons. First, between 1970 and 1975 when the fall in barriers was making an impact, the country's trade balance was being improved by strong agricultural export prices and by CAP transfers. Second, inward capital and direct investment flows further strengthened the balance of payments during this period. The net effect of these two developments was to mask the adverse price-incentives facing indigenous industry (which because of its weakness was unable to avail of the investment incentive grants as measured by Bond and Guisinger). The effect on indigenous firms could readily be analysed in terms of the Dutch disease literature (but has not been so analysed yet to my knowledge). The indigenous (declining) sector is crowded by the 'boom' sectors (CAP-supported agriculture and direct foreign investment).

The EMS added another twist to this story. Taking the period since 1979, it has been associated with (a) a severe decline in Ireland's competitiveness of over 40 per cent relative to Germany, (b) an improvement in competitiveness relative to the UK, up to a peak in mid-1981, which has since been eroded, (c) fluctuating fortunes relative to the US dollar, with a return to the 1979 *status quo ante* in 1986 (Walsh, 1986). The net impact of these trends is hard to subsume under any single aggregate index. Clearly, the loss in competitiveness of such a huge magnitude relative to continental European markets has made it difficult for indigenous entrepreneurs to break into these markets. Structural change in Britain and high Irish cost inflation have moderated the benefits that otherwise might have accrued as a result of the improvement in Ireland's labour costs position relative to Britain's. Using a GDP deflator and trade weights, Bacon (1986) shows a severe decline in aggregate competitiveness since 1979. It is inconceivable that changes of this order of magnitude, if sustained for any period of time, would not have a negative effect on the performance of formerly protected import-substitution industries.[7]

The general conclusion must be that exchange rate developments were such as to leave the Irish pound overvalued rather than undervalued, relative to its major competitors and, for a country as needful of economic growth as Ireland, this was to say the least unfortunate. The pound's unwarranted appreciation, which occurred during 1986 as a result of the decline in sterling and which the August unilateral devaluation within the EMS was designed to correct, must also be viewed with concern. Overvaluation has inhibited the economy's capacity to gain the most from the process of integration.

(iv) Direct investment

A liberal approach to foreign direct investment is not an essential prerequisite of outward-looking policies, but it has been a special feature of Ireland's development policy since the mid-1950s. During the protectionist period, strenuous but not altogether successful efforts were made to keep out foreign investors. From a theoretical point of view, this policy was the correct one at the time because it aimed to ensure that protectionist rents accrued to nationals rather than to non-nationals (Neary and Ruane, 1984). With outward-looking policies, a complete reversal of policy occurred: subsidies and grants were paid to export-orientated foreign corporations. This was the most singular and successful aspect of Ireland's export-promotion strategy.

However, the Industrial Development Authority faced competition for projects from industrial development organisations in other countries. In a sense it acted as a price-taker, i.e. failure to match other countries' incentives would result in loss of the project. A recent multi-country study (which includes Irish experience in its coverage) showed that, for roughly two-thirds of the investment projects that were surveyed, attributes of the host country other than investment policies were responsible for the location decision, but that for the other one-third the location decision was made because of government policies (Guisinger et al, 1985). If, however, a country refused to offer incentives, then the survey showed that it would suffer heavy project losses. This would be particularly true of a country of Ireland's size with no home market to offer as a bargaining counter. The survey strongly supports the view that incentives are an effective device to attract foreign investment.

The influx of foreign investment was not costless. Yet without it I doubt if the convergence towards European standards would have been possible. On the other hand, it is equally certain that if the liberalisation process had not ground to a halt the Irish pound would have had to be devalued more severely in real terms. Foreign borrowing would also have been more difficult, given the emphasis that lenders put on a strong export performance.

Direct investment outflows are also an intrinsic feature of

Ireland's outward-looking policies, but they still await a proper study. Most of Ireland's remaining large indigenous companies have expanded their overseas activities in recent years. Waterford Glass, James Crean, Irish Ropes, McInerneys, Cement Roadstone, Smurfits (and, in the services sector, Aer Lingus, Allied Irish Banks) are well-known instances. It is possible to argue that overseas investment by these firms strengthens the company as a whole and therefore makes the Irish operation more secure. What is good for the company is also good for the Irish economy.

While not disagreeing with this general conclusion, the issues are not that simple. There is a possibility that the direct investment outflow, representing 'exit' in Hirschman's terms, weakens the 'voice' of indigenous industry and allows policies to continue that ultimately are detrimental to the economy. To the extent that capital is mobile and its geographical spread diversified, the common interest is weakened between labour and capital in the declining sectors of the economy. If things go bad in Ireland, the firms survive by concentrating their entrepreneurial efforts on overseas locations. An overvalued pound, by making purchases of an overseas foothold less expensive, is not unwelcome in such a context. By contributing further to a weakening of Irish industry, the overvaluation makes overseas diversification all the more profitable in relative terms *ex post facto*. Similarly, the consequences of inflated labour costs, an excessively expensive social welfare system and the deplorable condition of Irish public finances are sidestepped rather than confronted. This may explain why the Confederation of Irish Industry, for all its eloquence and trenchant critiques, has been unable to halt decisively the drift towards economic mismanagement, which in so many ways has undermined the capacity of industry to reap the potential benefits of outward-looking policies.

Towards closer European integration
The economic themes running through the Single European Act debate are broadly the same as they have been in relation to the Irish government's past initiatives towards integration with the outside world. Market access, safeguards and transfers continue to occupy centre stage.

European Integration   165

The Confederation of Irish Industry's *Newsletter* of 22 May 1986 welcomes the objective of market unification:

Irish industry depends on exports for almost two-thirds of its industrial output. It is essential that all barriers to the free movement of goods between member states should be removed as quickly as possible.

The government takes the same view. Economic prosperity depends on exports, and exports can flourish only in the context of unambiguously open internal markets. Although there has been no published study of NTBs facing Irish companies that export to other member states, there is plenty of anecdotal evidence of their existence. Food and drink, health-care, pharmaceutical and electronics industries all have had their share of problems on this score. Even more insidious: prospective foreign investors, and the expansion of existing subsidiaries, have been deterred by implicit threats that access will be difficult if these companies establish in Ireland rather than in the country to which it is intended to make most sales. All grist to the market-access mill! Market access will be further assisted by a reduction in trade administrative costs, envisaged in the market unification measures. Although I believe that the Commission's estimate of a £1 billion gain for Ireland as a result of these economies is wildly optimistic, a figure of even £100m. a year, which would be closer to the mark, still represents a substantial gain (McAleese, 1986b).

Although concern has been expressed over the effect of liberalisation on certain parts of Ireland's financial sector, there has been no advertence to any damage which greater exposure to competition might cause to domestic industry. This contrasts with the situation before the signing of the Treaty of Accession. Perhaps the reason is that the vulnerable sectors constitute a smaller proportion of Irish industry than was the case in the early 1970s. Moreover, unlike other countries, Ireland has not had much recourse to the type of NTBs that the SEA is designed to negate. The result has been that the *safeguard* theme has been much less to the fore than was previously the case. However, it may be significant that in relation to fiscal approximation and tax incentives for industry, where Irish interests are likely to be closely affected, decisions are to be taken by unanimous rather than by qualified majority voting. The government has also been at pains to reaffirm the continued existence of the veto in matters where vital national interests are involved (White Paper, *The Single European Act*, 1986).

Resource transfers are given a high priority in the SEA. The Irish government doubtless pushed hard to secure this outcome. Given the prospective erosion of CAP price support, it is clear that something substantial will have to be put in its place. Article 130A of the Act promises that:

> the Community shall develop and pursue its actions leading to the strengthening of economic and social cohesion. In particular the Community shall aim at reducing disparities between the various regions and the backwardness of the least-favoured regions.

It will be crucial for Ireland, having played a prominent part in the framing of parts of the cohesion section of the SEA, to have a clear idea of what précise measures it considers necessary to secure this higher level of economic and social cohesion. At all costs, the government must avoid accepting 'aid' in the form of interest-subsidised loans for unprofitable capital-intensive ventures, or for the maintenance of levels of social services that are beyond the country's capacity to sustain. What is needed are carefully vetted programmes designed to help us overcome developmental constraints: targetted aid to help indigenous industry ('enterprise-friendly' activities), to improve the skills of our workforce, to encourage interaction between continental and Irish firms, and to reduce the costs of communication within Ireland and between Ireland and other member states.

Experience should warn us against placing too much hope on transfers from Brussels as a way out of our difficulties. We have already seen that these are unlikely to be forthcoming. Any transfers which do come Ireland's way will be based on the principle of mutual interest. Adam Smith's approach will be relevant to Irish negotiators:

> Man has almost constant occasion for the help of his brethren, and it is in vain for him to expect it from their benevolence

only. He will be more likely to prevail if he can interest their self-love in his favour and show them that it is for their own advantage to do for him what he requires of them. (*Wealth of Nations*, 1776)

Almost every serious review of Ireland's experience of Community membership has stressed the importance of *domestic* policy — not transfers, not tinkering with the details of external commodity and factors flows — in determining the extent to which the full potential of membership can be realised.

It would be wrong to blind ourselves to the ultimate consequences of the SEA. The Act's intention is to pave the way for closer union within the Community. This implies further erosion of the Irish government's autonomy in fiscal, monetary and trade policy. On the basis of the government's performance in economic affairs during the past decade, some might say that this erosion is no bad thing. But such a conclusion would be facile. The institutions of the European Community will be perfectly capable of making a mess of things too! The key to the resolution of this difficulty is to build greater economic strength in Ireland so that the strain of adhering to the guidelines for co-ordinated behaviour in an integrated Europe can be successfully withstood.

Conclusion

As has often been said, economic integration with the outside world is a means of escape for a small country, escape from the limitations of small size and small horizons. This article has tried to show how Ireland at first tentatively and then with increasing confidence changed from protectionist, import-substitution policies to outward-looking policies. Throughout the thirty-five year transition, the same themes have been debated: the desirability of greater market access, the need for transitional safeguards for weak sectors and the possibilities of resource transfers.

In retrospect, the really key factor has been market access. Without that, we would have an impoverished agriculture and a small-scale low productivity industry. Safeguard clauses were rarely sufficient to ensure a genuine adjustment from import substitution to export orientation. However, they helped to delay the process of attrition and provided a useful breathing space. Resource transfers have also been useful, but not as useful as was hoped, mostly because they have been used to postpone necessary adjustment (in farm structures and in government finances), rather than to promote structural change.

The European Community is now launching forward on further market integration. Obstacles to *factor* movements are now very much on the agenda. Sooner or later, therefore, Irish exchange controls will have to be eliminated. Attitudes to the mobility of labour will also have to change, and the new generation of Europeans will be better travelled and more educated than their predecessors. In such a highly interdependent economy, the Irish will have to be more conscious than they have been of the need to tailor Ireland's costs environment to European standards of competitiveness.

The year of the ratification of the Single European Act will be seen as one of low confidence and general pessimism in Ireland. Echoes of the 1957 memorandum cited earlier in this paper! The fall in manufacturing employment in the 1980s has been, in percentage terms, not that different from the rise in manufacturing employment during the 1930s. Superficially this might appear an indictment of outward-looking policies. But, as this lecture has argued, it is no such thing. Rather it reflects the fact that, without appropriate supporting policies, even the best designed external commercial policies will not secure economic advancement. It is reassuring to note, in the debate about the Single European Act, the welcome absence of any tendency to blame others for our own deficiencies in that regard.

Notes to article

[1] World Bank (1986), p. 33.

[2] Maher refers to the 'neutral attitude' adopted by Ireland in the free trade negotiations up to 1958, 'indicative of the uncertainty felt by the Government as to where the balance of advantage might lie' (p. 69).

[3] Sheehy (1982–83) argues persuasively that Irish farm incomes would be reduced far less by a quota system than by either price reductions or across-the-board co-responsibility levies. See also O'Connor, Guiomard and Devereux (1983).

[4] Sheehy (1985), p. 93.

[5] Commission of the European Communities, *Annual Economic Report 1986–87*, Brussels, October 1986 (mimeo). It is fair to note that comparison based on GNP would be less favourable since the latter takes account of the large outflow of interest and dividend payments abroad in the 1980s.

6 World Bank (1986), p. 23. Later estimates suggest that the coverage ratio may be even higher than this. The estimates of NTBs of Nogues *et al* show a Community coverage ratio of 22.3 per cent in 1983.

7 It is paradoxical that employment in British-owned subsidiaries — the country against which Ireland, along with all other countries, experienced a dramatic improvement in labour cost competitiveness — suffered the most severe cutback in this period. A number of possible explanations are suggested for this in McAleese (1986): the weak position of the British companies, the poor management of Irish subsidiaries, and Ireland's unfavourable general competitive position relative to Britain in terms of labour relations.

References

Bacon, Peter, 'Exchange Rate Policy', paper presented at Dublin Economics Workshop: Annual Policy Conference, Kenmare, October 1986.

Balassa, Bela, 'Economic Development in Small Countries', paper to Conference on Small Countries in the World Economy, Budapest, 25–27 August 1986.

Bond, E. W., and S. E. Guisinger, 'Investment Incentives as Tariff Substitutes: A Comprehensive Measure of Protection', *Review of Economics and Statistics*, February 1985.

Commission of the European Communities, *Report of the Study Group on the Role of Public Finance in European Integration* (the MacDougall Report), Brussels, 1977.

Coombes, D., (ed.), *Ireland in the European Communities*, Gill and Macmillan, Dublin, 1983.

Dornbusch, R., and F. L. Helmers, *The Open Economy: Tools for Policy Makers in Developing Countries*, World Bank, 1986.

Drudy P. J., and D. McAleese (eds.), *Ireland and the European Community*, Cambridge University Press, Cambridge, 1984.

Drudy, P. J., 'The Regional Implications of EEC Policies in Ireland', in Drudy and McAleese (1984).

Economic and Social Research Institute, *The Economic Consequences of European Union*, Policy Research Series, No. 6, April 1986.

Fogarty, C. P., 'European Union: Implications for Ireland', *Administration*, Vol. 33, No, 4, 1985.

Government Publications Office, *The Single European Act: An Explanatory Guide*, Dublin, 1986.

Guisinger, S. E., *et al.*, *Investment Incentives and Performance Require-ments*, New York, Praeger, 1985.

Guisinger, S. E., 'Do Performance Requirements and Invest-ment Incentives Work?' *World Economy*, March 1986.

Hederman, M., *The Road to Europe: Irish Attitudes 1948-61*, Dublin, Institute of Public Administration, 1983.

Kennedy, K. A., *The Unemployment Crisis*, The 1985 Busteed Memorial Lecture, Cork, Cork University Press, 1985.

Laffan, B., *The European Social Fund and its Operation in Ireland*, Dublin, Irish Council of the European Movement, May 1985.

Lee, J., 'Perspectives on Ireland in the EEC — a Review Essay,' *Economic and Social Review*, October 1984.

Lee, J., *Reflections on Ireland in the EEC*, Irish Council of the Euro-pean Movement, Dublin, 1984.

Maher, D. J., *The Tortuous Path: The Course of Ireland's Entry into the EEC 1948-73*, Institute of Public Administration, Dublin, 1986.

Matthews, Alan, 'The Options for Further EEC Integration — an Irish view', *Journal of the Statistical and Social Inquiry Society of Ireland*, Vol. XXV, Part I, 1983-84.

Matthews, Alan, 'European Union: The Economic Implica-tions for Ireland', *Irish Studies in International Affairs*, Vol. 2, No. 1, 1985.

McAleese, D., 'Anglo-Irish Economic Interdependence: Effects of Post-1979 Changes in the British Economy on Ireland', *Irish Banking Review*, Spring 1986.

McAleese, D., 'Completion of the Internal Market — Implica-tions for Irish Trade', *Irish Banking Review*, December 1986.

Neary, J. Peter and Frances P. Ruane, 'International Capital Mobility, Shadow Prices and the Cost of Protection', Working Paper No. 32, Centre for Economic Research, University College Dublin, December 1984.

Nogues, J., A. Olechowski and L. A. Winters, 'The Extent of Non-Tariff Barriers to Imports of Industrial Countries', World Bank Staff Working Paper No. 789, Washington D.C., February 1986.

O'Connor, R., C. Guiomard and J. Devereux, *A Review of the Common Agricultural Policy and the Implications of Modified Systems for Ireland*, ESRI Broadsheet No. 21, Dublin, October 1983.

O'Mahony, D., Foreword to the 1985 Busteed Memorial Lecture, Cork, Cork University Press, Cork, 1985.

Sheehy, S. J., 'Co-responsibility and the Future of Irish Agriculture', *Journal of the Statistical and Social Inquiry Society of Ireland,* Vol. XXIV, 1982–83.

Walsh, B. M., 'Irish Exchange Rate Policy', paper presented at Dublin Economics Workshop: Annual Policy Conference, Kenmare, October 1986.

World Bank, *World Development Report 1986,* Washington D.C., 1986.

Wrigley, L., 'Ireland in Economic Space', in J. Lee (ed.), *Ireland: Towards a Sense of Place,* Cork, Cork University Press, 1985.

[6]

Cambridge Journal of Economics 1985, 9, 141–154

The problem of late industrialisation and the experience of the Republic of Ireland

Eoin O'Malley*

The literature on industrialisation in developing countries has become strongly influenced by the view, derived from neoclassical economic theory, that outward-looking policies with reliance on free market forces and minimal State intervention are the key to success.[1] Reference to the experience of Japan, some Far Eastern NICs and Puerto Rico, and the supposedly free-market policies followed there, has increasingly been made in support of this view. The Republic of Ireland, which has experienced rapid industrial growth since adopting neoclassical-type policies in the 1950s, has also been referred to as a successful example (e.g., Farley, 1973).

There must, however, be considerable doubt about the validity of this view in respect of some of these countries, particularly Japan, South Korea and Taiwan. It is not at all clear that these countries relied on the pure outward-looking free-market strategy for industrial development. Rather their success may well be attributable to departing significantly from this strategy—by using protection against imports combined with selective state intervention and guidance to develop targeted industries to internationally competitive standards.[2]

This article examines the record of industrial growth in the Republic of Ireland and argues that it too offers no convincing support for a general recommendation of outward-looking free-market policies for late-industrialising countries. The reason for this conclusion, however, is different for Ireland than for the countries mentioned above. Ireland has undoubtedly followed a free market strategy more closely than these other countries, but arguably the success achieved by following this strategy has occurred only because of *exceptional* circumstances. Hence Ireland's experience does not offer general support for outward-looking free-market policies. Furthermore, future prospects for Ireland look less than favourable if the country persists with this strategy.

1. Barriers to entry for latecomers

The neoclassical prescription of an 'outward-looking' strategy consists of three specific policies—free international trade, the favouring of export industries (or at least non-

*Economic and Social Research Institute, Dublin. I am grateful to Professor Reginald H. Green and the late Professor Dudley Seers of the Institute of Development Studies at the University of Sussex for advice and comments on this research; responsibility for the views expressed and for any deficiencies remains my own.

[1] Little, Scitovsky and Scott (1970) and Balassa (1980) are good representatives of this neoclassical view.
[2] See, for example, Allen (1981) and Adams and Ichimura (1983) on Japan; Luedde-Neurath (1980 and 1984) on Korea; Wade (1984) on Taiwan.

0309–166X/85/020141 + 14 $03.00/0

142   E. O'Malley

discrimination against them), and freedom for foreign investors. The reliance on market forces which is also recommended would allow, at most, state intervention in the form of generalised, automatic incentives, such as tax concessions or investment grants. But it would not allow more active, selective intervention, such as the use of state enterprises to develop targeted industries or measures to encourage private firms to pursue objectives set by the state.

It may be seriously doubted whether such openness to international market forces can best serve to promote industrial development, given the competitive disadvantages faced by countries making a relatively *late start* to industrialisation. In various strands of the development literature it is recognised that the long-established industries of advanced industrial countries have built up competitive advantages so strong as to create serious barriers to entry into many manufacturing sectors. Such entry barriers take many forms, their nature and scale varying from industry to industry.

Significant barriers to entry into international markets can be created for late-industrialisers as a result of factors such as economies of scale in production, advantages of large established firms in marketing and raising capital, and the established technological strength of existing industries in advanced industrial countries. In industries where economies of scale are important, newcomers would have to produce and sell on a large scale to be competitive but may have great difficulty in capturing quickly the necessary market share. The marketing strength of established firms compounds such difficulties, while technological disadvantages can be even harder to overcome. Thus in many industries newcomers would have to go through a period of initial losses, which they may not be able to survive.[1]

For these reasons indigenous private firms in a late-industrialising country with outward-looking, free-market policies would generally tend to be deterred from trying to enter many internationally traded industries where entry barriers are important. This would leave them largely confined to investing in sheltered or non-traded industries, internationally traded industries with relatively insignificant barriers to entry, or simple, low value-added processing of local primary products. Since there is a good deal of evidence to suggest that imperfect competition and barriers to entry are prevalent in many important branches of manufacturing, this confinement to the accessible, 'easily-entered' sectors would present strictly limited opportunities for industrial development.[2] These limitations are all the more significant in view of the degree of competition between so many latecomers in the same limited range of industries.

These considerations are relevant to *indigenous* industries, but there is also the possibility of attracting direct investment from established firms in advanced countries, not subject to the constraints on newcomers. Foreign investment, however, can scarcely provide a general solution to the problem of late industrialisation since it tends to occur on a relatively small scale. Most firms are attracted to advanced industrial areas and relatively few are sufficiently mobile or footloose to move to less developed locations. Thus, in 1977, less than 15% of the assets of foreign subsidiaries of US manufacturing companies were located in developing countries. Nevertheless, the Republic of Ireland has attracted a very substantial share of the foreign manufacturing investment going to

[1] For more detailed discussions of barriers to entry see Bain (1956) and Porter (1980, ch. 1). In the development literature, the 'Dependency' school is particularly conscious of the problems caused for late-industrialisers by barriers to entry.

[2] The view that imperfect competition and barriers to entry are widespread is commonly held by Marxist writers, such as Baran (1973), and Bienefeld and Innes (1976). It also features, however, in basic textbooks on industrial or business economics.

late-industrialising countries—a share greatly disproportionate to the country's own small size.[1] But even with this major concentration of foreign investment, industry in Ireland still accounts for a significantly smaller proportion of output and employment than in the rest of Western Europe.

Although the overall impact of foreign investment in developing countries is limited, a few small late-industrialising countries, which are *exceptionally* attractive sites for mobile foreign investment, can achieve quite rapid industrial growth, sufficient to have a significant impact on their economies for some time, by attracting a greatly disproportionate share of such investment. This can occur even though their indigenous industrial development is seriously constrained. This article aims to show that, to the extent that Ireland has had some success with the outward-looking free-market strategy, it has been an exceptional case of this type (rather like Puerto Rico or Singapore). Rather than supporting the neo-classical view, the weak performance of Irish indigenous industry illustrates the serious difficulties faced by latecomers and suggests a need for different policies.

2. Irish industry before the 1950s

The early history of Irish industry is relevant here. For over a century up until the 1930s, Ireland was in a position analogous to that of present-day latecomers following outward-looking policies and relying on market forces. For most of this period, Ireland was part of the UK (then the world's most advanced industrial country) and had free trade with other parts and followed classic *laissez-faire*, free market policies; and for nearly ten years after the establishment of the Irish Free State in 1922 this did not change greatly. The consequences for most of Irish industry, except in the Belfast region in the north-east, were quite devastating.

Industry had developed to substantial proportions in Ireland by the early nineteenth century, suggesting that local conditions were not markedly unfavourable for industrialisation. But the decline in most areas thereafter indicates that the attainment of suitable local conditions, and reliance on market forces, are not sufficient to generate sustained industrialisation in a country making a late start on a small scale in developing mechanised industry (in relation to Great Britain's pioneering industrial revolution). As the development of mechanised industry proceeded, the growing importance of economies of scale, the external economies of large industrial agglomerations, and technological capabilities created ever stronger concentrated industrial centres in those areas of the UK (including the Belfast region) which began mechanised development on a large scale first, while those starting relatively late and/or on a smaller scale (including most of Ireland outside Belfast) were gradually eliminated by competition.[2]

When the Irish government introduced strong protectionist policies in the early 1930s, rapid growth of industrial employment followed for two decades, apart from during the Second World War when it was difficult to import inputs. Starting from only 62,000 in 1931, employment in manufacturing grew to 140,000 in 1951, an average

---

[1] The Republic of Ireland, with a population of little over three million or about 0·1% of that of the less-developed countries, had 4·8% of the assets of US manufacturing companies in developing countries in 1977 (US Department of Commerce, *Survey of Current Business,* October 1981); in addition, non-US foreign companies together account for more manufacturing employment in Ireland than US firms.

[2] A full discussion of the causes of the nineteenth-century decline of most of Irish industry, in contrast to the Belfast area, is beyond the scope of this article (see O'Malley, 1981).

144   E. O'Malley

growth rate of 4·2% a year. But labour productivity growth was sluggish and the volume of output per worker grew by only 1·4% a year in 1931–51.[1]

If the labour productivity trend suggests that the protected industries were inefficient, this impression is strengthened by the fact that sales were concentrated on the small protected domestic market and few industries were able to compete effectively in export markets. Leaving aside Food, Drink and Tobacco, which had been the only substantial export industries in the 1920s, the rest of manufacturing exported only 6% of its output in 1951. Further evidence comes from the reports of the Committee on Industrial Organisation, established in 1961, which noted that old equipment, small scale, short production runs and wide ranges of products (resulting from the prevailing orientation towards the small protected domestic market) commonly resulted in high production costs.[2]

The lack of export growth was important because economic growth depended on importing the many capital goods, components and materials still not available domestically. In these circumstances, a chronic balance of payments crisis emerged in the 1950s and the deflationary measures taken to reduce imports resulted in prolonged recession, rapid decline in employment and massive emigration.

It may be concluded that the industrial structure generated by protection was rather inefficient, largely unable to export and thus ultimately causing growth to be constrained by a lack of foreign exchange. This is not to say, however, that the introduction of protection was the *original* cause of industrial stagnation. Seen in a longer-term perspective, it is evident that free trade and reliance on market forces had already produced industrial decline or stagnation for more than 100 years before the 1930s when protection was introduced. Protection, for a time, probably generated greater industrial growth than would have occurred under continuing free trade and reliance on market forces. But it seems that protection alone was ultimately *inadequate* to overcome the entry barriers into international competition which had been raised to a high level by the mid twentieth century.

Seen in this longer-term perspective, it might have been appropriate to use stronger systematic and selective state initiatives to supplement protection as a means of building industries capable of overcoming international entry barriers. But the prevailing view favoured a return to the outward-looking free-market approach. General incentives to promote export industries and to attract foreign investment were introduced in the 1950s and the removal of protection began in the mid 1960s.[3]

3. Indigenous industry under the new policies

Roughly coinciding with this policy change, economic recovery began in the late 1950s, and industrial output in the 1960s and 1970s grew at over three times the rate of the 1950s. Manufactured exports grew particularly rapidly as Ireland's share of foreign markets increased and diversification occurred into a wider range of goods, including technically advanced products such as computers, and fine chemicals and pharmaceuticals. Irish industrial wages rose almost to equal UK levels by 1979. This experience

[1] These data are from the Census of Industrial Production. The output per worker data for 1931–51 refer to 'Transportable Goods' industries, which include mining and peat as well as manufacturing, but manufacturing accounts for over 90% of the total.
[2] See Committee on Industrial Organisation (1965).
[3] Details of the steps by which these policies were introduced are contained in O'Malley (1980).

of industrial growth since the 1950s has been widely regarded as a fundamental break-through, and Ireland is now conventionally classified as an advanced industrial country. As suggested above, however, these developments are largely attributable to Ireland's exceptional success in attracting a greatly disproportionate share of mobile foreign industry. Indigenous industry has shown signs of relative decline since the removal of protection began.

Table 1 shows that employment in industries other than new foreign ones grew by almost 20,000 in 1960–66 while protection still remained, but then declined slightly under freer trade after the mid 1960s. Output in these industries has grown since the mid 1960s, but they have experienced declining market shares—a trend which may be

Table 1. *Manufacturing employment in new foreign industry and the rest of industry, 1960–80 (thousands)*

	1960	1966	1973	1980
New foreign industry	3	10	36	61
Rest of industry	169	188	186	182
Total	172	198	222	243

Sources: Trend in Employment and Unemployment series for Total; *IDA Employment Survey* for New foreign in 1973 and 1980; New foreign in 1960 and 1966 estimated from *Survey of Grant-Aided Industry* (1967); Rest of industry by subtracting New foreign from Total.

Note: New foreign industry is defined to be majority foreign-owned firms grant-aided under the Industrial Development Authority's (IDA) New Industry scheme for projects started since the 1950s or their Small Industry scheme begun in 1967.

described as one of relative decline. Relative decline occurred in the domestic market, as shown by the growth of competing imports, which had gained only an extra 0·2% a year of the Irish market in 1960–67, but then gained an extra 1·5% a year in 1967–73, and 1·0% a year in 1973–79.[1] Since the new foreign industries are very highly export-oriented, they have always accounted for less than 5% of domestic market sales, so the rise in import penetration has taken market shares almost exclusively from other industries.

It might be thought, of course, that while a rise in import penetration was predictable under freer trade, the accompanying gain in export market shares would compensate (or more than compensate) for this. In fact, however, Irish industries other than new foreign industry showed no overall gain in export market shares. They accounted for an estimated 0·26% of the manufactured exports of all market economies in 1966 and the

---

[1] 'Competing' imports are imports of manufactured goods which are considered to be competing directly with existing producers of similar products in Ireland. Official data on competing imports for 1960–73 are published in the *Review of 1973 and Outlook for 1974*; for 1973–77 data were derived from the *Trade Statistics of Ireland* by summing up import items classified as 'competing' according to Matthews (1980); for 1977–79, data are as supplied by the Department of Industry, Commerce and Tourism for a study of industrial job losses by the National Economic and Social Council.

146   E. O'Malley

same percentage in 1976.[1] In the same period, the share of *total* Irish manufactured exports, including new foreign firms, rose from 0·33% to 0·48%.

It may be concluded from these aggregate trends that Irish indigenous industry suffered a net loss in market share as it lost out in the home market without a compensating increase abroad. It may be concluded, too, that rather little progress has been made in industrial development under outward-looking free-market policies, apart from the development of the country as a site for mobile foreign industries. The more detailed analysis which follows tends to support the view that the basic problem confronting indigenous industry is the existence of barriers to entry in many internationally traded industries which confine latecomers to a limited range of activities.

Certain types of Irish indigenous industry have, in fact, fared quite well under outward-looking free-market policies, while others have tended to decline rapidly. Table 2 illustrates this variation in experience. As columns 1 and 2 of Table 2 show, Clay, Glass and cement, Drink and tobacco, Food, and Paper and printing performed relatively well, resisting import penetration and suffering little or no loss of employment between 1973 and 1980 in firms established before 1973, while recording an increase in the total number of jobs in the industry. Chemicals, Textiles, and Clothing and footwear have the weakest record on these three indicators and show signs of significant decline. The performance of the remaining three sectors—Metals and engineering, Wood and furniture, and 'Other' manufacturing—was relatively weak in terms of the first two indicators, but total employment increased.

The strongest performances have generally oc :urred in industries which are *not* subject to the constraints imposed on latecomers by barriers to entry. These industries are characterised by either (a) low value-added processing of local primary products, or (b) being long established in Ireland, or (c) being the 'non-traded' sectors enjoying a degree of natural protection because of transport or logistical costs.

Thus the Irish Food industry consists mostly of very basic processing of local primary products: value-added in the main subdivisions ranges from 13 to 21% of gross output compared with 44% in non-food manufacturing. The Drink and tobacco sector, which has higher value-added, is largely composed of a few big firms which date back at least 160 years and which have not, therefore, had to face barriers-to-entry problems. Clay, Glass and cement and Paper and printing consist largely of virtually non-traded activities, as is demonstrated by their success in resisting import penetration without at the same time achieving success in exporting.[2]

Small-scale firms in Metals and engineering, Wood and furniture, and Other manufacturing have also fared quite well where they have been engaged in small non-traded activities such as carpentry, simple metal fabrication, structural steel, plastic moulding and tyre remoulding. However, these three sectors also include larger scale, internationally traded industries, which have lost ground to competing imports, so that the overall increase in import penetration in each of these sectors is in the intermediate range in Table 2. Overall employment growth was almost entirely due to small firms

---

[1] Exports of Irish industries other than new foreign industry are calculated by subtracting data on new foreign industry from national totals. Data on new foreign industry are derived from the *Survey of Grant-Aided Industry* (1967) and O'Farrell and O'Loughlin (1980). Exports of all market economies are derived from the UN *Yearbook of International Trade Statistics 1977*.

[2] The percentage of output exported by firms other than new foreign firms was only 15% in Clay, Glass and cement and 13% in Paper and printing in 1973—the last year for which data are available—slightly lower than in 1960 in both cases and well below the 1973 average of 26% for all industries other than new foreign industry.

Table 2. *Performance indicators for indigenous industry, by sector*

	Increase in competing imports' Irish market share 1967–79 (% p.a.)	Employment change (%) 1973–80 in firms existing before 1973	Total Employment change (%) 1973–80
Clay, Glass and cement	0·2	6·5	16·4
Drink and tobacco	0·3	1·1	1·6
Food	0·5	−2·1	4·9
Paper and printing	1·4	−2·0	16·0
'Other' manufacturing	1·4	−14·2	5·2
Wood and furniture	2·0	−16·0	6·8
Metals and engineering	2·3	−8·7	23·9
Chemicals	2·3	−27·1	−9·1
Textiles	2·8	−39·9	−33·4
Clothing and footwear	4·6	−36·3	−24·6
All sectors	1·2	−12·8	−3·0

Sources: Competing imports derived from *Review of 1973 and Outlook for 1974* for 1966–73, from *Trade Statistics of Ireland* for 1973–77 and from data supplied by the Department of Industry, Commerce and Tourism for 1977–79. Employment data, which refer to Irish-owned industries, are obtained from *IDA Employment Survey*.

Notes: Column 1 shows the average gain per annum in competing imports' percentage share of the Irish market (e.g. an increase from a 30% share held by competing imports in 1967 to 54% in 1979 would appear in column 1 as a 2% gain per annum). Column 2 shows the percentage change, in 1973–80, in employment by firms which already existed in 1973, while column 3 shows total employment change in 1973–80 including new firms set up *during* that period.

setting up (employment in plants with under 200 workers increasing by 32% in 1973–80) employment in large firms declining significantly (by 30% in plants with over 200 workers).

The sectors with the weakest overall performance, Chemicals, Textiles, and Clothing and footwear, enjoy little or no natural protection and were fully exposed to competition under free trade. Within Textiles and Clothing and footwear, however, there are activities with relatively low barriers to entry, as witnessed by their growth in many NICs. It might be expected that Ireland, as a latecomer, ought to have had some success in competing internationally in these areas. There have, in fact, been some successes in developing exports, with all of the eight largest Textiles and Clothing firms exporting exceptionally large proportions of output—ranging from 31% to over 90% in 1978.[1] But many Irish firms have not succeeded in developing the scale, degree of specialisation and marketing sophistication required for international competition even in these low-entry-barrier industries. Competition from low-wage NICs has also been a problem in certain areas, though the overall impact has been limited (Fitzpatrick, 1981).

To sum up, although growth occurred in certain indigenous industries which enjoyed natural advantages, there was a substantial decline in employment in most internationally traded sectors. By the early 1980s, there were few private indigenous firms in large-scale, traded industries except for basic processing and long-established companies which had not had to overcome entry barriers. Among the 100 largest private indigenous manufacturing firms, in terms of sales in 1981/82, 76 (accounting for 89% of sales and

[1] 'Irish Companies 1978', *The Irish Times*, 1 and 2 January 1979.

148   E. O'Malley

86% of employment) were mainly engaged in Clay, Glass and cement, Drink and tobacco, Food, and Paper and printing, and the relatively easily-entered Textiles and Clothing and footwear sectors.[1] Virtually none of the largest indigenous firms was mainly engaged in Metals and engineering, Chemicals, or Other manufacturing, which tend to be dominant among the activities of the biggest firms in advanced industrial countries (in branches such as transport equipment, metals, consumer durables, industrial chemicals, and so on, characterised by barriers to entry). Only one of the 23 Irish private indigenous manufacturing companies employing over 1000 people is in this sector, and it is more involved in construction and services than in large-scale manufacturing.

Rather than gradually developing larger-scale, more technically demanding, traded industries, the trend among Irish indigenous firms has been more in the opposite direction. Expenditure on R & D actually declined in relation to industrial output between 1971 and 1979.[2]

Irish indigenous industry has made little progress, if any, under outward-looking free market policies, in overcoming barriers to entry. Moreover, far from being hostile to industrial development, the rapid expansion of foreign industry in Ireland in the 1960s and 1970s demonstrates that local economic and social 'supply-side' conditions—in the form of the infrastructure, the political and bureacratic environment, financial and professional services, and the attitudes and commitment of the labour force—have been reasonably favourable. (Foreign companies have enjoyed no exclusive qualification for state support or assistance in Ireland, and grant assistance and advisory services have become more intensive, if anything, for indigenous firms since the early 1970s—see O'Malley, 1980).

Nor does an absence of entrepreneurial initiative seem to be a sufficient explanation for the problems of Irish industry. New Irish entrepreneurial activity has, in fact, been quite considerable, but this does not necessarily lead to satisfactory industrial development involving the growth of internationally traded industries. Thus many new indigenous manufacturing firms were established in the period 1973–80, accounting for as much as 37% of all Irish manufacturing firms operating by 1980, the rate of formation per 1000 employees being more than double that of the East Midlands of England in 1968–75, which then had a rate 50% above the UK average (O'Farrell and Crouchley, 1984). But the new Irish manufacturing firms are mostly small and (despite tax incentives to export up until 1981) in largely non-traded activities. The decline in older large firms has, therefore, meant a decline in employment in indigenous manufacturing and little export development.

It could be argued, however, that Irish entrepreneurship is deficient in the sense of lacking the *specialised skills and experience* required in specific traded industries. Such 'entrepreneurial' deficiencies could be seen as a form of entry barrier, rather than as a social-psychological deficiency, since specialised business competence based on experience is not easily acquired in an economy where the industries concerned do not already exist. Thus the fact that Irish firms have not attempted to develop in many traded industries with substantial entry barriers could reasonably be interpreted as rational and realistic behaviour for profit-seeking private entrepreneurs, who may be

[1] Derived from *Irish Business*, January 1983 list of top companies.
[2] According to the National Board for Science and Technology statistics, real expenditure on R & D increased by 3·7% a year as against a growth rate of industrial output of 5·5%. These figures include foreign subsidiaries, but the fact that the many new foreign firms established in the 1970s had, on average, a higher R & D intensity than Irish firms, means that R & D intensity in Irish firms must have declined significantly.

The Economic Development of Ireland II

conscious both of conventional entry barriers and the need for some familiarity with a complex area of business before setting up a new enterprise.

4. Foreign industries in Ireland

It is clear from the discussion above that industrial growth in the Republic of Ireland over the past two decades has been due largely to success in attracting mobile foreign industry. By 1982, foreign-owned firms accounted for more than one-third of manufacturing employment and over 70% of manufactured exports.

Some foreign firms had been set up before the 1950s, motivated mainly by Ireland's former protectionist policies to establish plants in Ireland to serve the local market, and these tended to decline at much the same rate (in terms of employment) as Irish-owned firms under the freer trade of the 1970s. But the new export-oriented foreign sector has expanded rapidly. Studies of new foreign industries in Ireland suggest that they are mostly similar to those established in low-wage LDCs or NICs during the 1960s and 1970s, in so far as they fall within the following two categories. First, there are technically mature, labour-intensive products (such as clothing, footwear, textiles, plastic products and toys) which, as Vernon (1966) has suggested, are capable of locating in industrially undeveloped countries because they have no great dependence on close contact with the specialised skills, knowledge, suppliers and services of advanced industrial centres. Second, there are newer and more sophisticated products (such as machinery, electronic products, chemicals, etc.) but typically only those *stages* of their production which make few demands on technical skills or local high-quality suppliers. These activities are roughly comparable to those which Helleiner (1973) regarded as the emerging growth area for foreign manufacturing investment in LDCs, again because of little dependence on the skills and external economies of advanced industrial centres.[1] However, in some cases (such as electronics) Ireland has more highly-skilled activities than most NICs, though still generally lacking key R & D functions or significant local linkages.

Consistent with these suggestions, a recent detailed assessment of new foreign firms in Ireland includes the following:

(On electrical and electronic firms)

Of the 60 companies surveyed, none have a truly stand-alone operation in Ireland, and only three have operations in Ireland which embody the key competitive elements of the company's business. All others are currently manufacturing satellites, performing partial steps in the manufacturing process. Skill development and linkages in Ireland have been limited. The electronics industry is a high-skilled industry worldwide, but the activities in Ireland's electronics industry do not now reflect this.

(On mechanical engineering firms)

Ireland's foreign-owned mechanical engineering companies consist mainly of sub-assembly and assembly shops of the sort commonly found in newly-industrialising countries . . . Of the 34 shops surveyed, about half had only one or two skilled blue-collar workers and one or two engineers.

(On foreign-owned firms in general)

Foreign-owned industrial operations in Ireland with few exceptions do not embody the key competitive activities of the businesses in which they participate; do not employ significant numbers of skilled workers; and are not significantly integrated into traded and skilled sub-supply industries in Ireland (Telesis Report, 1982).

[1] Studies of new foreign industries in Ireland which would suggest that they mostly fall into these categories include Cooper and Whelan (1973); Buckley (1975); Teeling (1975); and Stanton (1979).

150   E. O'Malley

Although foreign firms have made a major contribution to industrial growth in Ireland, the nature of their activities means that their impact in encouraging indigenous development is minimal. Future industrial growth remains heavily dependent, therefore, on the continuing growth of new foreign industry.

This point has been made by earlier studies which have shown that the new foreign firms set up in Ireland have not developed close linkages with indigenous industry and have contributed rather little in the way of skill development, technology transfer, or the generation of 'spin-offs'. New foreign industries (excluding Food) purchased only 11.2% of their inputs of materials and components from Irish sources in 1974 (McAleese, 1977, Table 5.4), which means that their purchases amounted to less than 3% of the sales of indigenous industry. McAleese and McDonald (1978) found that the proportion of purchases by foreign firms from Irish sources had been increasing, but only by about two or three percentage points per decade up to 1974, and O'Loughlin and O'Farrell (1980) found no evidence of this increase continuing. With such low levels of local purchasing, foreign firms can have done little to stimulate development of an indigenous plant and machinery industry, which is one significant secondary benefit that might have been expected. The extracts from the Telesis Report (1982) quoted above suggest that new foreign firms have contributed little to the development of indigenous skills and technological capabilities.[1]

On the more positive side, McAleese (1977) has investigated and rejected the hypothesis that new foreign firms might have actually damaged indigenous industry by paying wages above the national norm, thus raising wage expectations generally and causing a worsening of cost competitiveness. And they have earned foreign exchange and thereby facilitated the growth of domestically-oriented indigenous industries (which need to import many inputs, quite apart from the spending on imports from the income generated by them). But this particular contribution to indigenous industrial growth itself implies a state of continuing dependence since (unlike technology transfer, skill development, or spin-offs) it is not a lasting benefit which could continue independently of developments in the foreign sector. The survival and growth of indigenous industries remain heavily dependent on the ability of other sectors—agriculture and foreign borrowing by the government as well as foreign firms—to push back the foreign exchange constraint.

The continuing viability of the country's current development strategy depends mainly on the prospects for future growth of the foreign-owned sector. An important factor tending to create increasing difficulties in securing a high rate of growth in the foreign-owned sector is the fact that new foreign firms in Ireland show a tendency eventually to decline, at least in terms of employment. Thus, according to the IDA Employment Survey, employment in new foreign firms fell by 2.4% in 1973–80 in the case of those established before 1973 and by over 10% in those established before 1969.

This decline probably reflects in part increasing difficulty in competing with producers of similar products in low-wage NICs. However, it probably also reflects the sectoral composition of the foreign industries concerned, many of which tend to be maturing industries which have experienced weak growth internationally. Both of these factors may well continue to apply with each succeeding generation of foreign investment, since industries generally only become sufficiently mobile to move to a less advanced industrial environment as they mature. When an industry reaches a stage

[1] See also Cooper and Whelan (1973) and Buckley (1975) on the question of transfer of skills and technology; and see Cogan and Onyenadum (1981) on the low level of 'spin-offs' from foreign electronic firms.

Problem of late industrialisation 151

where it can readily locate a plant in Ireland, it can soon do so in low-wage NICs as well. And it would also be drawing closer to the phase of slower growth commonly faced by mature industries.[1]

The declining trend in the longer-established foreign firms means that Ireland has depended on *new first-time* foreign investors for manufacturing employment growth. If the newcomers themselves tend eventually to go into decline, there will be a gradually increasing proportion of relatively old declining plants, necessitating continuous increases in new first-time investment to attain net employment increases of any given amount.

It looks very doubtful, at present, whether such continuous increases can be achieved. In the 1960s and 1970s, the Republic of Ireland was able to attract many mobile industries successfully, despite having much higher labour costs than most LDCs, because of a combination of advantages such as political 'reliability', proximity to the European market, free trade with the UK and later the EEC, tax and grant incentives, effective promotion work by the Industrial Development Authority, and other institutional and cultural factors which reduce information costs, uncertainty and perceptions of risk. And Ireland's attractions, as compared with other European locations, have lain mainly in tax and grant incentives and cheaper labour costs.

However, the development of a number of low wage NICs as 'reliable', relatively risk-free sites since about the mid 1960s, combined with rising labour costs in Ireland, have to some extent eroded the attractions which brought many of the labour-intensive mobile foreign investors to Ireland up to the late 1960s. But this appears to have been offset by Ireland's improved market access to the UK market since the mid 1960s and to the EEC market since 1973—which brought new foreign investors seeking secure access to those markets. This advantage, however, may now be diminishing as a result of stronger competition from other EEC members for foreign investment. An important factor here is the relative decline of the UK economy, which has led to increased efforts by the UK to attract foreign investment. The recent or imminent accession of Greece, Spain and Portugal to the EEC may also be creating new sources of stronger competition for the type of mobile foreign investment for which Ireland had special attractions in the 1970s.

Coupled with this increasing competition, relatively slow growth in European markets in the 1980s has led to greater difficulties in attracting new foreign firms to Ireland. New US manufacturing investment in Ireland peaked in 1979–81 and then declined until 1983, with only a small recovery in 1984. Furthermore, Ireland's *share* of new US manufacturing investment in Western Europe also declined after 1979–81 (after rising almost continuously since 1972.[2] Although there maybe some recovery, it is still very doubtful whether it will be possible to achieve continuous increases in new foreign investment.

---

[1] The decline in employment in longer-established firms in 1973–80 is at least consistent with this hypothesis of a recurring pattern of eventual decline, but the available data are limited to too short a period to establish this point firmly. However, data on employment in new overseas firms in Northern Ireland clearly show this pattern in every five-year cohort going back as far as the late 1940s (Northern Ireland Economic Council, 1983, Figure 5).

[2] Ireland's share of new US manufacturing investment in the EEC (nine countries) fell from 2·5% in 1979 to 1·7% in 1983, whereas the UK's share rose from 26·4% in 1977 to 29·2% in 1983. Ireland's share of new US manufacturing investment in the 'EEC twelve' (including Spain, Greece and Portugal) fell from 2·4% in 1979 to 1·6% in 1983, whereas Spain's share rose from 2·4% to 3·9%, and Portugal's share from 0·2% to 0·4%, although Greece's share did not increase in 1979–83 (US Department of Commerce, *Survey of Current Business*, October 1981 and September 1984).

152   E. O'Malley

5. Conclusion

It has been argued above that industrial growth in the Republic of Ireland under outward-looking, free-market policies offers no general support for such policies. The growth of industry in Ireland has been mainly due to the attraction of an *exceptionally* large share of a globally limited amount of mobile foreign industry, while indigenous industry was in relative decline. Furthermore, the continuation of the relatively high overall industrial growth rates of the 1960s and 1970s under these policies is now in some doubt, because of the difficulties of securing a continuous high rate of expansion of foreign industry, while the fundamental problem of overcoming barriers to entry facing indigenous industry remains to be addressed effectively.

Singapore and Puerto Rico are two other late-industrialising countries which are often referred to as examples of the success of the neoclassical strategy, but the validity of these two cases can be doubted on much the same grounds as in the case of Ireland. Both of these countries appear to have depended even more heavily than Ireland on attracting *exceptionally* large shares of mobile foreign industry, which was sufficient to have a major impact on industrial growth. By 1980, 52% of industrial employment, 71% of industrial output and 90–95% of industrial exports were accounted for by foreign firms in Singapore (Cheah, 1980; Telesis, 1982, p. 367). In Puerto Rico, foreign firms accounted for 73% of industrial employment and 90–95% of industrial exports (Villamil, 1979; Telesis, 1982, p. 367).

By contrast, indigenous industry in South Korea, Taiwan and especially Japan has made significant progress in overcoming the barriers to entry faced by latecomers in international markets, but it is very doubtful whether this has been achieved (as is sometimes claimed) through relying on a pure outward-looking, free-market strategy. Rather, success may be attributable to significant departures from this strategy.

The type of policy adopted by these countries is summed up by a Japanese policy-maker (quoted by Allen, 1981) who said the policy was to (a) select industries carefully, (b) prevent ruinous competition at the infancy stage, (c) nurse them to competitive stature and then expose them to outside competition. All three stages of such a strategy involve departures from fully outward-looking, free-market policies. At the same time, the element of selectivity and the measures taken to develop a fully competitive stature distinguish this strategy from the simple, indiscriminate protectionism which has ultimately failed in many countries, including Ireland in the 1950s.

If the analysis of Ireland's experience in this article shows that an outward-looking, free-market strategy has proved inadequate to overcome barriers to entry for late-developing indigenous industry, the experience of countries such as Japan and South Korea seems to indicate that an efficient selective and directive state policy can help to achieve better results. Protection, however, would obviously be of less value as a means of ultimately developing internationally competitive industries in Ireland, in view of the small domestic market of only a few million people. There are, of course, many reasons why the Japanese or Korean approach might not be fully transferable to a different culture. But it seems reasonable to conclude that Irish policy makers should develop some variant of a more active, directive approach, aiming to build up selected industries (along the lines, for example, proposed in the Telesis report, 1982).

It would be essential for Ireland to focus mainly on developing traded *export* industries in adopting such a strategy, since such a small economy will inevitably continue to depend heavily on imports of many kinds for further growth. The development of exports to pay for the necessary imports is thus the key constraint to be tackled in promoting economic development, and industry should play a major role in exporting since many non-industrial activities are largely oriented to local markets. The target export industries would have to be selected on the basis of careful analysis of the specific requirements for international competitive success in the industries concerned, together with a realistic assessment of the potential and constraints arising from Ireland's existing skills, resources and size. This would tend to mean that Ireland would have to select quite specialised industries, whether these are specialised by product, customer, geographical area, or a combination of these. Such specialised, or 'niche' industries, have the advantage of avoiding direct competition with very large firms, which are not interested in, or may not be flexible enough to compete in these activities.[1] The actual development of the selected industries would then require active state initiatives and concentrated support to sustain them, while policies and resources would need to be focussed on building up the necessary characteristics for competitive success—such as scale, skills, technology and marketing.

The current thrust of policy in Ireland, however, as presented most recently in the White Paper *Industrial Policy* (1984), continues to focus mainly on creating the right environment and providing quite generalised incentives for industry, rather than on implementing an active, selective and directive approach.

Bibliography

Adams, F. G. and Ichimura, S. 1983. Industrial policy in Japan, in Adams, F. G. and Klein, L. R. (eds), *Industrial Policies for Growth and Competitiveness*, Lexington, Wharton Econometric Studies

Allen, G. C. 1981. Industrial policy and innovation in Japan, in Carter, C. (ed.), *Industrial Policy and Innovation*, London, Heinemann

Bain, J. S. 1956. *Barriers to New Competition*, Cambridge (Mass.), Harvard University Press

Balassa, B. 1980. *The Process of Industrial Development and Alternative Development Strategies*, World Bank Staff Working Paper No. 438, October

Baran, P. A. 1973. *The Political Economy of Growth*, Harmondsworth, Penguin

Bienefeld, M. and Innes, D. 1976. Capital accumulation and South Africa, *Review of African Political Economy*, No. 7

Buckley, P. J. 1975. The effects of foreign direct investment on the economy of the Irish Republic, Ph.D. thesis, University of Lancaster

Cheah Hock Beng, 1980. Export-oriented industrialisation and dependent development: the experience of Singapore, *IDS Bulletin*, Sussex, vol. 12, no. 1, December

Cogan, J. and Onyenadum, E. 1981. Spin-off companies in the Irish electronics industry, *Journal of Irish Business and Administrative Research*, vol. 3, no. 2, October

Committee on Industrial Organisation 1965. *Final Report*, Dublin, Stationery Office

Cooper, C. and Whelan, N. 1973. *Science, Technology and Industry in Ireland*, report to the National Science Council, Dublin, Stationery Office

Farley, N. 1973. Outward-looking policies and industrialisation in a small economy: some notes on the Irish case, *Economic Development and Cultural Change*, vol. 21, no. 4, pt 1, July

Fitzpatrick, J. 1981. *Industrialisation, Trade and Ireland's Development Co-operation Policy*, Dublin, Advisory Council on Development Co-operation

Helleiner, G. K. 1973. Manufactured exports from less developed countries and multinational firms, *Economic Journal*, vol. 83, no. 329, March

Industrial Policy 1984. Irish Government white paper, Dublin, Stationery Office

Little, I., Scitovsky, T. and Scott, M. 1970. *Industry and Trade in Some Developing Countries—a Comparative Study*, London, New York and Toronto, OUP

[1] See National Board for Science and Technology (1983), for further discussion of this point.

154   E. O'Malley

Luedde-Neurath, R. 1980. Export orientation in South Korea: how helpful is dependency thinking to its analysis? *IDS Bulletin*, Sussex, vol. 12, no. 1, December

Luedde-Neurath, R. 1984. State intervention and foreign direct investment in South Korea, *IDS Bulletin*, Sussex, vol. 15, no. 2, April

McAleese, D. 1977. *A Profile of Grant-Aided Industry in Ireland*, Dublin, Industrial Development Authority

McAleese, D. and McDonald, D. 1978. Employment growth and the development of linkages in foreign-owned and domestic manufacturing enterprises, *Oxford Bulletin of Economics and Statistics*, vol. 40, no. 4, November

Matthews, A. 1980. *EEC External Trade Policy: Its Relevance to Ireland*, Dublin, Irish Council of the European Movement

National Board for Science and Technology, 1983. *Technology and Irish Industrial Policy*, Dublin, NBST

Northern Ireland Economic Council, 1983. *The Duration of Industrial Development Assisted Employment*, Belfast, Northern Ireland Economic Development Office

O'Farrell, P. N. and Crouchley, R. 1984. An industrial and spatial analysis of new firm formation in Ireland, *Regional Studies*, vol. 18, no. 3, June

O'Farrell, P. N. and O'Loughlin, B. 1980. *An Analysis of New Industry Linkages in Ireland*, Dublin, Industrial Development Authority

O'Loughlin, B. and O'Farrell, P. N. 1980. Foreign direct investment in Ireland: empirical evidence and theoretical implications, *Economic and Social Review*, vol. 11, no. 3, April

O'Malley, E. 1980. *Industrial Policy and Development: A Survey of Literature from the Early 1960s to the Present*, National Economic and Social Council, Paper No. 56, Dublin, Stationery Office

O'Malley, E. 1981. The decline of Irish industry in the nineteenth century, *Economic and Social Review*, vol. 13, no. 1, October

Porter, M. 1980. *Competitive Strategy—Techniques for Analyzing Industries and Competitors*, New York, Free Press

Stanton, R. 1979. Foreign investment and host-country politics: the Irish case, in Seers, D., Schaffer, B. and Kiljunen, M. (eds), *Underdeveloped Europe: Studies in Core-Periphery Relations*, Hassocks, Harvester

Survey of Grant-Aided Industry 1967. Survey team's report to the Industrial Development Authority, Dublin, Stationery Office

Teeling, J. 1975. The evolution of offshore investment, DBA thesis, Harvard University

Telesis Consultancy Group 1982. *A Review of Industrial Policy*, National Economic and Social Council, Paper No. 64, Dublin, Stationery Office

Vernon, R. 1966. International investment and international trade in the product cycle, *Quarterly Journal of Economics*, vol. LXXX, no. 2, May

Villamil, J. J. 1979. Puerto Rico 1948–1976: the limits of dependent growth, in Villamil, J. J. (ed.), *Transnational Capitalism and National Development*, Hassocks, Harvester

Wade, R. 1984. Dirigisme Taiwan-style, *IDS Bulletin*, Sussex, vol. 15, no. 2, April

Excerpt from Frank Litton (ed.), *Unequal Achievement: The Irish Experience 1957–1982*, 1–18.

Society and Culture

NA

JOSEPH LEE

If Lonergan's definition of culture as 'the set of meanings and values that informs a way of life' be adopted, then T. K. Whitaker's *Economic Development* must loom as a landmark in the mid-twentieth century cultural landscape. Ireland had not enjoyed the instructive experience of wartime occupation. There was little post-war feeling of a new era inspired by the spirit of the Resistance. It took the frightening emigration figures of the 1950s to generate an Irish substitute for the shame of Sedan. Responses varied. There were those like Whitaker whose sense of honour, outraged at the humiliation, drove them to embrace an Irish version of the Resistance mentality. Whitaker belonged to a Department of Finance long suspicious of what it deemed the reckless initiatives emanating from the Industry and Commerce of Sean Lemass. In 1957, in the major revolution in Irish administrative history, Whitaker adopted something of the Lemass approach. Though no instinctive gambler, Whitaker found himself cast in the role of the conservative revolutionary from above, launched on a struggle to restore the vanishing self-respect of his country.

The economic growth of the 1960s, bringing a dramatic decline in emigration and a corresponding rise in national morale, silenced the sceptics, at least temporarily. But there remained many who had been quietly accommodating their interests to the stagnation of the 1950s. They were the collaborators in the wasting away of Irish society. The collaborationist mind with which the Resistance mentality had to wrestle, considered emigration 'a useful safety valve', on the grounds that 'when all that can be done has been done to absorb the supply of labour locally, it is better to allow the unemployed surplus to move to areas of rising demand than to condemn it to chronic unemployment'. By definition, 'all that can be done' had, of course, always been done.

1

Unequal Achievement

Emigration was due to the unreasonable expectations of the natives. 'If Irish people could be induced to refrain from measuring economic progress by British standards, they might take a much more cheerful view of their condition'. Once they abandoned presumptuous Anglo-American criteria, 'they might be content to pursue their own way of life that would conform closer to the patterns and the standards of other European countries.[1]

The maturity of a culture, no less than of an individual, is reflected in the urge to search for, and the capacity to confront, the truth about itself. Behind its sober prose, *Economic Development* extended an invitation to Irish society to embark on a search for self-knowledge, and not to flinch from the findings. There was much territory to be explored. A 'Hidden Ireland' – hidden by the Irish from themselves – awaited investigation. 'We are only beginning to produce good native studies of our formal decisionmaking institutions like the Oireachtas, and of the state sponsored bodies . . . we have not a single study of the informal decision making bodies, like pressure groups, and virtually none of the community 'elites', a vital subject in the analysis of power. We have no large scale study of class structure in Ireland . . . we have not as yet any professional study of the Catholic Church in Ireland as a social and political influence. . . ' wrote David Thornley in 1957.[2] The list might have been expanded almost indefinitely. There was scarcely a solitary standard general work on subjects or topics like anthropology, constitutional law, contemporary history, economics, education, management, politics, public administration, social policy, social psychology, sociology, trade unionism. The standard works had yet to appear. Many still remain to be written. Nevertheless, intellectual activity in most of these areas has increased significantly. Ritualistic invocation of emotively elastic terms like 'spiritual', 'tradition', 'family', 'materialism', have now begun to be subjected to scholarly scrutiny, as research probes, however hesitantly, the realities shrouded in the comfortable drapery of ignorance or hypocrisy.

That it is now difficult to recapture the bleakness of the intellectual terrain of twenty five years ago itself testifies to the change that has occurred. Promising inter-war initiatives, usually by foreigners, like Kohn on constitutional law, Moss on political parties, Arensberg and Kimball on social anthropology, remained isolated, sad reminders of the harvest the natives failed to reap. There were some hopeful, if still sporadic, signs of the coming Spring. *Christus Rex* began in 1947, *The Furrow* in 1950, *Administration* in 1953, *Irish Banking Review* in 1957.

2

Society and Culture

No Irish weekly has reached the level of sustained intellectual power to be found in the *Leader* in the early 1950s under the editorship of Desmond Williams. But there was still in 1957 no ESRI, with its impressive publication list, no NIEC or NESC, no Foras Forbartha, no NBST. There was no *Crane Bag*, no *Irish Economic and Social History*, no *Irish Educational Studies*, no *Irish Journal of Education*, no *Irish Jurist*, no *Scríobh*, no *Studia Hibernica*, to name only a few of the more stimulating subsequent arrivals.

Though the world of scholarly publication has been transformed since 1957, fundamental gaps remain, above all at the level of general comprehension. Of the relevant intellectual disciplines, as conventionally organised, it is history, anthropology and sociology that most aspire to a holistic perspective, however much individual practitioners may remain content to burrow in their own holes. Unfortunately, if understandably, the most institutionally advanced discipline, history, tended to shirk the challenge of the contemporary until the 1970s. The flight of the historians imposed a burden on sociology and anthropology which they were institutionally too under-developed to bear. Indeed fifty years after Arensberg and Kimball began their researches in Clare, there is still no chair of anthropology in a southern Irish university. Subsequent sectoral advances, particularly in economics and more recently in politics, have not yet been fully incorporated into total perspectives.

Sustained scholarly activity in the social sciences in the 1950s would have found itself quickly frustrated by glaring gaps in the official supply of information, itself a revealing index of the complacency of the collaborationist mentality. Nevertheless, it would be unhistorical to indict civil servants exclusively for this. When scholars subjected so little of the available information to systematic analysis, they could hardly complain about shortage of information. The supply, however many specific gaps continue to be identified as research frontiers pushed forward, has increased rapidly in the past twenty five years. Unfortunately, the civil service has managed to provoke widespread suspicion that it fails to disseminate information that may provoke expert criticism of its policies.[3] Tussing's sources generously attributed the shortage of useful information on the Irish educational system to conspiracy rather than incompetence. 'We have been told, again and again, by people within the educational system, and even by people within the civil service, that the State will resist publication of the kinds of information called for here, not because of any administrative

Unequal Achievement

costs or difficulties, but because they fear that public knowledge will limit their own freedom of action'.[4] That would be a reassuring tribute to the intelligence, if not necessarily the benevolence, of the state. More disturbing reservations arise where crucial information is not even collected, as appears to be the case in the field of social policy where the lack of adequate information 'about the distribution of income and wealth . . . prevents any evaluation of trends in inequality and therefore any overall assessment of the impact of social policy'.[5]

In its great years, Finance actually felt sufficiently self-confident to invite a scholar to examine its archives and write a detailed history down to the fairly recent past.[6] Other departments, most unhappily Foreign Affairs which has done so much to achieve a respected voice for Ireland internationally, have shown an unfortunate reluctance to open their archives in the manner now accepted as normal in western cultures.[7] The very publication of *Economic Development* indicated a reappraisal of the role of the civil servant. That an official should put his name to a virtual manifesto dismayed those whose power lay partly in their ability to stifle dissent behind the amiable facade of 'ministerial responsibility'. By venturing to publish, Whitaker showed he had come to accept the view of Patrick Lynch that public confidence in the quality of the official mind was itself an important prerequisite for national progress.[8] That this attitude has failed to permeate the civil service may contribute to what seems to be a growing lack of public confidence in the calibre of the official mind.

The civil service attitude, however, merely reflects instincts common to the wider culture. 'We markedly lag behind other industrial countries', for instance, 'in disclosure of information on company profitability'.[9] A leading liquidator, echoing the words of a bishop,[10] asks 'Why are people so chary of the workers and investors knowing the financial facts?'. He suggests a cultural rather than a technical explanation: 'There is involved here a whole morass of status seeking and pursuit of self-interest'.[11] The peasant residue in the Irish psyche confuses the distinction between necessary confidentiality and furtive concealment. This confusion is reinforced by suspicions grounded in the face to face nature of society and the petty scale of activity.

Lack of adequate evidence often makes it difficult to advance confident generalisations about cultural trends over the past twenty five years. The impact of television, especially since 1962, is a perennially controversial subject, and 'if the sociologists had been on

4

Society and Culture

the ball, a survey of attitudes and behaviour then would have provided us with valuable information against which a comparison could be made now. . . '[12] as Colm O Briain observed. But they were not, partly because there were so few sociologists, partly perhaps because the urge for self-knowledge was still underdeveloped. Claims to the effect that 'our latter day affluent society' is 'incomparably richer, also incomparably more selfish and greedy' than the Ireland of forty years ago,[13] or that 'economics has quietly but inevitably replaced religion as the dominant value in Irish society',[14] however plausible on impressionistic evidence, must remain unproven. So must the hypothesis that circumstances have changed much more than attitudes.[15]

Comparative perspective is required to make the most effective use of the growing corpus of information. In 1957 comparative perspective meant comparison with Britain. The ignorance of continental languages produced by the school syllabus made systematic comparison with continental countries virtually impossible and left Ireland, in many respects, a European country only in a geographical sense. Exposure to the EEC and the OECD came as a culture shock to Irish officials and directly stimulated the seminal enquiry, *Investment in Education.*[16] But the later cultural impact of the EEC has been muted. The prediction that 'within the EEC, we shall continue to have a derived or provincial British culture with a diminishing Roman Catholic tinge and diminishing relics of a Gaelic past'[17] has proved broadly correct. The Brussels connection has been largely domesticated to reinforce the powerful sponger syndrome in the Irish value system while leisure patterns have become, if anything, even more responsive to Anglo-Saxon influence in the age of television. However stimulating the potential western European cultural impact in the broader or narrower sense of Ireland, the harnessing of that potential demanded political vision and leadership on a grand scale. If there was a historic opportunity it was scarcely perceived, much less seized.

Ireland entered a period of rapid economic change with little grasp of the criteria by which it might assess and guide its own performance. This poverty of perspective was peculiarly unfortunate at a time when the cult of technological determinism became increasingly fashionable. The technology lobby succeeded in blurring central issues about the nature of future society by skilful propaganda which convinced credulous observers that technology was not only an indispensable tool

5

Unequal Achievement

for enhancing the potential national welfare, but that it held the secret of all socio-economic progress, that there was a crock of gold buried at the end of the technological rainbow, and that if one looked after the technology the society would look after itself. There seems to be a danger that even the Department of Education may be succumbing to the cult. The chapter on third level education in the latest White Paper fails to contain a solitary mention of the significance of the quality of social thought, or indeed of any thought, for the well-being of society. Yet the Department of Education has deserved well of public opinion in the past two decades. It has suffered much abuse, often selfish, often ignorant, in a period when it has itself changed from a centre of stagnation to a centre of activity. Nor has there been much sustained outside reflection on higher education on which it could draw. Nevertheless, the Department may be in danger of slithering from one set of axioms concerning the nature of higher education to another set of directly contrary axioms, without offering a sustained defence of either set.

The cult of technology has discouraged serious thought about its own social consequences. The technologists were, qua technologists, unqualified to provide that thought, lacking training in the relevant areas of social and political analysis. The 'something for nothing' syndrome attached to the cult appealed to the instincts of some of the consumers. It served as an alternative to serious social analysis, offering yet another alibi to avoid grappling with enduring problems of social structure, social justice, and public morality.

If 'the true locus of the problem' in post-industrial society 'is not in the technology *per se* but in the social system in which that technology is embedded',[18] more Irish thought has to be devoted to that problem. If Patrick Lynch's fundamental contribution, 'Whither science policy?'[19] does not appear to have yet exerted the full influence it deserves, at least the introduction of technology assessment under the aegis of the National Board for Science and Technology (NBST)[20] suggests an encouraging, though belated, recognition of the problem. The success of this programme may determine whether the NBST will play a central role as the umbrella organisation for reconciling 'the two cultures'. The first futurist enquiry conducted under the auspices of An Foras Forbartha and the NBST concluded that 'as Irish society will become more pluralistic, heterogenous and socially fragmented than in the past, the major problems will hinge on political and social issues rather than on the technological concerns themselves'.[21] The contents,

Society and Culture

however, generally revealed the distance still to be travelled in technology assessment. As a perceptive reviewer commented, the enquiry conveyed the impression that 'technology ordains that a happy future is our destiny . . . but 'social factors' could cheat us of this happiness . . . the prevailing belief appeared to be that individuals were not up to the technology which would guide their affairs; recalcitrant civil servants blocked the reforms required if the public sector is to effectively plan us; selfish workers demand ruinously high wages and distort the labour market; people everywhere are individualistic, given to sectional interests and altogether unplannable'.[22] This attitude was eloquently expressed in the observation that 'people often go berserk for no good reason at all'.[23] 'No good reason at all' simply means, of course, a reason that cannot be comprehended within the thought processes of technological determinism!

Research might appear to be urgently required into those alien creatures, 'people'. The futurist enquiries have refrained from this suggestion, unlike the major OECD investigation which, identifying the main 'trouble spots' as 'values and the organisation of society', logically concluded that 'thorough and comparative studies on the evolution of values in the advanced industrial societies'[24] was likely to prove a rewarding investment, even by the most mercenary criteria.

Values deeply influence that key variable in any society, the relationship between individuals and institutions. It is encouraging that so much analytical work has been devoted to the study of institutions in the past fifteen years, at least in connection with the public sector, especially through the stimulus of the Devlin Report and the work of the Public Service Advisory Council. But it is apparent too that the forces of inertia remain powerfully entrenched. If a small open society must largely live on its wits, if its main weapon in improving the quality of its life is the calibre of its own mind, then sustained analysis of the quality of decision-making, and action based on that analysis, are crucial to the overall performance of the society. This becomes even more the case if 'the alleviation of our problems will, in large measure, be dependent on the ingenuity, enterprise and development capacity of the policy formulators within our public service',[25] for a glaring characteristic of Irish decision-making elites is an extraordinarily uneven range of ability among individuals who have reached posts of similar level. If, in the French public service, 'one is struck again and again by the gulf between the small elite at the top,

Unequal Achievement

vigorous and efficient, and the junior employees whose muddle or lethargy simply sabotages the technocratic',[26] in Ireland one is struck again and again by the gulf *within* the elite. If the gap between the best and the second best can be so wide in Irish institutions, this increasess the urgency of making the most effective use of scarce talent and of removing obstructionists.

The constraints of the domestic intellectual market have already driven some outstanding minds abroad. A striking proportion of research in the social sciences has relied on imported investment, whether in the form of private scholarly enterprise or of consultancies. There is, however, no conclusive evidence that imported talent is generally superior to the domestic product. Dangers as well as advantages arise from the heavy intellectual dependency on imported thought, whether in the form of persons or of models. It can be argued that Ireland, no more than Italy, 'cannot be interpreted by using the same models as are currently applied to western societies'.[27]

Obsession with personal animosity ranks high among the diseconomies of small scale. Many derive as much satisfaction from dragging others down to their own level as from getting things done themselves. Nor does the prevailing culture decisively discourage such attitudes. It is not only trade union resistance, but inherited values, that still preclude the measures necessary to burn, or at least chop off, dead wood or poisoned limbs. The indulgence displayed towards leeches remains a cultural phenomenon. A vigorous chairman of the RTE authority, having asserted that 'RTE has more than its share of excellent, creative and dedicated people . . . its fair share of people who, though dedicated, will never set the world alight, and . . . a number who would cause trouble wherever they were', concluded resignedly that 'it will always be so, because RTE, like all organisations, has to settle for what is available'.[28] The culture does not yet demand that 'troublemakers' should be rendered unavailable. An attempt by the Irish public service to emulate the American approach towards 'a rigorous weeding out of those who do not measure up to requirements'[29] would create culture shock. But until that happens, one cannot confidently assert that 'there is an overall culture which seeks to attain excellence'.[30]

A strange hesitancy appears to afflict normally decisive minds on the crucial question of the quality of the public service. The National Economic and Social Council (NESC) has sponsored much valuable research. Yet, when confronted with the verdict of its own

Society and Culture

subcommittee on enterprise in the public sector that 'the central theme of this report is that within the public sector in this country there are many talented, able and willing people, who would contribute much more effectively to economic and social developments in Ireland', if given the opportunity, the NESC simply evaded the question with the plea that 'it is difficult to take a view on this issue, since entrepreneurship is a most elusive factor'.[31] 'Entrepreneurship', in the heroic Schumpeterian sense, may be an elusive factor. Talent, ability and willingness are not. The small scale of Irish organisations makes it a simple matter to identify the thrusters, and the sleepers, as well as the not inconsiderable class of dozers. Identification is not the difficulty. Stimulation is. It is puzzling that the NESC should shy away from this problem, which is central not only to the public service, but to the entire culture. If it gets the answer right, many of its reports would be unnecessary. If it doesn't get it right, many of the reports, however worthy their individual merits, may be doomed to remain monuments of futile endeavour.

This attitude also appears to influence the approach of the Review Body on Higher Remuneration in the Public Service. Its recommendations reinforce the view that it is status, not merit, that should be remunerated. Where Lemass stated bluntly that 'the performance of a state corporation depends, in our experience, on the capacities of the individual holding the chief executive post . . .'[32] the Review Body would only concede that 'the scope of a job can be influenced by the personal qualities of the person filling it'. But it went on to insist that 'we evaluate the demands of the job',[33] not the merits of the man. Whatever the practical difficulties involved in matching merit and reward in the civil service, and that too may be more a question of cultural attitude, as the Americans demonstrate, than of technical difficulty, this approach seems strange where the calibre of the decision making can have a major influence on the performance of the whole enterprise. If the Reports of the Review Body are not necessarily monuments of mindless diligence, the culture-bound nature of their assumptions nevertheless deserves sceptical scrutiny.[34]

The view that status rather than merit should be rewarded also affects the response of the comfortable classes to the demands of the less privileged. It is characteristic of a society where objective equality of opportunity appears to be somewhat limited by western standards[35] to disproportionately blame the poor for their poverty.[36] Equality of

9

Unequal Achievement

opportunity does not hold irresistible appeal for those who have a shrewd suspicion of just where they themselves would be if objective merit were the criterion for material success. The view that women suffer disproportionately from lack of opportunity makes little impact on those whose own pockets are lined with the rewards of inheritance, seniority, contacts, influence, and luck. The less a culture emphasises merit, the more resistant to equality of opportunity for women are the males likely to be (and perhaps many females also, clinging to their own 'successful' males), if only because the supremacy of the dominant males does not depend on superior merit. They are therefore likely to feel vulnerable to what they perceive as a threat posed not so much by women, as by ability in women.

A cluster of historically conditioned reflexes continues to influence the work ethic. From the Land Acts to Common Agricultural Policy, many farmers have reaped a higher return from investment in politics than investment in agriculture. Livestock farmers felt themselves heavily dependent on 'luck' when it came to the fortunes of the fair, where the market price might bear no obvious relation to productive efforts. The assumption that return on investment was a function more of bargaining skill than of objective merit etched itself deeply on Irish consciousness. The influence of professional norms reinforced this assumption. The view remains widespread that the fees charged by professional people bear 'little or no relationship to the value of what they actually do'.[37] Further along the social scale, entry to the craft unions was historically as closed as was entry to university professional faculties. The main industry in which the Irish flourished at home and abroad, construction, was even more heavily dependent on contacts, politics, and luck, than was much of manufacturing industry. It was claimed sixty years ago that 'success in Dublin . . . is not the prize of ceaseless toil. It is the fruit of influence widely used'.[38] The morality of the 'just price' had difficulty taking deep root in the Irish psyche in those circumstances. When Alec Wrafter expressed himself 'struck by the apparent lack of any qualitative set of criteria by which results can be judged . . . we are not a nation of managers – we are a nation of fixers',[39] he identified one conspicuous element in Irish attitudes. His conclusion that 'we would have to change our attitudes because we are not living in the real world' may underrate the resilience of the sponger syndrome. While Lemass asserted in 1957 that 'the world does not owe us a livelihood on our terms'[40] much effort, though less than in the 1950s, continued to be devoted to the proposition that it did.

10

Society and Culture

Controversy about work ethics revolves essentially around concepts of public morality, an area in which the Catholic Church became increasingly involved during the 1970s. Fr Liam Ryan has argued, in the course of a brilliant survey, that 'the Church is increasingly becoming an institution of social criticism . . . '[41] It might perhaps be contended that the Church had always been an institution of social criticism, but that it saw little to criticise in many earlier social or moral conditions that it had accepted with complacency, but that now seem to some bishops to outrage the Catholic version of the christian conscience. If it was not until the pastoral on Justice in 1977 that the bishops chose to refer to jobbery as a moral issue, this was hardly because jobbery had been hitherto unknown but because their concept of public morality was changing in the face of the challenges posed by economic growth, the end of emigration, television, and the Vatican Council.

The institutional church has naturally always been vulnerable to short term manipulation by the dominant elements in society. The hierarchy faced widespread incomprehension, at least from the older generation, once it expanded the concept of conscience in the direction of public morality. The beauty of 'traditional' morality was that the area to which it applied was so conveniently circumscribed. 'Traditional' Irish society achieved singular success in excluding ethics from the sphere of religion, largely confining the concept of morality to sexual morality and banishing from the agenda of moral discourse doctrines potentially subversive of the material interests of the dominant social elements. 'Traditionalists' naturally strove to divert hierarchical concern away from the dangerous area of public morality, and revert to the safe ground of sexual morality.

Opinions vary on how effectively the Church has responded to the challenge of 'the materialism of affluence' and 'political violence',[42] which have been identified as the two most serious threats to the christian witness. The decline in the number of recorded vocations restricted the room for manoeuvre of the institutional church on educational issues in particular. Just when the number of children began to increase, the number of available clergy began to decline. It must remain conjectural, however, whether this can be equated with a decline in *real* vocations. It may even be that the number of true vocations increased after the Council. 'Traditional' Irish culture exerted enormous pressure on the child in the seminary to stay in the seminary. Popular castigation of the 'spoiled priest' reflected the bitter

11

Unequal Achievement

disappointment at a gilt-edged family investment turned sour – incomprehensibly, wilfully, ungratefully sour. That attitude would seem to be much less prevalent now than twenty five years ago, if only, the cynic might say, because the investment no longer appears gilt-edged, and alternative investment prospects have become more attractive.

There was, as ever, much that did not change. A glance at the 'agony' columns, making all appropriate allowance for the limitations of the genre, conveys some sense of the torment still inflicted on the sensitive young by hell fire preachers. Nevertheless, the fear of hell may not now be as central to the Catholic vision as it was a generation ago, being superseded by 'the optimistic view of one's own salvation . . . the Church's role is today increasingly seen not as that of the agent of salvation but as an instrument which enables people to live out the salvation which Christ has bestowed on them.'[43]

At the level of high politics, potential church/state conflict has been mediated with remarkable skill. The potentially explosive education issue was largely resolved in the 1960s, following an extraordinary surge of activity by the previously moribund Department of Education. If the strong feelings roused on both sides have not yet fully subsided, the observer must remain impressed with the relative smoothness of so striking a change in educational power structures. The contraception issue has also been handled with considerable political sophistication. Mr. C. J. Haughey's cunningly contrived 'Irish solution to an Irish problem', however abhorrent to the purists, was a nimble piece of political gymnastics.

The demographic data indicate that a growing proportion of the younger generation of Irish women are planning their families. The longer term consequences of the silent revolution of the sixties, which has resulted in a sharply reduced average completed family size, and in a much younger age of mother at birth of the last child, have yet to work themselves fully through. The implications for women will only begin to be felt in the next two decades. Then, for the first time, a substantial number of Irish women will have reared their families by their mid-40s rather than their mid-50s. Better educated than any previous generation of Irish women, they may not be prepared to suffer in silence the sense of unfulfilled lives that some of their mothers apparently felt.[44]

Formal religious observance remains high. Nevertheless, evidence indicating a sharp decline among the younger urbanised generation has

Society and Culture

deeply disturbed some observers, who detect 'shallow' religious roots and a church suffering from 'spiritual malnutrition'. The more comforting conclusion that 'what the Church is experiencing is less a crisis of faith than a crisis of culture' may be a shade optimistic in a society where faith and culture are so intimately intertwined. It is precisely this close connection that makes the civic culture so vulnerable to a sudden decline in the role of institutional religion. However confined the role religion may play in shaping standards of public morality, however long it may have been domesticated in Ireland as 'convention rather than conviction',[45] the very shallowness of 'traditional' civic culture leaves religion as the main bulwark between reasonably civilised social control and the untrammelled predatory instincts of sectoral and individual selfishness. If religion no longer fulfils its historic civilising mission as a substitute for internalised values of civic responsibility, the consequences for society no less than for the institutional church are potentially disruptive, particularly at a time when 'exit' no longer offers an alternative to 'voice' as a 'solution' to Irish problems.[46]

A sense of cultural identity itself constitutes a bonding power in most societies. Ireland suffers from a peculiarly weak sense of identity by European criteria in this respect. The failure of the language revival may have cost the country more than it realises in the meanest mercenary terms. Recent policy appears to have been increasingly geared towards the euthanasia of the language. The abolition of 'compulsory Irish' in the Leaving Certificate and civil service examinations since 1973 has at least reduced the level of hypocrisy, and did not mark any significant change of trend in teaching practices. Of course were there any serious political commitment, the procedure would have been to build on 'compulsory Irish' in the wider society, rather that to abolish it in the schools. The decline of Irish in the training colleges means that many teachers will soon be incapable of properly teaching the language.[47] Television offered the revival a chance as well as a threat, if only there were a national revival policy.[48] There was none. RTE has done rather better than the Review Group on Higher Remuneration in the Public Service, which revealed its sense of values by recommending 'after weighing all the evidence' that the remuneration of the chief executives of Bord na nGaeilge and Bord na gCon should be identical.[49] It rated the language every bit as important a national asset as the greyhound! Out of the mouths of Review Groups. . . !

Unequal Achievement

The speed with which 'traditional' society succumbed to the temptations of affluence provides an eloquent commentary on the resilience of 'traditional' values. One may wonder how wholesome the 'traditional' culture was when such modest prosperity – for Ireland remains the poorest country in northern Europe – went so quickly to so many heads. The combination of shallowness, selfishness and exhibitionism is nicely caught in the ad man's philosophy, 'If you've got it – flaunt it'. This is also, of course, a recipe for rousing resentment among those who haven't[50] – a resentment which may in turn threaten to upset the social stability necessary for those who 'have it' to enjoy 'it' – but then the social consequences of the ad man's philosophy have not yet impinged on the horizons of our leaders.

But this refrain threatens to become too recriminatory. Skilfully though it has concealed it from itself, Ireland has been an extraordinarily lucky country since the tragedy of the Great Famine. It has been put to the stretch of its own vivid imagination to continue fertilising its sense of grievance when in reality it has had a charmed existence, thanks to the accident of geographical location, compared with most countries in Europe, not to mention the less fortunate continents. As a scathingly sympathetic critic observed in 1957, 'the truth is that Ireland has had an almost fatally easy time of it, at least in this century'. While the Ulster problem has since assumed a new degree of virulence, thanks in large measure to the primitiveness of the British nationalistic tradition, it remains as true in 1982 as in 1957 that 'Ireland has no right to be sick'.[51] The leadership cadre of 1957 did make a historic breakthrough. It did succeed in bringing to an end the emigration that for more than a century had been the main scar on the social anatomy. Since 1957 a bridgehead has been established in the direction of a viable community. The past twenty five years have seen the creation of a dual society, a dualism that has resulted from the, however halting, advance of the productive forces and despite the resolute resistance of the parasitic forces. A new Irishman does not have to be forged. He already exists. But there is still much travail ahead before he establishes his dominance. In business, agriculture, administration, scholarship, politics, or the media – right across the main areas of Irish life – high class achievers jostle cheek by jowl with high class dossers.[52] No society can be all one or all the other. It is a question of where the balance falls. In 1982 that balance falls far more than in 1957 on the productive side, but not yet sufficiently decisively to wrench the limpets clinging to their free ride completely loose from

14

Society and Culture

the ship of state.

The result of the past twenty five years is that Irish experience in 1982 is much less unrepresentative of the European norm than in 1957. The nature of Irish problems has shifted towards 'normalcy'! Consider the following remarks selected at random from recent literature:

> We seem to be . . . in a cultural crisis which may be the greatest challenge that confronts western society, in as much as our incapacity to develop appropriate decision making mechanisms – the ungovernability of our society – is a cultural failure.[53]

> Policy orientated research seems to have little or no direct impact on policy making.[54]

> The inability of parliaments to offer constructive comments upon economic plans or public expenditure plans is well known.[55]

> The political economy of the welfare state . . . is now confronted with new problems and demands which seem to challenge its continuing viability. The resulting crisis of transition may lead into political regression and even catastrophe unless political systems increased both their capacity for policy innovation and their ability to avoid dramatic policy failures.[56]

> The individual's loyalties are traditionally towards family rather than community, and civic cooperation in the Anglo-Saxon sense is not highly developed. Public initiatives are expected to come from the state and the authorities, rather than from ad hoc citizen groups . . . [57]

> Institutionally we have become spastic, and culturally we have lost our way.[58]

None of these comments was made with specific reference to Ireland, but all obviously apply with considerable force to our current circumstances.

Ireland now shares serious problems with other countries.

The prospects, however, are far more promising than in 1957. The problems are at least partly the problems of success rather than of almost unbroken failure. The dual culture offers a major opportunity to a leadership cadre capable of grasping it. That a variety of values are

Unequal Achievement

jostling side by side in a malleable culture, selflessness and selfishness, dedication and opportunism, energy and laziness, intelligence and stupidity, the psychology of tidy towns as well as dirty dumps, makes leadership vital in moulding the ethos of the wider society. 'We can manage our way out of our problems provided the leadership is there to create the *will,* unleash the *energy* and support the *courage* that coming times will require'.[59] Whether the political and administrative systems can now throw up the creative leadership to harness the potential is the major question mark hanging over Irish society in the early 1980s.

Our politicians have often been wiser than their media critics. The political stability of Irish society in the past twenty five years, as in the previous thirty five, has been no mean achievement. The potential disruption inherent in both economic change and in the northern problem has been incubated remarkably successfully within the existing party system. Irish politicians have continued to prove masterly party managers. And party management, however distasteful fastidious spirits may find the techniques of management, has a central role to play in maintaining political stability in an ideologically vacuous society. The pressures placed on Irish political leaders, even if partly of their own making, should not be underrated and may be all the greater for the feeble cultural bonding in the society. The lack of a hard core of Irish identity compels the politicians to work even harder at creating communities of interest. It is in this sense that the state now bears so heavy a burden in sustaining the identity of the society, rather than vice versa.[60] It is therefore particularly disturbing that the ship of state seems to have begun to drift increasingly out of control, in rather rudderless fashion, in recent years. Some would even fear that profligate leadership may be squandering the national capital that had begun to be stored up between 1957 and the mid 1970s.

It has been always an exciting, and sometimes a disturbing twenty five years. Whether it will historically come to be seen as a self-contained time period, or whether historians will date a significant shift – the ebbing of the rising tide of the sixties – from some time in the seventies, remains to be seen. Only then will it be possible to determine whether the culture was too fragile to cope with the shock of rapid economic change, with the challenge posed by the end of emigration. Or could a fugitive sense of identity survive only in a culture of national poverty? That would be a sad epitaph for even 'a trouble of fools'.

16

Society and Culture

Notes to Article

1 'Favourable aspects of the Irish economy', *Irish Banking Review*, (Dec. 1958) pp. 5-9

2 David Thornley 'Ireland: the end of an era' *Studies* (Spring, 1964) p. 3

3 Mary Robinson, in M. Healy and J. Davis (eds) *The control and management of technology in society* (Dublin, 1981) p. 91

4 A. Dale Tussing *Irish education expenditures – past, present and future* ESRI Paper No. 92 (Dublin, 1978) p. 178

5 NESC *Irish social policies: priorities for future development* No. 61 (July 1981) pp. 3, 48

6 R. Fanning, *The Irish Department of Finance 1922-58* (Dublin, 1976)

7 D. F. Keogh 'Ireland: the Department of Foreign Affairs' in Z. Steiner (ed.) *The Times Survey of Foreign Offices of the World* (London, 1982)

8 P. Lynch, 'The economist and public policy' *Studies* (1953)

9 P. J. Mooney 'Incomes policy' in B. R. Dowling and J. Durcan (eds) *Irish economic policy: a review of major issues* (Dublin, 1978) pp. 260-1

10 J. Kavanagh 'Reflections on some areas of Irish society' in *ESRI The economic and social state of the nation* (Dublin, 1982) p. 66

11 L. Crowley *Cork Examiner* 1 May 1982

12 C. O Briain 'Broadcasting today: a status report' *Irish Broadcasting Review* 1 (Spring 1978) pp. 5-6

13 *Irish Times* 18 June 1979, p. 9

14 M. P. Gallagher 'What Hope for Irish Faith?' *The Furrow* xxix, 10 (October 1978) p. 608

15 As the present writer is inclined to argue! See J. J. Lee 'Continuity and change in Ireland, 1945-70' in J. J. Lee (ed.) *Ireland 1945-70* (Dublin, 1979) p. 177

16 E. Randles *Post primary education in*

Ireland 1957-1970 (Dublin, 1975) pp. 77-80

17 D. Fennell 'The Irish cultural prospect' *Social Studies* 1 (December 1972) p. 684

18 D. Bell 'Communication technology – for better or for worse' *Harvard Business Review* (May-June 1979) p. 36

19 P. Lynch 'Whither science policy?' *Administration* 27, 3 (Autumn 1979) pp. 255-81. See also C. Cooper and N. Whelan, *Science, Technology and Industry in Ireland* (Dublin, 1973)

20 M. Healy and J. Davis (eds) *The control and management of technology in society* (Dublin, 1981)

21 An Foras Forbartha *Ireland in the year 2000* (Dublin, 1980) p. 80

22 *Administration* 28, 2 (1980) p. 236

23 Quoted in E. M. Walsh 'Science, technology and education' in *Ireland in the year 2000* (Dublin, 1980) p. 32

24 OECD *Facing the future* (Paris, 1979) p. 187-8

25 N. Whelan 'Ireland's National and Regional Development – Issues for Consideration' *Administration* 28, 4 (1980) p. 380

26 J. Ardagh *The new France* (London, 1977) p. 679

27 G. E. Rusconi and S. Scamuzzi 'Italy: an eccentric society' *Current Sociology* 29, 1 (Spring 1981) p. 1

28 P. J. Moriarty 'My experience in Irish broadcasting' *Irish Broadcasting Review* xi (Summer 1981) p. 7

29 S. Gaffney 'A look across the Atlantic: how the Americans are pursuing public service reforms' *Seirbhís Phoiblí* 1, 2 (Samhain (1980) p. 19

30 Moriarty, 'Irish Broadcasting' p. 8

31 NESC *Enterprise in the public sector* No. 49 (1980) pp. 24-5, 79

32 S. F. Lemass 'The role of state sponsored bodies' *Administration* 6, 4, (1959) reprinted in B. Chubb and P. Lynch (eds) *Economic Development and Planning* (Dublin, 1969) p. 189

Unequal Achievement

33 Review Body on Higher Remuneration in the Public Sector *Report No. 20* (Dublin, 1979) 10.45, 10.70. The occasional references to merit scattered through the text seem rather meaningless in the overall context.

34 For a wide-ranging review of many relevant issues, see K. Murphy 'Raising productivity in the civil service' *Seirbhís Phoiblí* 3, 1 (Meitheamh 1982) pp. 2-14

35 D. B. Rottman, D. F. Hannan, N. Hardiman, M. M. Wiley, *The distribution of income in the Republic of Ireland: a study in social class and family-cycle inequalities* (Dublin, 1982) p. 2

36 S. O Cinnéide 'Poverty and inequality in Ireland' in V. George and R. Lawson (eds) *Poverty and inequality in Common Market countries* (London, 1980) p. 156

37 *Cork Examiner* 1 May 1982

38 G. A. Bermingham *An Irishman looks at his world* (London, 1919) p. 236

39 *Cork Examiner* 1 May 1982

40 *Irish Press* 18 January 1957

41 Liam Ryan 'Church and politics: the last twenty five years' *The Furrow* xxx, 1 (1979) p. 7

42 Peter R. Connolly 'The Church in Ireland since Vatican II' *The Furrow* xxx, 12 (December 1979) p. 755

43 Liam Ryan 'The Church now' *The Furrow* xxxii, 2 (Feb. 1981) p. 82

44 M. Finucane 'Making women real' *Irish Broadcasting Review* 9 (Autumn/Winter 1980) p. 35

45 M. P. Gallagher 'What Hope for Irish Faith?' p. 609, 611. See also P. R. Connolly 'The Church in Ireland' pp. 756-8; L. McRedmond 'The Church of the visit' *The Furrow* xxx, 10 (Oct. 1979) pp. 620-4

46 To use the now familiar Hirschman vocabulary. See, in particular, 'Exit, voice, and the state' in A. Hirschman *Essays in trespassing: economics to politics and beyond* (C.U.P., 1981) pp. 246-65

47 S. O Buachalla, 'The language in the classroom' *Crane Bag* 5, 2 (1981) p. 29

48 Nollaig O Gadhra 'Craoladh i nGaeilge: fadhb no faill?' *Irish Broadcasting Review* 1 (Spring, 1978) p. 28; Breandán O hEithir 'Thuas seal, thíos seal' *Irish Broadcasting Review* 9 (Autumn, 1980) p. 47; Liam O Murchú 'An Ghailge sna seirbhísí craolta' *Irish Broadcasting Review* 11 (Summer, 1981) p. 57

49 Review Body on Higher Remuneration in the Public Service pp. 192-3

50 J. Kavanagh 'Some areas of Irish Society' pp. 62, 71

51 John V. Kelleher 'Ireland . . . and where does she stand?' *Foreign Affairs* 35 (April, 1957) p. 491

52 For the situation in agriculture, a graphic case of dualism, see T. F. Raftery *The Dr Henry Kennedy Memorial Lecture* (1982)

53 M. Crozier 'Western Europe' in M. Crozier, S. P. Huntington and J Watanuki *The crisis of democracy* (New York, 1975) p. 30

54 B. Wittrock 'Social knowledge, public policy and social betterment' *European Journal of Political Research* xx (1982) p. 83

55 P. Self 'Planning: rational or political?' in P. R. Baehr and B. Wittrock (eds) *Policy analysis and policy innovation* (London, 1981) p. 224

56 F. W. Scharpf 'Public organisation and the waning of the welfare state' *European Journal of Political Research* 5 (1977) Abstract, p. 334

57 J. Ardagh *The new France* p. 28

58 S. MacRéamoinn 'Crisis and challenge' *Irish Broadcasting Review* (Summer, 1981) p. 47

59 H. Kilroy quoted in *Cork Examiner* 1 May 1982

60 L. de Paor 'Ireland's identities' *The Crane Bag* 3, 1 (1979) p. 29

[8]

MONEY IN AN ECONOMY WITHOUT BANKS: THE CASE OF IRELAND*

by ANTOIN E. MURPHY†

Trinity College, Dublin

Ireland is unique in the financial world for the prevalence and duration of its bank closures. Between 1966-76 industrial disputes resulted in the closures of the Associated Banks[1] on three occasions in the Republic of Ireland. These closures, totalling in aggregate almost a year, provide economists with a unique opportunity of examining an economy functioning for long periods without the direct use of the major part of the money supply, bank deposits.

Against the background of the six and a half months closure of 1970, it is intended:

(1) to examine the alternative "money" structure that arose during the closures;

(2) to investigate the extent to which the closures affected economic activity;

(3) to discuss the implications for monetary theory of these events.

THE ALTERNATIVE MONEY STRUCTURE

Current and deposit accounts with the Associated Banks formed 82 per cent of M_2 (currency and Bank deposits) in 1966, 85 per cent in 1970 and 86 per cent in 1976. The bank closures therefore deprived the public of the direct use of, on average, well over 80 per cent of the money supply.

*Manuscript received 10.8.77; final version received 27.2.78.

†I am indebted to Dr. Roger Craine (University of California, Berkeley) and Mr. Terence Ryan (Trinity College) for their suggestions and assistance in preparing this paper. The usual disclaimer applies.

[1]These disputes involved the closure of all the offices and branches of the clearing banks in the Republic of Ireland. The Associated Banks are the Bank of Ireland, Allied Irish Banks, the Northern Bank and the Ulster Bank. The dates of the closures were:

> May 7—July 30, 1966
> May 1—November 17, 1970
> June 28—September 6, 1976.

Unfortunately, for purists in these matters, the closures did not result in the suspension of all the means of payment within the country. Irish currency and sterling continued to circulate. Some of the North American and merchant banks provided current account facilities to major companies, and in some cases alternative banking facilities were availed of in Northern Ireland and Great Britain. Table 1 shows the changes in currency and current accounts with institutions that remained open during the 1970 closure.

Table I

Changes in Currency and Demand Deposits During 1970 Closure (£millions)

	(I) Irish Currency	(2) Sterling	(3) Current Accounts with Non-Associated Banks
May	+9		+3
June...	+1		+2
July	+1		+1
		+35	
August	−3		+3
September	−4		+2
October	0		+2
Overall Change	+4	+35	+13

Source:

Column I   *Quarterly Bulletins* of the Central Bank of Ireland.

Column 2 and 3   Central Bank of Ireland *Survey of Economic Effects of Bank Dispute 1970.*

Column 1 shows changes in the amount of currency outstanding. The Central Bank was concerned to ensure that adequate supplies of currency were made available to the public. Currency was transferred from the Central Bank to government departments so as to meet the wages and salaries of employees in the public sector and also to meet social welfare payments. After the initial jump in currency in May of £9 million the demand for currency slackened off considerably.

In the months of August and September the volume of currency outstanding fell by £7 million and at the end of the dispute there was only £4 million of currency more in circulation than at the start.

Offsetting part of the additional demand for currency was the increased amount of sterling in circulation. Sterling is freely accepted as a means of payment in the Republic. It has been estimated by the Central Bank that there was a total of about £5 million in circulation in April 1970 and that this built up to £40 million by November with

Money in an Economy without Banks: the case of Ireland   43

most of the increase coming from tourist expenditure during the Summer months.[2]

In remaining open the non-Associated Banks, an amalgam of merchant and North American banks, did provide some transactors with an alternative source for current account transactions. However, their ability to provide alternative means of payment was very limited, as these banks had no branch network system to operate within so that they found themselves physically incapable of dealing with the new volume of business presented to them. By the end of May most of them refused to handle new accounts. Current accounts with these non-Associated Banks only rose by £13 million during the closure.

Some transactors were able to utilize bank accounts held in Northern Ireland and Great Britain. Unfortunately, there are no statistics available on these deposits. However, any outflow of funds to build up bank deposits outside the State in the weeks prior to the closure would have been reflected in a fall in the Republic's official external reserves. No significant fall in the reserves was recorded indicating that such activity did not occur on any sizeable scale. Between the end of March and the end of May 1970 the official external reserves fell from £304 million to £301 million.

In some cases bank accounts outside the State were established and built up with the proceeds of export payments during the closure. These accounts were used to finance part of the import bill.[3]

Aggregating the known alternative sources of payment money outlined in Table 1, it may be seen that by November 1970 there was an additional £52 million of currency plus deposits in circulation. This does not include deposits held by residents outside the State. Taking it as a rough approximation it still only constituted less than one twelfth of the Associated Banks' current and deposit accounts. This indicates that the alternative standard "money" made available in the form of currency and deposits cannot be held to have filled the gap created by the withdrawal of the direct use of the banks' deposits from the system.

The total of £5 billion of uncleared cheques at the end of the bank closure was, by definition, the exchange medium that was used to finance most transactions. Cheques drawn on the Associated Banks

---

[2] As this sterling currency would normally have been collected by the Central Bank and invested in interest bearing bills and bonds in London, the dispute resulted in a saving of over £1 million for the British Exchequer (assuming average excess sterling holdings of £17·5 million and an average Treasury Bill rate of 6·9 per cent).

[3] Central Bank *Survey* (1971).

continued to be the main transaction instruments used during the closure.

However, it is important to note that the substance of the chequing transaction changed during the closure. In a normal banking system cheques are readily acceptable because it is believed that they are drawn against known accounts and will be cleared quickly. During the bank disputes they were drawn, not against known credit accounts or allowed overdraft limits, but against the value of other uncleared cheques and/or the transactor's view as to his creditworthiness.

Cheques cleared within a few days and against known accounts have little default risk attached to them or, if they are dishonoured, the mistake will not be repeated. Cheques accepted against uncleared cheques, debits issued against uncleared credits, greatly increased default risk.

The acceptor of a cheque depended not only on the issuer's creditworthiness but also on the creditworthiness of the latter's payers. One transactor's credit was contingent on another's. A break in the credit link could, it was recognized, have a cumulative impact on the creditworthiness of other transactors.

Uncertainty also existed because it was not known when the banks would re-open.[4]

In summary a highly personalized credit system without any definite time horizon for the eventual clearance of debits and credits substituted for the existing institutionalized banking system.

The nature of the economy greatly facilitated the emergence of this new system. The Republic of Ireland has a population of only 3 million inhabitants. The small size of the population meant that there was a high degree of personal contact amongst members of the community. Where information was lacking at the personal level substitute information "storage units" existed in the form of retail shops, numbering around 12,000 and, that well-known Irish institution, the public house, 11,000 of which exist in the Republic—a pub population (over eighteen) ratio of 1 : 190.

It appears that the managers of these retail outlets and public houses had a high degree of information about their customers—one does not after all serve drink to someone for years without discovering

---

[4]The public knew from the outset of the 1970 closure that it would be a prolonged one. The *Irish Times* of May 16, 1970 reported that roughly 3,500 out of the total of 7,000 bank employees had taken up alternative work in London. Planes, seemingly, were chartered to bring groups of bank employees to work in Britain! The speed with which employees accepted alternative temporary work was indicative of the magnitude of the impasse between employers and employees.

something of his liquid resources. This information enabled them to provide commodities and currency for their customers against undated trade credit. Public houses and shops emerged as a substitute banking system.

RISK CATEGORIES OF CHEQUES (GOVERNMENT VERSUS PRIVATE)

All cheques were not universally accepted. Cheques were graded into various risk categories. Cheques drawn on the government and on well established institutions were readily accepted by the alternative banking system. In many cases these cheques acted like certificates of deposit in that they changed ownership often during the closure.

The negotiability of personal cheques depended on the degree of information and personal contact that the acceptor had about the issuer of the cheque. The high credit information content possessed by transactors in the community, a major factor facilitating the use of personal cheques, is borne out by the Central Bank's *Survey*.

"The number of firms (retailers) who expressed concern at the prospect of a large volume of unpaid cheques was small, despite the fact that a very large number of cheques was accepted by them."

"Through the dispute, Associated Bank cheques were freely accepted both within the country and, to a lesser extent, in respect of external payments. There is little evidence that firms or individuals experienced much difficulty in initiating domestic payments by drawing cheques on closed banks, but there was a reluctance to accept third party cheques."

These types of statements run right through the *Survey*. They indicate the substantial amount of information transactors possessed about one another. The ease with which transactions were carried out using this system is also exemplified by the fact that there was little evidence to indicate that bankers' cards or similar facilities were used more intensively during the dispute of 1970. In addition some printing houses found that there was an active market for blank cheque books which they supplied to the general public through newsagents.

ECONOMIC ACTIVITY DURING THE CLOSURE

To what extent did these three bank closures affect economic activity? For the 1970 closure the Central Bank and the Economic and Social Research Institute carried out a *Survey* of the economic effects of the bank dispute. The general picture derived from that *Survey* was that economic activity remained quite resilient throughout the six and a half month closure:

". . . the level of economic activity continued to increase, though at a reduced pace . . ."

The conclusion reached by the Central Bank/ESRI was qualitative in nature. We wished to test the quantitative impact of the closure on expenditure.

The monthly Retail Sales Index 1961-76 was taken as the best indicator of consumer expenditure.[5] Having detrended this series, the average sales for each month between 1961-76, excluding the bank closure years of 1966, 70 and 76, were calculated.[6] The average sales for each month were taken to represent the expected retail sales. The recorded monthly retail sales for bank closure years were then compared with the expected retail sales to see if, as a result of the closures, there was any statistically significant divergence of retail sales from what would have been expected—see Table 2.

Table 2

Percentage Changes in Actual as Against Expected Retail Sales in the Bank Strike Years 1966, 1970 and 1976

(Strike Months are underlined)

Year	January	February	March	April	May	June
1966	+2·0%	1·4%	−1·5%	+2·1%	−2·3%	−4·9%
T Statistics ...	·9	·5	·6	·6	1·07	3·5*
1970	+1·6%	−·14%	+1·9%	+3·8%	−5·3	−3·9%
T Statistics ...	·7	·1	·8	1·1	2·4*	2·8*
1976	−·3%	+5·3%	−4·9%	−1·4%	+·4%	+·2%
T Statistics ...	1·	1·8	2·0	·4	·2	1·

Year	July	August	September	October	November	December
1966	−1·1%	+1·4%	+6·1%	−1·0%	+2%	1·4%
T Statistics ...	·4	·4	3·4*	·3	·1	·3
1970	·3%	−3·1%	+3·1%	−·8%	−·8%	+3·5%
T Statistics ...	·1	·8	1·7	·2	·3	·9
1976	−10·4%	−4·2%	+2·8%	+·1%	+7·7%	+4·9%
T Statistics ...	3·8*	1·1	1·6	·02	2·6*	1·2

* Significant at the 5% level.

[5] The emphasis had to be on retail sales because output statistics were available only on a quarterly basis and a further strike in the cement industry during the first half of 1970 caused major difficulties in interpreting the unemployment statistics.

[6] The months were normalized by the yearly total and expressed at annual rates.

The results may be summarized as follows:

(1) In eight out of the twelve bank closure months, actual retail sales did not significantly diverge from expected retail sales.

(2) In four cases—June 1966, May and June 1970 and July 1976—there was a significant fall in actual retail sales below expected retail sales.

(3) Caution needs to be exercised in interpreting the 5·3 per cent (May) and 3·9 per cent (June) fall in retail sales below expected sales in 1970. On May 1st of that year wholesale tax was doubled from 2½ per cent to 5 per cent. Transactors had been notified of this change in taxation in April. It seems plausible to assume that the tax change caused transactors to push forward purchases of cars and heavy consumer durables to April so as to avoid the tax increase. This change in taxation was a contributory factor to the downturn in retail sales in May and June.

(4) In the case of the "shorter" closures of 1966 and 1976, there was a pick up in retail sales some time after the re-opening of the banks. The deflationary effects of the 4·9 per cent (June 1966) and 10·4 per cent (July 1976) downturns in retail sales were offset by the 6·1 per cent (September 1966) and 7·7 per cent (November 1976) increases in actual above expected retail sales. There was no significant upturn in retail sales at the end of the 1970 closure.

It would seem reasonable to assume that if the public is deprived of the direct use of over 80 per cent of the money supply such a situation would create substantial deflationary forces in the economy. The evidence collected from the monthly Retail Sales Index suggests that this did not happen during the three bank closures. In eight out of the twelve bank closure months retail sales were not significantly affected by the changed monetary circumstances. In the other four months it is noticeable that the downturn in retail sales took place at the start of the closures. A similar learning process seems to have been at work in each case with the initial desire on the part of buyers to maintain liquidity, allied with the reluctance on the part of sellers to extend credit, giving way to the development of a huge multilateral system of credits and debits which permitted the smooth functioning of exchange activity as the closures lengthened.

IMPLICATIONS FOR MONETARY THEORY

It may be contended that there was no fundamental change in the money system as a result of the closures. Transactors drew or accepted cheques of the Associated Banks in the belief that they would eventually re-open their doors to the public. Is there any fundamental distinction between cheques drawn on closed as against open banks?

As was pointed out above, the substance of the chequing transaction underwent a fundamental change during the closures. Depositors were not drawing cheques against known accounts.[7] They were drawing against their pre-closure accounts plus the cheques they themselves had accepted. The payees accepted the cheque, not on the basis of a known bank deposit, but by virtue of the information they possessed about the creditworthiness of the issuer and the latter's payers.

Consider the case of a payee faced with the following:

(1) A cheque issued against a known credit account which may be cleared with little delay through the clearing system.

(2) A one/three/six months post dated, from the viewpoint of clearing, cheque.

The former is the type of transaction that takes place when the banks are open. Payment and exchange take place simultaneously. The second represents the situation payees faced during the closures—indeed transactors did not know at what date in the future cheques could be cashed, if at all.

Shackle (1971) recently pinpointed this essential distinction between money as a means of payment and money as a medium of exchange. Defining money in a payments context, Shackle maintained that one needed to define payments first:

"Payment has been made when a sale has been completed. Payment has been made when the creditor has no further claim. Payment is in some sense final . . . the stock of money can be defined as the means of strictly simultaneous payment."

Money, as *a means of payment* is, therefore, defined as that which finalises a transaction either immediately (currency) or within the period required to clear a cheque (bank deposits).

[7]The assumption that transactors issue cheques against known accounts when the banks are open is not strictly accurate as cheques can and do on occasion "bounce". The point made here is that the degree of trust and information required was far greater during the closures.

Money, as *a medium of exchange* does not finalise immediately the transaction process. It leaves the transactor and/or the accepting agency with some liability or contingent liability. Exchange takes place but payment is deferred. Time separates the act of payment from the act of exchange.

As long as exchange takes place, one can define as money the instruments which have facilitated the exchange of goods and services. By using the concept of money as a medium of exchange, the range of items defined as money may be broadened to include instruments such as bills of exchange, IOUs and trade credit.

Money in its means of payment role is largely required because it acts as an information substitute. Once payment money is used the transaction is finalised and information on the creditworthiness of the payer is not required. On the other hand, money as a medium of exchange embodies an information factor which allows exchange to take place prior to payment for goods and services. It is the information possessed by the payee on the creditworthiness of the payer which is vital to the transaction. Without adequate information the payee will demand means-of-payment money in return for his goods or services.

This means that as information on the public's creditworthiness improves and as institutionalized arrangements reduce the cost of acquiring information, exchange becomes less dependent on payment money.[8] In this way improved information may tend to increase the potential money supply by monetizing bills of exchange, IOUs, trade credit, etc. Due to improved information transactors may be more prepared to exchange goods and services on a deferred payments basis. In other words, exchange may take place without the means of simultaneous payment.

CONCLUSION

It is held that the bank closures in Ireland illustrate empirically the validity of the distinction between money as a medium of exchange and money as a means of payment as well as the importance of information in the exchange process. The direct use of means-of-payment money (bank deposits) was removed from the transaction process. In the absence of this money, exchange activity remained relatively unaffected because the public was prepared to use undated trade credit

---

[8]It is of interest to note in this respect that some firms ". . . . particularly in manufacturing, feel following the dispute that they can manage their affairs with relatively lower money balances in future". Central Bank *Survey*, *op. cit.*, p. 51.

as the instrument of exchange. The public's ability to do so was based on the vast stock of information available to transactors on the credit-worthiness of fellow transactors. Faced with the necessity for finding alternative exchange instruments, the public used undated trade credit, finding it a close substitute for payment money because of the information content on creditworthiness available in the economy.

REFERENCES

Central Bank of Ireland (1971). *Survey of Economic Effects of Bank Dispute 1970*.

Shackle, G. L. S. (1971). Discussion Paper on R. Clower's "Theoretical Foundations of Monetary Policy" in G. Clayton, J. C. Gilbert and R. Sedgwick (eds.), *Monetary Theory and Monetary Policy in the 1970s*, Oxford University Press, pp. 32-34.

Excerpt from John F. McCarthy (ed.), *Planning Ireland's Future: The Legacy of T.K. Whitaker*, 128–50.

The Legacy of Economic Development: The Irish Economy 1960-1987

John Bradley

052

AN ECONOMY OR A NATION?

There is an understandable tendency for newly emerging countries to confuse national *autonomy* with national *sovereignty*. Sovereignty is the ability of a nation to act on its own rather than under the coercion of other nations.[1] National autonomy, on the other hand, describes the ability of a nation to attain its desired objectives, such as economic growth or full employment, if necessary through unilateral action. In the economic sphere the autonomy of small nations is heavily circumscribed and the recognition of this truth represents a wise exercise of national sovereignty. James Connolly's prophecy[2] that Irish independence might amount to a switching of flags and symbols was amply demonstrated in the first four decades of the new Irish state.[3]

Looking back at the first decades of a sovereign Ireland, its lack of economic autonomy is truly startling: the dominance of agriculture and the almost total dependence on the UK market; the problems of functioning in a world dominated by protectionist policies and the need to copy these policies; the absence of an independent monetary authority; a conservative commercial class notable for its lack of progressive entrepreneurial instincts; the partitioning of the country with its consequential political 'tunnel vision' and economic disruption; massive dislocation of international trade by a world war (euphemistically referred to in Ireland as the *Emergency*), which brought on a period of isolation which seems to have persisted, in one form or another, up to the late fifties.

A new age of economic planning was ushered in by *Economic*

ECONOMIC DEVELOPMENT IN HISTORICAL PERSPECTIVE

Development and the *First Programme*. Economic policy over the period 1922-32 had been characterised by Irish adherence to the modified form of *laissez-faire* and free trade which prevailed in the UK at the same time. Orthodoxy in economic and financial matters prevailed as the new state established itself. The period 1932 to the mid-fifties had been marked by a drive to construct an indigenous Irish industrial base behind high tariff barriers. However, in relation to economic planning, political economists writing even as late as the fifties felt the need to justify state intervention in the economy against prevailing views hostile to such intervention.[5] Nevertheless, the economy from 1922-58 was not 'unplanned'. Anybody who has read accounts written by contemporary observers[6] will be aware of the state's role in creating such basic infrastructural business organisations as the ESB, Bord na Móna, Aer Lingus, etc. What was missing from that earlier period was the Keynesian language and inspiration which had characterised economic policy in the UK[7] and the US[8] from the immediate aftermath of the war, and the ability to take a broad overview of the supply potential of the economy. This latter notion of 'Ireland Inc' has always caused problems for Irish intellectuals, who were happier with more lofty concepts of Irishness. When these spiritual concepts were blended with Éamon de Valera's vision of frugal self-sufficiency, the outcome was unlikely to be a dynamic entrepreneural capitalism either in the public or private sectors.

The revolution in economic thinking, when it belatedly came, was swift and comprehensive. While in opposition during the fifties, Seán Lemass had immersed himself in new economic thinking and guided Fianna Fáil away from its Sinn Féin roots towards acceptance of a dependency on foreign capital and expertise and of an explicit Keynesian public policy framework. The progress of the parallel creative dynamic within the public sector has already been described in John McCarthy's essay. The dire state of the economy (low growth, massive emigration, balance of payments crises), the perceived failure of the policies of protection in bringing European-type growth to Ireland, and the failure of indigenous industries to reorient towards export

129

PLANNING IRELAND'S FUTURE

markets from behind tariff barriers led directly to a fundamental policy revaluation, the details of which were codified and articulated in *Economic Development* and the *First Programme*. In this essay I review briefly the planning or programming process as it took root and propagated within Ireland, the particular form it took, its relationship to shifting views and fashions on economic theory and policy and its influence on Ireland's economic progress. A comprehensive evaluation of the complete Irish experience with economic planning has yet to be written, although excellent accounts of the origins and early stages are available.[9]

THE FIRST PROGRAMME: A NEW BEGINNING

From the publication of the *First Programme for Economic Expansion* in 1958 to the *Programme for National Recovery* in 1987, Irish economic policy-making has generally been formulated within the published guidelines of medium-term planning frameworks. We need not dwell too much on what precisely is a 'plan' or 'programme'. Dr Whitaker's definition will suffice: 'a coherent and comprehensive set of policies for economic and social development over a period of four to five years ahead'. He insists that any such plan 'must be consistent with the availability of resources and its various parts must be well integrated'. Great importance attaches to the notion of a plan, since it is 'the supreme policy document of the government'.[10]

More formally, a plan must have all of the following four elements. Firstly, an explicit choice of targets ranked in order of priority. The range of targets would typically include unemployment, inflation, the growth and level of real incomes. Secondly, a clear statement of the internal and external constraints facing the economy. Typical constraints would include the likely state of the world economy, the public sector's ability to borrow to finance its activities, and the nation's ability to 'pay its way' in the world (i.e. the balance of payments deficit).[11] Thirdly, the availability and selection of suitable policy instruments. Typical policy instruments include public sector employment, direct and indirect tax rates, income support schemes such as unemploy-

THE LEGACY OF ECONOMIC DEVELOPMENT

ment benefits and public sector investment. Finally, a thorough evaluation of the likely consequences of the proposed policy actions in attempting to achieve the stated targets without violating the known constraints.

Responsibility for drawing up plans and monitoring them has varied over the last three decades. Some have originated directly from within the Department of Finance; others from a special department with responsibility for planning functions and one originated, at least in part, from outside the civil service in an independent Planning Board. The somewhat ambivalent public and private attitudes to these plans has tended to conceal the important, if subliminal, role they play within the economy. In particular, their relationship to the annual budgetary process has always been left a little ambiguous. There is a sense in which the 'plan' represents what the government would ideally like to do, or what would be 'good' for the country in some normative and medium-term sense, but that the annual budget needs to be pragmatically flexible when buffeted by circumstances outside our control, or when political exigencies become too important to ignore, for example, near election time.

Economic Development and The First Programme

As we have seen in the earlier essays, *The First Programme* grew out of the crisis of the late fifties and, although motivated by a spirit of pragmatism, it represented the arrival of Keynesian macroeconomic thinking and policies in Ireland. Of crucial importance was the role staked out for the public authorities in the planning process. Speaking in 1961, Seán Lemass asserted that,

> In Irish economic development, the role of the Government is predominant. Nobody believes that, in the circumstances of this country, economic progress on the scale which is needed is likely to be realised otherwise than through the medium of a strong and sound Government policy directed to that result. . . . The vast dynamic of growth which is inherent in free private enterprise cannot be fully availed of without Government drive and leadership.[12]

However, there were differences between the enthusiastic, explicit

PLANNING IRELAND'S FUTURE

and unbridled Keynesianism of Lemass and the more guarded and exacting approach of Whitaker. For example, Whitaker's critique of Keynesian policy prescriptions as applied to a small exposed economy like Ireland and his insistence on the primacy of what we would today call 'supply-side' policies, were prophetic, particularly in the light of the subsequent explosive growth of the public sector.[13] Nevertheless, the portrayal of Whitaker as an ideological right-wing free-marketer[14] is far off the mark given the documented record of his commitment to the need for state intervention to manage aggregate demand and not leave the economy to the mercy of market forces.[15]

Certain aspects of *The First Programme* are of interest from the point of view of the subsequent development of planning in Ireland. Nature abhors a vacuum and *Economic Development* filled such a vacuum. It is to the credit of the politicians of the day that, however reluctantly, they acknowledged this and shared the limelight with its author, the head of the civil service. Also, we have become so used to the passionless language of later plans that the honesty, directness and clarity of *Economic Development* should be remembered.[16]

The 'psychological' aspect was emphasised in *Economic Development*, although the real meaning of this remains obscure. Clearly the programme was intended to be the vehicle of decisive political action, not a substitute for it, and from Lemass's leadership this political action was forthcoming. The population recognised this new sense of direction and purpose and responded positively to its ambition and vision. A justification for the duration of the plan (1959-63) was that the traditional budgetary year was too short a time frame for strategic policy-making. A much broader framework was needed. However, planning over a long time horizon brought its own problems. For example, the expectation that the agriculture sector would provide the 'engine' of growth proved to be wrong, and that role was played by the new burgeoning foreign-owned industrial sector. Much attention was paid to the domestic sources of capital financing and the necessity to increase domestic savings. In the event, the large inflows of private foreign capital eased the domestic financing

THE LEGACY OF ECONOMIC DEVELOPMENT

constraint.[17] Even the projections of public capital spending were exceeded, so the plan did not serve well as a guide to the evolution of a key set of its own policy instruments! Overall economic growth of 23 per cent for the duration of the programme (1959-63) exceeded the 'target' of 11 per cent. Understandably, this was not the subject of criticism. Quite the reverse! However, it opened up a gap between the planner's projections and the outturn which was ill-understood. This would return to haunt the policy-makers in later programmes.

THE DECLINE OF PLANNING

The Second and Third Programmes: 1964-72
The loose framework of the *First Programme* contrasts sharply with the complex methodological structures of the *Second* and *Third*. Developments in national accounting statistics, partially initiated as a result of the *First Programme*, provided a comprehensive national accounting framework which imposed a formal discipline and consistency which was lacking in the earlier plan. A further innovation in these programmes was the use of formal economic techniques, including a mathematical model of the Irish economy, to perform economic computations and consistency checks. The target of both later programmes was to obtain a profile of the Irish economy at a specified terminal date (1970 for the *Second*, 1973 for the *Third*), which reflected the highest growth rate which could be achieved in the light of 'policy possibilities, the probable development of the external environment and resource availability'. In both programmes, a target aggregate growth rate of approximately 4 per cent for national output was broken down into internally consistent sub-targets for the sectoral components.[18]

It may seem paradoxical to describe this period as representing the decline of planning. However, the very ambition of the planners to quantify at a high level of sectoral and institutional detail contained the seeds of its own destruction. With hindsight, the methodological underpinnings of the plans were flawed and the economic tools of analysis inadequate to capture the market

PLANNING IRELAND'S FUTURE

dynamics of a rapidly developing small and open economy.[19]

As unfolding international and domestic developments rendered the projections of the *Third Programme* increasingly unrealistic, the planning process was gradually abandoned. Paradoxically, during the most turbulent period of the post-war world economy, in the lead into, and immediate aftermath of, the first OPEC oil price crisis, there was no plan or programme formally in place. The extent of planning's fall from grace is captured by the remarks of the coalition government's Minister for Finance, Mr Richie Ryan, in the 1975 budget speech, when he said: 'Of all the tasks which could engage my attention, the least realistic would be the publication of a medium or long-term economic plan based on irrelevancies in the past, hunches as to the present and clairvoyance as to the future'. Such an approach 'would not be meaningful in the context of the unsettled world situation'. As a result of this lack of foresight, a policy change of crucial future consequence went through without a comprehensive economic analysis of its medium-term consequences. Starting in 1972, the government planned for, and incurred, deficits on its current account and these deficits on day-to-day expenses were financed by borrowing, mainly abroad.

In summary, the first phase of economic planning in Ireland covered the period 1958 to the end of the sixties. The extent to which the obvious increased growth of the Irish economy, towards rates prevailing in mainland Europe, was a result of these programmes remains an open issue. Neary concludes rather pessimistically that 'the programmes were not really the cause of the economic progress which occurred in the 1960s and the early 1970s. They accompanied it and charted its course'. He surmised that it was the new outward-looking policies towards foreign trade and investment, rather than the programmes, which caused the economy to take off.[20] However, this is a somewhat artificial distinction since the policy of openness, together with the tax and capital incentives designed to attract foreign industry, were fundamental parts of the programmes.

THE LEGACY OF ECONOMIC DEVELOPMENT

Planning Briefly Revived: National Development 1977-1980

The decade of the seventies was characterised by fluctuations in the world economy of a kind which had not been experienced in peacetime since the thirties. Even with the wisest and most prudent fiscal and monetary policies it would have been impossible to protect the Irish economy fully from the world-wide recession. This period also marked the onset of an extensive disenchantment with the Keynesian policies of state intervention and demand management which had been widely used in the fifties and sixties in most western economies. Instead in market-oriented economics revived and, towards the end of the seventies, governments in the western world came to power with political mandates to roll back state interference and to deregulate and liberalise markets. It is truly ironic that it was in just such a hostile international intellectual climate that economic planning was revived here in Ireland.

Whereas the *First Programme* originated from within the civil service in a relatively non-political way, the seeds of a revival of economic planning over the period 1977 to the end of the decade came from a party political manifesto. On entering into office in June 1977, the new Fianna Fáil administration set up a Department of Economic Planning and Development, a decision which was opposed strongly by the author of *Economic Development* in his role as Senator.[21] Two publications in particular serve to characterise this period: *National Development 1977-1980* and *Development for Full Employment*. Did these documents have all the necessary attributes of a 'plan'? They were explicit and ambitious in terms of their growth and unemployment targets, and their massive use of public expenditure increases and tax cuts. On the analysis of the constraints facing the achievement of these targets, the planners could not use the excuse of earlier workers – that of a dearth of quantitative knowledge about the functioning and properties of the economy. *Even* within a Keynesian framework of analysis, the limited influence of state intervention in a small open economy was well known by this time. On the evaluation of the consequences of policy actions, the work reported in the published documents was excessively

PLANNING IRELAND'S FUTURE

optimistic, unconvincing and singularly failed to build any consensus within the pool of economic experts in the country.[22]
Consequently, the planning process, which had started out in
1958 commanding wide professional and popular consensus,
became the subject of much public and political controversy.

PLANNING WITH BINDING CONSTRAINTS: 1981–1987

The second OPEC oil price crisis of 1979 spelled the end of the
final period of 'optimistic' planning which had started in 1977.
It also ushered in a period of political instability, there being
three general elections between June 1981 and December 1982.
The Way Forward, published in October 1982 marked the start
of a transition to a more sombre and realistic appraisal of the
nature of the new constraints facing policy-makers in Ireland. It
emphasised the economic problems besetting most developed
countries: slower growth, high inflation, high unemployment
and balance of payments deficits. However, quite optimistic
assumptions were made about the future international environment and within these assumptions it planned to eliminate the
now burgeoning current deficit completely by 1986. The instruments selected included a combination of expenditure cuts
(mainly through public sector employment cuts combined with
wage moderation) and charges for state services. Off-setting positive employment growth was to come from manufacturing and
services through a process of wage moderation. Although targets
and instruments were clearly isolated in the plan, its evaluation
of the constraints — both political and economic — facing the
achievement of these targets proved unduly optimistic. In the
event, the general election called immediately after the publication of *The Way Forward* returned a new administration, and a
centre-left coalition government of Fine Gael and Labour was
formed.

The plan which covered the term of the coalition administration of 1982–86 came in two stages: the *Proposals For Plan
1984–87* in April 1984 and *Building on Reality* in the Autumn
of 1984. The National Planning Board was established in March

THE LEGACY OF ECONOMIC DEVELOPMENT

1983 with the task of drafting a medium-term programme for the economy within which short-term economic planning could proceed. The Board consisted of seven members, all from outside the civil service, two of whom were professional economists, and had a director and secretariate of professional economists. Their report, a comprehensive document containing 241 recommendations, was used as an input into the production of the actual government plan, *Building on Reality*, which was drawn up within the Departments of Finance and of the Taoiseach. This latter document, beneath its optimistic rhetoric, was probably the most sober planning document of all published in the period since 1958. Essentially, it was a manifesto on how to deal with the burgeoning fiscal imbalance without being seen to deflate the economy excessively, a process roughly akin to squaring the circle. It was perceived as a political rather than as an economic document and, in the absence of political consensus on economic policy (to some degree even within the coalition government itself), it was the subject of much controversy over its period of operation. With an unfavourable international climate (in particular, historically high real interest rates) the political will seems to have been lacking to wind back the large-scale state involvement in the economy and reduce a level of state indebtedness which has reached crisis proportions. During these years the political air was filled with mutual and bitter recriminations.

After a change of government in February 1987, the plan in operation at present, the *Programme for National Recovery*, was published in October 1987, and included a detailed pay agreement for both public and private sectors for the period to 1990. By this time, the precarious size and nature of the fiscal imbalance was acknowledged to be so serious that major and immediate surgery was needed. The overriding objective had become the stabilisation of the inexorably rising debt-GNP ratio so as to break out of a vicious circle of intensifying debt, an increasingly intolerable tax burden on wage income, loss of international competitiveness and spiralling unemployment and emigration. However, the fundamental ambivalence that characterises Irish

PLANNING IRELAND'S FUTURE

plans endured. The *Programme* was relatively silent on the draconian expenditure cuts being contemplated by the government, the details of which were published *after* the plan in the public expenditure *Estimates* for the year 1988. This nice sense of timing ensured that a crucial element of the *Programme*, the national wage agreement, could be concluded with the Trades Unions before the nature and extent of the cuts were widely understood.

MEANWHILE, BACK AT THE ECONOMY

How did the Irish economy fare over the thirty-year era of economic planning? Were we promoted or relegated in the league of international comparisons? If we were promoted, was it because of, or in spite of, the activities of the economic planners?

Two key economic measures capture the overall story of the Irish economy over the last thirty years: real growth and the unemployment rate. Figure 1 shows the growth rate of real gross national product (GNP) since 1958 while Figure 2 shows the unemployment rate. By the standards of the late seventies and the decade following *Economic Development* was truly a golden age of sustained high growth and low unemployment. However, just as Lemass's rising tide lifted all domestic ships, could it be that there was an international rising tide? In other words, did Ireland manage to grow *relative* to other similar European countries? Tables 1 and 2 show how Ireland fared relative to Denmark, Belgium, Norway and Finland, four of the club of small rich countries. All five countries had broadly similar growth rates on average. Hence, while Ireland singularly failed to converge upwards towards the *per-capita* GDP of its initially richer neighbours, neither was there any systematic tendency towards further deterioration. Turning to comparative unemployment, Figure 3 shows Ireland's unemployment rate in 1985 compared with the rest of the OECD countries.

So, Ireland not only failed to catch up with the wealthier European countries but by 1985 it had the second highest rate of unemployment in the OECD (after Spain). However, behind this

THE LEGACY OF ECONOMIC DEVELOPMENT

simplistic comparison in terms of aggregate growth and unemployment lay good and bad developments. For example, the industrial sector grew while the importance of agriculture declined (Figure 4) and within industry the modern sector came to dominate the traditional sector[23] (Figure 5). Not only did exports from the modern industrial sector outstrip agricultural exports (Figure 6) but also their destinations were considerably more diversified than in the early decades of the state when the UK was totally dominant (Figure 7).

All these were good developments and were foreseen in the economic plans. However, there was a dark side to the story. A large proportion of net employment creation was in the public sector (Figure 8) and total public expenditure steadily monopolised a growing proportion of GNP. With few exceptions taxes grew steadily every year as a proportion of GNP (Figure 9). Yet even as she became heavily taxed, Ireland simultaneously became heavily indebted, and the total national debt as a percentage of GNP reached the dizzy heights of 150 per cent in 1987. The really worrying aspect of this debt was that a sizable fraction of it (over a third by 1987) had been borrowed from foreigners, the interest payments on which represented a net loss to the economy.

Finally, a feature of industrial growth in recent years has been an increasingly high level of profit repatriation by multinational industries producing in Ireland. Such outflows are a normal feature associated with foreign direct investment. However, multinational high-technology firms that have located in Ireland over the last few decades tend to be intensive in terms of capital and research, source most of their inputs abroad, have relatively weak downstream links with the rest of the economy and repatriate the major part of their profits. Public policy has not yet succeeded in building on existing Irish industrial strengths to develop firms which will generate and retain a greater portion of added-value within the economy. The dilemma of policy remains particularly acute: low wage costs and an adequate supply of trained workers are a key element serving to attract industry to Ireland but the low downstream linkage and the

PLANNING IRELAND'S FUTURE

high rate of profit repatriation means that the domestic wage bill is the main benefit received from such activity. The foreign-led industrial growth strategy developed into, at best, a *zero-sum* game (i.e. of little *net* benefit to the economy).

THE LESSONS OF ECONOMIC PLANNING

Any detailed attempt to attribute success or failure to individual plans would be impossible. In the first place, it is the annual budget that actually implements government economic policy decisions, not the plan. The budgetary process involves a multitude of policy instruments, complex timing of changes, is spread over the whole year and embodies a high degree of continuity with past policies.[24] In addition, the assumptions made *ex ante* in the plans about, say, the international environment may not be realised *ex post*. Irish planners can hardly be blamed for not forecasting the Yom Kippur and Iran-Iraq wars, the depth and duration of the recession of the early eighties or the extraordinary bad weather of 1985/6. These assumptions are made by both politicians and public servants. Politicians are usually, by nature and selection, assertive, optimistic people. Public servants in general are calculating risk-averse pessimists, while those in the Department of Finance are expected to be downright gloomy Scrooges. Out of the creative tensions between these different personalities our plans are born and the best plans have been those which achieve an elusive balance. The *First Programme* had this balance. The plans of the 1977-80 period had not.

To some extent, the dominant features of Irish economic plans (in particular, the nature and degree of state activity) arose from their broadly accepted Keynesian intellectual underpinnings. One of the results of the Keynesian revolution had been to play down the significance of resource allocation issues and to stress the limitations rather than the uses of markets. However, today we are faced with a situation where economic planning by the state is unfashionable and no longer holds the 'high ground' of national concensus. Past planning experience has taught us that in a small open economy the ability of state intervention to achieve policy

THE LEGACY OF ECONOMIC DEVELOPMENT

goals is extremely circumscribed, no matter what view of economics one holds. More recent developments have broken with the previous Keynesian tradition and the underpinnings of present policies and plans have taken on aspects of a more market-oriented economics.

The concept of the market is central to economics since in a market economy this is the mechanism by which scarce resources are efficiently allocated. Economists can be classified in terms of their attitudes to market forces and to market intervention by governments. A free-marketer holds that the role of governments should be restricted to setting the ground-rules or laws required by the system of private property. The opposite Marxist position replaces markets by a system of central planning where resources are entirely allocated by government *diktat*. What is interesting about the Irish political party system, shaped as it was by the civil war, is that it bears little resemblance to the right/left or conservative/socialist divide that characterised British and European politics in the twentieth century.[25] The main Irish political parties try to keep to the ideological centre and the closer they are to office the more they consolidate a moderate centre position in their actions. During a period of strong economic growth, policy changes are less controversial since it is easier to divide up a growing cake than a fixed or shrinking one. The Lemassian *dictum* of 'rising tides' eases political tension.

The 1987 general election took place after a period of unprecedented stagnation of growth, historically high unemployment and chronic imbalances in the state finances. While all political parties acknowledged these problems, they disagreed strongly on apportioning blame and proposing solutions. If the 1951 election has been described as the first Irish 'pork barrel' election,[26] 1987 could be characterised as the first ideological one, where the previous economic consensus showed a distinct tendency to break down in the face of unpleasant policy choices.

Through a Glass Darkly

In looking ahead to the next Irish economic plan, both our experience of the past and that of other small European states is rele-

PLANNING IRELAND'S FUTURE

vant.[27] Almost without exception, the small European states have
carved a path between liberalism and statism, and have evolved
towards indirect forms of economic control. What characterises
the economic and political experience of small European states
and sets them apart from the large industrial countries is the
'premise' of their planning efforts: adaptation to external market
forces. They have generally come to find detailed comprehensive
sectoral planning efforts increasingly inapplicable, simply because
of the openness and vulnerability of their economies. Their problem is one of selecting the devices of planning that are in har-
mony with their social objectives. Hence, the *rationale* for state
intervention depends on the ability or otherwise of market forces
to yield results consistent with these social objectives. Because
of their lack of autonomy, their strategy must be flexible, reactive
and incremental. They cannot oppose adverse change by shifting
its costs to others abroad. Instead, they must continually impro-
vise in living with change. The success or otherwise of this continual process of improvisation will depend in large part on the
efficiency with which they learn the lessons of their previous
planning efforts.

Is the time ripe for the emergence of a new *Economic Development* to map out Ireland's future over the next thirty years? The
world is a much more complex place now than it was in 1958 and
every aspect of economic and cultural life in Ireland is exposed
to international influences to an extent that would have seemed
unbelievable to the planners of that earlier period. The imminent
arrival of the Single European Market represents the logical cul-
mination of this trend. It would be wise to assume that these
changes are irreversible. In addition, attitudes to public sector
intervention in the economy have changed, not only in the western world but also in the centrally planned economies of Eastern
Europe and China. For better or for worse, the previous spirit of
what David Henderson has called 'unreflecting centralism'[28]
(i.e. the readiness to assume that decisions have to be taken by
governments and that governments can pick winners) has faded
and been replaced by a willingness to rely on a more Darwinian
outcome based on the survival of the fittest in the cut and thrust

THE LEGACY OF ECONOMIC DEVELOPMENT

of market forces. If Seán Lemass and Dr Whitaker were the popular heroes of the sixties and seventies, this role is now played by prominent personalities from the business world.

The core of any new *Economic Development* will be the manner in which it can reconcile the twin goals of efficiency and equity. For economic policy to be successful it must be hardheaded but soft-hearted.[29] But the very success of the policies of the past thirty years has given rise to what Mancur Olson calls 'distributional coalitions', powerful lobbies among employers, employees and the state who are more oriented to struggles over the distribution of income and wealth than to the production of additional output.[30] Consequently, it has become increasingly difficult in Ireland to negotiate and implement policies where there are winners and losers, and the sense of frustration this engenders risks leading to a breakdown of the already fragile consensus between the social partners. The single most important criterion of success of any new *Economic Development* will be the extent to which it can chart the way towards the elimination of the social evil of mass unemployment, probably the root cause of much of the social inequality in Ireland today. Nothing in the last thirty years, either here or abroad, convincingly demonstrates that this task will be accomplished without active and fruitful co-operation between the private and state sectors.

Table 1. *Average Growth Rates of Gross Domestic Product Per Capita*

	1951–73	1974–85	1951–85
Belgium	3.6	1.9	3.0
Denmark	3.1	2.0	2.8
Finland	4.2	2.3	3.6
Norway	3.3	3.9	3.5
Ireland	3.0	3.9	3.5

PLANNING IRELAND'S FUTURE

Table 2. *Gross Domestic Product Per Capita Relative to Ireland*

	1950	1973	1985
Belgium	1.7	1.9	1.9
Denmark	2.1	2.2	2.1
Finland	1.4	1.8	1.8
Norway	1.9	2.0	2.4

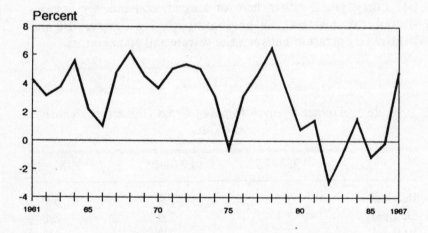

Figure 1. *Growth Rate of Real GNP*

144

THE LEGACY OF ECONOMIC DEVELOPMENT

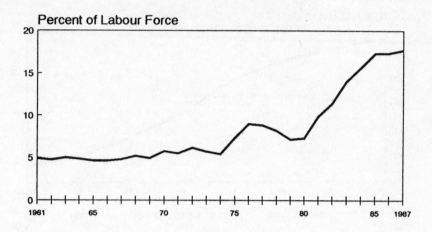

Figure 2. *Rate of Unemployment*

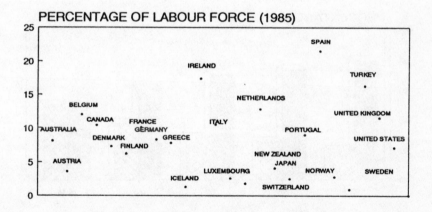

Figure 3. *OECD Unemployment Rates*

PLANNING IRELAND'S FUTURE

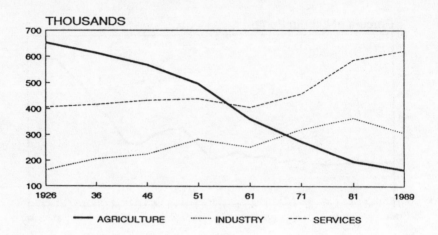

Figure 4. *Sectoral Employment: 1926-1989*

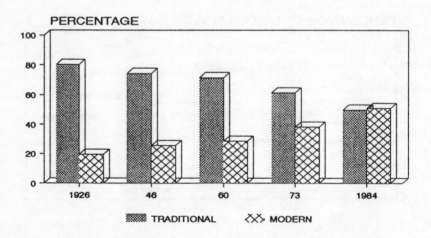

Figure 5. *Shares of Manufacturing Employment*

THE LEGACY OF ECONOMIC DEVELOPMENT

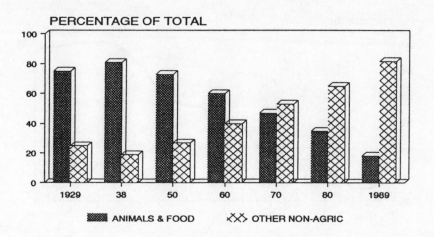

Figure 6. *Composition of Irish Exports*

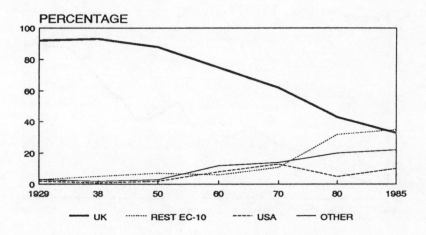

Figure 7. *Irish Exports: Geographical Destination*

PLANNING IRELAND'S FUTURE

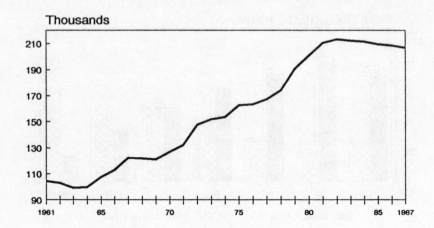

Figure 8. *Public Sector Employment*

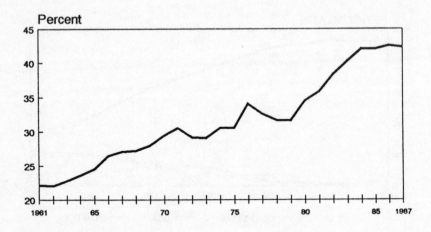

Figure 9. *Total Taxes as Percent of GNP*

148

THE LEGACY OF ECONOMIC DEVELOPMENT

NOTES

1. To take a modern example, Ireland could leave the EC but would have to suffer some unpleasant adjustments if she did so.
2. 'If you remove the English army to-morrow and hoist the green flag over Dublin Castle, . . . England would still rule you. She would rule you through her capitalists, through her landlords, through her financiers, through the whole array of commercial and individualist institutions she has planted in this country . . .;' James Connolly, *Socialism and Nationalism* (Dublin, 1948). This article first appeared in 1897.
3. Ronan Fanning, *The Irish Department of Finance 1922-58* (Dublin, 1978).
4. This sense of isolation after the Second World War, and the difficulties in overcoming it, are documented in Miriam Hederman's book *The Road to Europe: Irish Attitudes 1948-61* (Dublin, 1983).
5. F.C. King, 'Drifting to Absolutism', *Journal of the Statistical and Social Inquiry Society*, 1952; Patrick Lynch, 'The Economist and Public Policy', *Studies*, Autumn, 1953.
6. For example, C.S. Andrews, *A Man of No Property* (Cork, 1981).
7. W.H. Beveridge, *Full Employment in a Free Society* (London, 1944).
8. Employment Act, 1946.
9. B. Chubb and P. Lynch, *Economic Development and Planning* (Dublin, 1969); R. Fanning, *The Irish Department of Finance, 1922-58* (Dublin, 1968); O. Katsiaouni, 'Planning in a Small Economy: The Republic of Ireland', *Journal of the Statistical and Social Inquiry Society of Ireland*, vol. xxiii, 1977.
10. T.K. Whitaker, 'The Department of Economic Planning and Development', *Interests* (Dublin, 1983).
11. Constraints can, alas, mutate into binding targets. A decade-and-a-half of public sector profligacy has resulted in the debt/GNP ratio making this transition!
12. Quoted in P. Bew and H. Patterson, *Seán Lemass and the Making of Modern Ireland 1946-66* (Dublin, 1982).
13. For example, the section of his Statistical and Social Inquiry Society paper in 1956 dealing with the limited role of the Keynesian multiplier in a small open economy.
14. Bew and Patterson, *op. cit.*
15. R. Fanning, *The Irish Department of Finance, 1922-58* (Dublin, 1978).
16. In the light of present-day sensitivities to the nuances of every interest group, a certain political naïvety characterised the references to 'the virtual satisfaction of needs' in housing and other forms of social investment. This was an attitude which would be carefully excised from all future plans.

PLANNING IRELAND'S FUTURE

17. In part these capital flows were the result of the process of dismantling trade barriers, which was well under way even before the publication of the *First Programme*.

18. The 4 per cent growth rate chosen was never justified satisfactorily, but was broadly in line with projected OECD growth rates.

19. A pool of applicable empirical research was developing, in the then newly founded Economic & Social Research Institute and elsewhere. However, it is worth remembering that the *Economic & Social Review*, the main vehicle of economic publication in Ireland (together with the older *Journal of the Statistical & Social Inquiry Society*) was not founded until 1969. The first full-scale Keynesian macroeconomic model for Ireland was not constructed until 1966, but was not available for operational use by policy-makers.

20. J.P. Neary, 'The failure of Irish Nationalism', in *Ireland: Dependence and Independence, The Crane Bag*, vol. 8, 1984.

21. T.K. Whitaker, 'The Department of Economic Planning and Development', *Interests* (Dublin, 1983).

22. Whether this failure was political or economic in nature remains an open question. Given the Irish propensity towards imitative social behaviour, perhaps if Margaret Thatcher and Ronald Reagan had come to power three years earlier all would have been different.

23. The traditional sector includes food, drink, clothing, footwear, etc., while the modern sector includes chemicals, engineering, metal products, etc.

24. For the technically minded, a detailed analysis of the budgets of the 1967–80 period is provided in Bradley *et al.*, *Medium-Term Analysis of Fiscal Policy in Ireland* (Dublin, Research Paper No. 122, 1985).

25. The historian, Ronan Fanning, writing about the Labour Party's stance of principled neutrality in response to the Treaty split of 1922, commented: 'Labour, by standing aside on what became and remained the great divide in Irish politics, recognised the continuing irrelevance of socialism for the majority of Irish voters and effectively admitted that Ireland, as Engels had remarked to Marx fifty years earlier, "still remains the Holy Isle whose aspirations must on no account be mixed with the profane class struggles of the rest of the sinful world" '(R. Fanning, *Independent Ireland* (Dublin, 1983).

26. R. Fanning, *op. cit.*

27. P. Katzenstein, *Small States in World Markets* (Ithaca, 1985).

28. D. Henderson, *Innocence and Design: the Influence of Economic Ideas on Policy* (Oxford, 1985).

29. A. Blinder, *Hard Heads and Soft Hearts: Tough-Minded Economics for a Just Society* (New York, 1987).

30. Mancur Olson, *The Rise and Decline of Nations* (New Haven, 1982).

[10]

Excerpt from P.J. Drudy and Dermot McAleese (eds), *Ireland and the European Community*, 173–90.

8 · Ireland's membership of the European Monetary System: expectations, out-turn and prospects

BRENDAN M. WALSH

Membership of the European Monetary System (EMS) had a more dramatic and tangible impact on Ireland than membership of the EEC itself. This is because within weeks after the formation of the System our currency departed from the one-to-one no-margins parity that had been maintained with sterling since 1826. Ironically, the most immediate consequence of the new institutions whose goal was the creation of a wide 'zone of monetary stability' was the break-up of the oldest currency union between sovereign states in Europe. In the three years since the EMS was formed, the absence of the United Kingdom has made Ireland's membership somewhat of an anomaly in view of our continued close economic ties with that country.

In this review of the impact of the first three years of membership on Ireland, the background debate and expectations in the period leading up to the decision to join the System are reviewed, and then our experience since joining is assessed. In the final section, the prospects for Ireland's continued membership of the EMS are discussed. In an area of rapid change and development, it is important to bear in mind that this chapter reflects the situation as it was at the time of writing, that is, June 1982.

THE STERLING LINK

Before 1979 the only episode of Irish exchange rate independence from the UK was that which occurred during the Napoleonic Wars. When the currency instability that characterised this period subsided, a stable exchange rate was re-established between the UK and Irish pounds. The old 12:13

parity was adopted once again in 1821, but as part of the process of integration of Ireland into the United Kingdom envisaged in the 1800 Act of Union, the independent Irish pound was abolished in 1826. All transactions, debts, contracts, etc. were converted to UK pounds on the basis of 12/13 the amount reckoned in Irish currency.

During the rest of the nineteenth century, and until the establishment of an independent Irish State in 1922, the absence of an independent Irish currency did not figure among the economic grievances complained of by nationalist writers. Nor were currency matters high on the priorities of the fledgling Irish Free State. New token coins were issued in 1926 and a consolidated Note Issue gradually replaced the private banks' notes, without any fundamental change in the currency system. A Commission on Banking, Currency and Credit set up in 1934 was the only initiative in this area by a new administration that had taken radical steps in the field of industrial protection. The Majority Report published in 1938 firmly rejected various radical proposals and schemes regarding the Irish currency and emphasised that maintaining the sterling link was of paramount importance in view of the high degree of economic integration between Ireland and the United Kingdom, the pre-eminence of the UK as a trading nation, and the difficulty that would be faced in establishing international confidence in an independent Irish currency.

A Central Bank was established in 1942 with limited powers that were only gradually taken up and eventually extended in 1971 into those of a fully fledged Central Bank. During the devaluation of sterling against the dollar in 1949 and 1967, the Irish pound was also devalued against the dollar not as a deliberate beggar-my-neighbour policy but rather as an inevitable consequence of a largely unquestioned adherence to the sterling link.

The first systematic discussion in the post-war era of the costs and benefits of maintaining the sterling link, as opposed to alternative currency arrangements, is an essay written in 1973.[2] Although the analysis was conducted in the light of new ideas about optimal currency areas, the author re-

IRELAND AND THE EUROPEAN MONETARY SYSTEM 175

affirmed the view of the Commission that reported in 1938 regarding the advisability of maintaining the sterling link. However, although strongly of the view that a devaluation would not bestow any real gains on the Irish economy, he held out the possibility that a re-valuation 'would tend to be a powerful anti-inflationary weapon'.[3]

The link between our exchange-rate policy and our inflation rate began to pre-occupy Irish commentators as the rate of inflation in Ireland accelerated *pari passu* with that in the United Kingdom. Over the entire period 1955–78, the Irish consumer price index rose at an annual average of 6.7 per cent compared with the 6.5 per cent annual increase in the UK retail price index.[4] Although in individual years there were significant deviations between the inflation rates in the two countries, there was no trend in these deviations and no tendency for an enduring gap to emerge between the two. The Irish economy therefore seemed to fit extremely well the small open economy model of inflation.

It was a small step from this finding to the inference that a change of exchange-rate peg would bring about a change in our inflation rate. Specifically, it was argued by a growing body of opinion that a change of exchange-rate policy was at least a necessary condition for lowering our rate of inflation. Some economists went further and implied that a change in the exchange-rate peg would be sufficient to ensure, by some unspecified mechanism, the convergence of our inflation rate on the rate experienced in the country to whose currency we pegged the Irish pound. The spirit of this argument is conveyed by the following quotation from an introductory textbook that achieved a wide circulation in Ireland just as we entered the EMS:

so long as we maintain a fixed exchange rate with *any* major country with which there is relatively free trade, we will tend in the long run to have that country's rate of inflation. The reasoning amounts to little more than recognising that markets do exist . . ..[5]

This line of reasoning can be seen to have influenced official, as well as academic views about exchange-rate policy. The Governor of the Central Bank summarised the arguments that influenced the Irish decision to join the EMS as it became likely that the UK would not participate in its exchange rate mechanism under the following headings:

1   the inappropriateness of an indefinite prolongation of the sterling link;
2   the benefits in terms of a reduction in inflation to be obtained from adherence to a hard currency régime;
3   a commitment to a major Community initiative; and
4   Community support in the form of a significant transfer of resources.[6]

In the White Paper issued in December 1978 one of the reasons advanced in favour of Ireland's membership of the EMS was the belief that 'the discipline involved in membership of a zone of monetary stability acts as a powerful aid in the fight against inflation'.

Underlying these arguments was, of course, the implicit assumption that sterling would remain a high inflation, depreciating currency. This was made explicit in statements such as 'it would be prudent for us to proceed on the asumption that, in the longer run at any rate, membership of EMS involves a harder currency régime than non-membership'.[7] This, of course, represented the consensus view of sterling at the time, and one which was so deeply ingrained that the initial appreciation of sterling relative to the EMS tended to be dismissed as a short-term aberration.

Commentators who anticipated a dramatic moderation of our inflation rate subsequent to entry into the EMS did not intend to convey the impression that this would come about without supportive domestic policies. The need for appropriate income, monetary and fiscal policies was emphasised. Warnings emanating from the Central Bank and the Economic and Social Research Institute drew attention to the inappropriateness in our new situation of rates of increase in money incomes as large as had been the rule in the pre-EMS days. For example, the Governor of the Central Bank warned that 'for the first time since the establishment of the State, the effects of ill-advised domestic policies and actions will be seen quickly and obviously in the market's judgement of the Irish pound'.[8] But it was assumed in many quarters that appropriate action on these fronts would be inevitable because it was implicit in our decision to join the EMS. It seemed to be widely believed or hoped that membership of the newly formed club would lead to a fundamental change of national attitudes despite the events of the early months of membership when the promise of a substantial 'transfer of resources' fuelled expectations of higher living standards and, if anything, militated against the adoption of an appropriate incomes policy.

It is interesting to speculate whether prescience of the strength of sterling during the period 1979–82 would have affected the willingness of Irish officials and politicians to join the EMS without the UK. It would have been difficult, in view of the acceptance of the argument that a weak exchange rate resulted in increased domestic inflation, to have consciously chosen the EMS as a soft currency option relative to sterling. As events unfolded, this option was in fact accepted but in the guise of following a strong-currency EMS exchange-rate peg!

THE IRISH POUND IN THE EMS

With high hopes of dramatic benefits in terms of reduced inflation and 'convergence' of our economic performance to that of the stronger European countries, we joined the EMS at its formation in March 1979. Within weeks sterling had risen to the point where maintaining the sterling link would have entailed re-valuing the Irish pound against the other EMS currencies. Rather than take this step, we opted to stay within our band against the EMS currencies and towards the end of March 1979 the Irish pound floated against sterling for the first time in over 150 years.

The break with sterling was one of the most important consequences of joining the EMS. Almost half our trade, and probably a larger share of our foreign transactions, now entailed foreign exchange dealings. The transactions costs

178   BRENDAN M. WALSH

involved have been estimated at IR£5.5 million in 1979, equivalent to a current cost of about 2.5 per cent of Gross National Product (GNP).[9] The EMS interest subsidies which figured so prominently in our entry negotiations amounted to IR£44m, IR£45m and IR£46m in 1979, 1980 and 1981 respectively, and represent a 1979 value of less than 2 per cent of GNP. Thus, although at the time the question was not explicitly raised, it seems that the 'transfer of resources' which was one of the attractions of joining the System no more than offset the cost of the additional foreign exchange transactions incurred by breaking the sterling link.

There were other gains, however. The break with sterling set Gresham's Law in motion and the substantial quantity of United Kingdom legal tender that had circulated in Ireland was rapidly replaced by Irish currency. There was, therefore, a seigniorage gain to the Irish authorities. It has also been suggested that the break-up of a currency union increases the demand for money. The combined impact on holdings of Irish currency of these two effects has been put at about IR£34m.[10] The modest gain in terms of interest saved on the national debt as a result of this increase in the demand for Irish currency should be included among the benefits from membership of EMS.

During three years of EMS membership there has been an upsurge in the importance of foreign exchange dealings in the Irish economy, and the speed and efficiency with which this new complication to commercial life has been handled are impressive, although sophistication in foreign currency dealing hardly represents a net gain to the economy!

In the three years since the EMS was formed there have been six exchange-rate re-alignments but none of these involved a decision by the Irish Government to alter the value of the Irish pound against its EMS partners. As a consequence of changes in other countries' exchange rates, the Irish pound's central rate has appreciated relative to the Italian lira (+13%), the Danish kroner (+11%) and the Belgian and French francs (+9%), and depreciated relative to the Dutch guilder (−10.2%) and German mark (−10.8%). It has

IRELAND AND THE EUROPEAN MONETARY SYSTEM 179

remained virtually unchanged against a trade-weighted average of the EMS currencies. A very different picture emerges, however, from a broader index of the external value of the currency since 1979. In Fig. 8.1 the trade-weighted exchange-rate index is shown. From this, it is clear that the stability that has been maintained relative to the EMS has not been sufficient to achieve an overall stabilisation of our exchange rate. Since joining the EMS the index shows that the external value of the Irish pound fell by 14 per cent. This is due above all to the appreciation of sterling relative to the ECU during 1980–1, and the continued dominance of the UK in Irish trade. Even more disappointing in view of the expectation that the new exchange-rate policy would ensure stability and reduce uncertainty has been the volatility of the Irish exchange rate since 1979. The combination of re-alignments within the EMS and the instability of sterling relative to the EMS currencies has led to increased rather than diminished volatility in Ireland's foreign exchange rate.

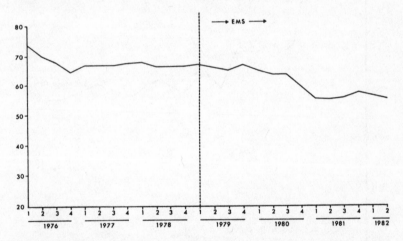

Fig. 8.1. Effective exchange-rate index, December 1971 = 100, (Quarterly averages).

The benefits of membership in terms of increased stability and reduced uncertainty would, of course, have been greater if the widely anticipated change in the pattern of our trade

180   BRENDAN M. WALSH

flows had in fact followed our entry into the System. One of the most extraordinary features of our experience since 1978 has been the absolute stability of the share of our EMS partners in our trade: these seven countries accounted for 20.8 per cent of our imports and 30.3 per cent of our exports in 1978, and in 1981 the EMS share was 21.2 per cent of our imports and 29.8 per cent of our exports. We remain in the extra-

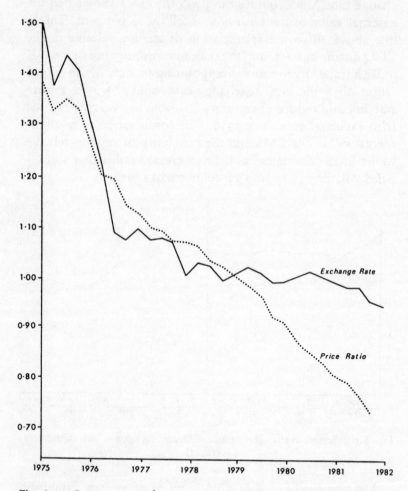

Fig. 8.2. German mark/Irish pound exchange rate and ratio of German/Irish price indices (Quarterly averages, 1975–82; first quarter 1979 = 100).

IRELAND AND THE EUROPEAN MONETARY SYSTEM 181

ordinary situation of maintaining an exchange-rate peg with countries that account for only 25 per cent of our trade. If we can conclude little else with certainty about the experience of the past three years, we can affirm that a commitment to fixed exchange rates between groupings of countries is not sufficient to result in a restructuring of trade flows.

But more important from every point of view is the equally striking failure of the inflation rates of EMS Member States to converge. This story is by now familiar and most strikingly illustrated by the contrast between Irish and German inflation rates (as measured by consumer price indices) since 1979 (Fig. 8.2). A similar, if somewhat less dramatic, picture emerges from a comparison of Gross Domestic Product (GDP) deflators or unit labour costs. A broader evaluation of these issues shows that the standard deviation of EMS inflation rates was larger in 1980 and 1981 than in 1976, 1977 or 1978, and will remain very high in 1982.

It has to be said that in reviewing the Irish experience since the formation of the EMS we tend to take a rather parochial view of our currency's performance. We speak, for example, of the performance of the Irish pound against sterling as if this bilateral market had a significant life of its own when in fact since March 1979 we have held a quasi-fixed rate against the EMS currencies while sterling has floated. Consequently, the trend of the Irish pound against sterling is mainly a reflection of the trend of sterling against the EMS currencies. Viewed from this perspective, the really major development since 1979 has been the extraordinary real appreciation of sterling against all its trading partners, as its exchange rate rose despite a persistence of relatively high inflation. Between mid-1978 and mid-1980 the real effective exchange rate of sterling rose by between one-third and one-half, depending on whether the nominal rate is deflated by retail prices or unit labour costs. We broke with sterling in the early stages of this dramatic rise, and consequently participated along with other EMS countries, but to a lesser extent, in the real depreciation against sterling, as may be seen from Fig. 8.3. We have thus steered a middle course between sterling and the EMS cur-

rencies, experiencing a major real depreciation relative to
sterling and an almost equally large real appreciation relative
to the EMS currencies. During 1982, however, the decline in
the UK inflation rate and the weaker trend in sterling have
begun to reverse the real appreciation of sterling and we are
now entering a phase in which maintaining our EMS exchange rate entails a loss of competitiveness not merely
relative to other members of the EMS but also relative to the
UK.

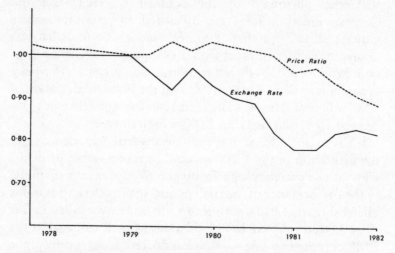

Fig. 8.3. Sterling/Irish pound exchange rate and ratio of UK/Irish price
indices (Quarterly averages, 1978–82; first quarter 1979 = 100).

A marked feature of the Irish economy since joining the
EMS has been the magnitude of the balance-of-payments
deficits that have been incurred. Table 8.1 sets out the
balance-of-trade broken down by area for the years 1978–81.
The current account balance of payments actually
deteriorated much more sharply than is indicated by these
figures, due to the rapid increase in net factor payments to the
rest of the world (see Table 8.4). It is striking that the
depreciation of the Irish pound relative to sterling in 1980–1
led to a marked increase in the value of imports from the UK,
suggesting a relatively inelastic demand for imports from

IRELAND AND THE EUROPEAN MONETARY SYSTEM 183

that source. On the other hand, exports to the UK grew only slowly, due no doubt in large part to the severity of the UK recession, but perhaps also to a lack of price sensitivity among some Irish exports. The result was a trebling of our balance-of-trade deficit with the UK between 1978 and 1981, despite the enormous gain in competitiveness relative to sterling. A similar train of events occurred following the decline of the Irish pound relative to the dollar in 1981, the value of imports rose by 57 per cent but exports rose by only 43 per cent, with the result that the trade deficit increased by 72 per cent.

Table 8.1. *Balance of trade by area for the period 1978–81 in IR£m*

	1978	1979	1980	1981
EMS				
Imports	771	1040	1088	1393
Exports	896	1084	1310	1444
Trade balance	+125	+44	+222	+51
UK				
Imports	1832	2414	2754	3268
Exports	1396	1625	1763	1920
Trade balance	−436	−789	−991	−1348
USA and Canada				
Imports	344	458	548	863
Exports	221	207	274	393
Trade balance	−123	−251	−274	−470
Rest of World				
Imports	760	916	1029	1051
Exports	446	580	784	1089
Trade balance	−314	−336	−245	+38
Total				
Imports	3707	4828	5419	6575
Exports	2959	3496	4131	4846
Trade balance	−748	−1332	−1288	−1729

Source: Trade Statistics of Ireland.

The current account balance-of-payments deficits in the three years 1979–81 have equalled 10, 8 and 13 per cent of

GNP. While some of these extraordinarily large deficits may be attributable to the loss of competitiveness relative to the EMS countries, public sector deficit spending in excess of revenue that can no longer be financed from the private sector's financial surplus must bear the brunt of the blame for the sustained excess of national spending over national income.

The clearest evidence of a loss of competitiveness may be seen in the sharp fall in net exports to the EMS countries in 1981. These figures exclude the effect of a deterioration in net foreign exchange earnings from tourism, which has also been adversely affected by the real appreciation of the Irish pound. The slow growth of exports to the EMS countries during 1981 is all the more striking in view of the increased exports attributable to the high level of overseas investment undertaken up to 1982 to avail of the tax advantage of Ireland as a base for exports to Europe. Data are not available for exports from these new industries, but the pattern of industrial growth between early 1980 and early 1982 strongly suggests a marked decline in the older, more labour-intensive Irish industries which are most vulnerable to the adverse developments on the competitiveness front. While industrial production as a whole grew by 2 per cent over this period, production in clothing and footwear, textiles, paper and paper products, metal articles, and several other sectors, declined.

In the longer run, a continued real appreciation of the Irish currency relative to the EMS could act as a deterrent to foreign investment. The Committee on Costs and Competitiveness, established in mid-1981 to recommend rates of increase in domestic costs consistent with maintaining Ireland's international competitiveness, documented the extent to which Ireland's advantages as a relatively low cost location in Europe had been eroded in the period since joining the EMS. Developments in labour costs during 1982 intensified this trend, as may be seen from Table 8.2. The transformation of the country to a high wage, high productivity economy has been proceeding at a pace that is not consistent with the ex-

IRELAND AND THE EUROPEAN MONETARY SYSTEM   185

tremely rapid growth of our working age population, and some of the 60 per cent increase in the level of registered unemployment since March 1979 must be due to these factors.

Table 8.2. *Trend in unit wage costs in manufacturing industry,*
1978–82

	In national currencies			In ECU		
	Ireland	EMS excl. Italy	EEC-8	Ireland	EMS excl. Italy	EEC-8
1978	100	100	100	100	100	100
1979	113	104	110	113	103	110
1980	133	112	129	132	110	133
1981ᵉ	145	118	140	140	115	151
1982ᶠ	159	125	148	153	122	156

e = estimate; f = forecast.
Source: Based on OECD data. EMS and EEC countries are weighted by importance in Irish trade.

The process by which Ireland has succeeded in holding a more or less fixed exchange rate within the EMS despite the massive balance-of-payments deficit is set out in Table 8.3. This summarises the main public sector financial aggregates for the years 1977–82. The extraordinarily high level of public sector borrowing in recent years and the dependence on foreign sources of finance to sustain this borrowing are clear from this table. In 1981 the Government financed more than four-fifths of its borrowing through monetary channels, mainly by borrowing abroad. The repercussions on the country's net indebtedness are shown in the last column of the table. Inevitably the rise in indebtedness to the rest of the world has meant a steady growth of foreign interest payments. The trend in factor payments to and from the rest of the world are shown as a percentage of GNP in Table 8.4. The

186   BRENDAN M. WALSH

sharp increase in interest payments on foreign debt in 1982
will pre-empt all the forecast growth in GDP and lead to a
slight decline in GNP. Projection of the budgetary situation
in 1983 suggests that it will be extremely difficult to prevent a
further rise in the ratio of foreign interest payments to the
GNP.

Table 8.3. *Public sector financial aggregates,* 1978–82 *as a*
percentage of GNP

	Exchequer borrowing requirement	Public sector borrowing requirement	Net increase in foreign debt		Level of official external reserves	
			Government	Total public sector	Gross	Net[a]
1977	10.0	12.9	0	0.2	22.0	− 5.0
1978	12.6	15.3	0.1	1.5	19.6	− 2.2
1979	13.6	16.6	6.7	7.3	13.2	−14.7
1980	14.1	18.0	7.7	11.7	15.6	−20.0
1981	17.0	21.8	15.0	17.6	14.5	−33.7
1982f	15.0	20.0	10.9	14.3	15.5	−39.1

Notes: a Net = gross reserves less public sector foreign debt.
        f = forecast
Source: Central Bank of Ireland, Annual Reports

The non-fulfilment of the widely-held expectation that
inflation rates would converge within the EMS is more
comprehensible in the light of the developments in relation to
the public finances since 1979. No one could have anticipated
the scale of external borrowing that has taken place in the last
three years. This borrowing has been facilitated by membership of the EMS, and in its turn it has facilitated the maintenance of our exchange rate at its original EMS parity by
financing the massive balance-of-payments deficits incurred
since 1979. Another strand in the explanation of our experience since joining the EMS is a possible shift in the ratio of
non-tradeable goods to tradeable goods prices. Although

Table 8.4. *Net factor income from abroad, 1976–82 as a percentage of GNP*

	Government interest payments	Net non-government factor payments	Net factor income
1976	−1.4	+1.4	0
1977	−1.8	+1.2	−0.6
1978	−2.0	+1.0	−1.0
1979	−2.1	+1.2	−0.9
1980	−2.6	+1.2	−1.4
1981[e]	−3.1	+1.0	−2.1
1982[f]	−4.8	+0.9	−3.9

e = estimate; f = forecast
Source: The Economic and Social Research Institute, *Quarterly Economic Commentary*, May 1982, Table 12.

conclusive data are not available, it is generally believed that the rate of pay in the public sector has accelerated more rapidly than that in the private sector since 1979. In addition, the growth of public sector employment has aggravated the growth of the public sector pay bill and of public sector spending in general. Taxation has been steadily increased although, as we have seen, not rapidly enough to match the upsurge in expenditure. The total tax burden has risen from 33 per cent of GNP in 1979 to 42 per cent in 1982. Indirect taxes have risen from 15 per cent of GNP to 20 per cent in the same period. Undoubtedly much of the excess of Ireland's inflation over that experienced elsewhere in Europe in recent years can be attributed to the direct and indirect repercussions of this increased taxation.

CONCLUSION

In reviewing Ireland's experiences since joining the EMS it is inevitable that broad issues concerning the conduct of economic policy are raised. The technical achievement of maintaining our exchange rate within the System is about the

188 BRENDAN M. WALSH

only aspect of membership that has operated according to our aspirations in 1979. The disappointments and drawbacks associated with our experience within the System can be summarised under the following headings:

1 The continued absence of the UK from the exchange rate arrangements of the EMS. This has meant that maintaining our exchange rate relative to the EMS has not resulted in stability in a broadly defined index of the external value of our currency.

2 The frequent re-alignments of the System have in fact allowed the high and low inflation countries to adjust their exchange rates to their inflation rates, rather than vice versa. Ireland is unique among the high inflation countries in not adopting this pragmatic approach and is, as a consequence, suffering a marked loss of competitiveness relative to other EMS countries. Up to 1982, the rise of sterling (and the dollar) relative to the EMS offset this trend and led to a slight gain in our trade-weighted index of competitiveness, but during 1982, the stability of sterling relative to the EMS implies that the exchange-rate peg with the EMS entails a loss of competitiveness in all our markets.

3 The failure of the EMS to develop into the hoped-for monetary union, with a convergence of economic performance between members, has meant that the long-term benefits from membership which weighed heavily in our decision to join have not materialised.

4 Maintaining a quasi-fixed exchange rate despite extremely high inflation has been facilitated by massive foreign borrowing, which has replenished our foreign exchange reserves at the cost of a steady rise in external indebtedness and consequently in the ratio of foreign interest payments to GNP.

5 It could be claimed that membership of the EMS, far from forcing the adoption of appropriate macro-economic policies, actually encouraged the inappropriate fiscal and incomes policies that have been pursued in recent years by raising expectations of higher living standards as a result of

IRELAND AND THE EUROPEAN MONETARY SYSTEM   189

the widely publicised 'transfer of resources' that formed part of our terms of entry and the improved access to lines of foreign credit that membership of the System provides.

Two concluding comments seem warranted. First, the EMS as it has evolved since 1979 cannot be said to provide a satisfactory solution to Ireland's need to define an appropriate exchange-rate target. As long as sterling floats against the EMS currencies, we may experience major uncertainty and instability even if we successfully adhere to an EMS exchange-rate target.

Secondly, the attempt to impose the discipline of low inflation, monetary, fiscal, and incomes policies on the economy through a strategy of pegging the exchange rate within the EMS has all the characteristics of putting the cart before the horse! Lasting exchange rate stability between members of the EMS presupposes a willingness on the part of national monetary authorities to adopt rates of monetary expansion in line with that adopted by the hegemonial country, which we may assume is Germany. As Korteweg remarked early in the life of the EMS 'it is highly unlikely that those countries (whose monetary policies have been most expansionary in the past) would indeed adjust their monetary policies as required in the short-run, given the negative effects on employment and economic activity transitorily produced by such adjustments'.[11] In fact, this prediction proved incorrect because the author included the UK among those countries whose monetary policies he believed would remain expansionary. (The change in the UK's policy was not of course attributable to the influence of the EMS!) But in the Irish case, entry into the EMS had no discernible influence on the public sector's contribution to monetary expansion, as was shown in Table 8.3. The need to implement domestic policies consistent with reducing inflation to the target rate must henceforth receive priority.

Acknowledgement: The research for this chapter was supported in part by the Committee for Social Science Research in Ireland.

190　　　　　　　BRENDAN M. WALSH

REFERENCES

1. Parts of this chapter draw on the author's contribution to Marcello de Cecco (ed.), *International Economic Adjustment: Small Countries and the European Monetary System*, (Oxford, 1982).

2. T. K. Whitaker, 'Monetary Integration: Reflections on the Irish Experience', *Central Bank of Ireland Quarterly Bulletin*, Winter 1973, pp. 64–80.

3. Whitaker, 'Monetary Integration', p. 72.

4. These figures are taken from P. T. Geary, 'How Much Inflation is Imported?', in D. F. McAleese and W. J. L. Ryan (eds.), *Inflation in the Irish Economy: A Contemporary Perspective* (Dublin, 1982).

5. D. A. G. Norton, *Economic Analysis of an Open Economy: Ireland* (Dublin, 1980), p. 190.

6. C. H. Murray, 'The European Monetary System: Implications for Ireland', *Central Bank of Ireland Annual Report*, 1979, pp. 96–108.

7. Murray, 'The European Monetary System', p. 105.

8. Murray, 'The European Monetary System', p. 107.

9. C. McCarthy, 'EMS and the End of Ireland's Sterling Link', *Lloyds Bank Review*, no. 136, April 1980, pp. 30–42.

10. P. Honohan, 'The Break-up of a Currency Union Increases the Demand for Money', *Central Bank of Ireland, Technical Paper* 1/RT/1981.

11. Pieter Korteweg, 'The European Monetary System – Will it Really Bring More Monetary Stability to Europe?', *De Economist*, vol. 128, no. 1, 1980, pp. 15–48. The quotation is from p. 42.

DO TARIFFS MATTER? INDUSTRIAL SPECIALIZATION AND TRADE IN A SMALL ECONOMY

By DERMOT McALEESE[1]

THE purpose of this paper is to examine the effects of protection on industrial specialization and trade, using Irish experience as a case study. Inferences about the effects of protection, and the consequences of its removal, are drawn on the basis of a comparison between the industrial sectors of Northern Ireland and the Republic of Ireland. These two economies are similar in practically every respect except that the Republic's manufacturing sector has been highly protected. The present study contrasts with previous empirical work on protection in being based on a comparison between observed patterns of specialization and trade rather than between an observed pattern on one hand and some hypothetical *ex-ante* or *ex-post* situation on the other.[2]

The manufacturing sectors of the Republic and Northern Ireland have expanded under radically different trade regimes during the last four decades. From the early 1930s to the mid-1960s, the Republic's manufacturing sector was one of the most highly protected in Europe. The average nominal tariff on industrial goods in 1966 was estimated at 25 per cent while effective rates averaged 85 per cent (McAleese, 1971). Northern Ireland, by contrast, experienced uninterrupted conditions of free trade during this same period.[3] Apart from this contrast, however, the two economies share many features in common, which could be expected to throw into sharp relief the consequences of their different commercial policies.

First, the absolute size of their manufacturing sectors is roughly the same. Numbers employed in manufacturing in Northern Ireland in the mid-sixties totalled 180,000 compared with 200,000 in the Republic. Second, market access for exports has been broadly similar in the two economies.

[1] I am indebted to Dr. W. M. Corden and Mr. John Martin, both of Nuffield College, for their invaluable comments on an early draft of this paper. Thanks for helpful criticisms and encouragement are also due to Professors Noel Farley (Bryn Mawr College), Herbert Grubel (Simon Fraser University), Thomas Wilson (University of Glasgow), Dr. G. C. Hufbauer (Office of the Secretary of the U.S. Treasury), Dr. K. A. Kennedy (Economic and Social Research Institute, Dublin), John O'Hagan (Trinity College, Dublin), and John Simpson (Queen's University, Belfast). The usual disclaimer applies.

[2] The approach is similar to Hufbauer and Chilas (1974) who compare the degree of specialization in Europe and the United States in order to deduce something about the long-term consequences of trade liberalization in Europe.

[3] Northern Ireland received some protection from the U.K. tariff, but as most of its trade is with Great Britain this was not of much practical importance.

118   DO TARIFFS MATTER ?

The Republic enjoyed free access to the British market for most manufactured goods since the Second World War and faced much the same tariff
barriers in non-U.K. markets as Northern Ireland. Since both parts of
Ireland are cut off from the British mainland, transport costs are also
similar. Finally, the two economies have reached a broadly comparable
level of economic development, share a common language and a similar
institutional background, and have currencies whose one-to-one parity
has never been broken. These similarities are sufficiently pronounced to
justify our contention that, while historical factors and the smaller size of
Northern Ireland's domestic market would account for some differences,
any pronounced divergence in the degree of specialization found in the two
economies can be attributed to the different trading conditions under
which their manufacturing sectors have operated.[1]

Under these circumstances, international trade theory would predict
a much greater degree of 'specialization' in the manufacturing sector of
Northern Ireland than in that of the Republic. According to the orthodox
(classical or Heckscher–Ohlin) theory, Northern Ireland will have a greater
degree of inter-industry specialization in the sense of higher export/gross
output ratios in export industries, higher import/consumption ratios in
import-competing industries, and a higher degree of industrial concentration. The modern theory of intra-industry specialization generates a
rather different set of predictions, namely, that the distinction between
export industries and import-competing industries will be blurred and
that the chief point of contrast between the free trade economy and the
protected economy will consist in the former's higher export and import
ratios in each industry. Higher aggregate trade ratios are, however, predicted by both theories.

This paper submits these various hypotheses to empirical test. First,
the degree of industrial specialization in the two economies is examined,
using data on trade flows and gross output for twenty-nine industries.
Second, changes in industrial specialization associated with the Republic's
movement towards free trade during the period 1964 to 1971 are analysed.
Thirdly, standard indices of intra-industry trade are computed and their
implications examined.

I. Trade ratios, concentration coefficients, and industrial specialization

Using 1963 as reference year for Northern Ireland and 1964 for the
Republic, two 'trade ratios' are calculated in Table I for twenty-nine

---

[1] It would require a very strict set of assumptions about demand and production
conditions to ensure identical degrees of specialization in Northern Ireland and the
Republic.

TABLE I. *Northern Ireland and Republic of Ireland manufacturing industry: gross output and trade ratios*

Industry	Northern Ireland 1963			Republic of Ireland 1964			Republic of Ireland 1971		
	GO £mn	X/GO %	$\frac{M}{GO-X+M}$ %	GO £mn	X/GO %	$\frac{M}{GO-X+M}$ %	GO £mn	X/GO %	$\frac{M}{GO-X+M}$ %
1. Grain milling and animal foods	50·61	2·88	20·6	38·88	3·5	12·4	65·04	1·5	2·7
2. Meat and fish products	28·38	76·0	10·8	60·55	59·8	4·6	146·74	64·3	1·7
3. Milk products	17·72	52·0	32·9	51·79	40·2	0·3	105·96	43·4	0·5
4. Bread and biscuits	13·98	—	2·8	23·33	2·9	1·3	38·11	5·4	3·9
5. Fruit, vegetable products, and misc. foods	2·91	66·4	77·5	14·22	16·1	21·4	31·64	20·3	22·5
6. Chocolate and confectionery	1·4	97·8	98·6	12·44	19·6	11·7	21·75	21·2	7·7
7. Drink and tobacco	55·87	95·8	90·0	73·31	11·7	3·6	127·32	12·6	3·2
8. Spinning, weaving, textile printing	45·81	36·7	38·1	9·37	21·8	57·3	11·94	39·4	70·1
9. Carpets and textile products	29·22	91·6	50·6	4·56	18·4	20·7	13·54	40·6	20·8
10. Woollen and worsted	4·72	87·6	69·8	16·47	17·6	33·0	21·61	32·4	30·9
11. Hosiery and knitted goods	6·69	77·8	58·2	14·12	18·8	14·0	31·92	30·7	35·6
12. Canvas goods, rope, twine	7·85	70·4	32·1	10·32	16·3	8·5	22·58	18·2	9·8
13. Leather	1·85	89·4	93·4	8·46	57·7	21·0	13·86	69·3	39·7
14. Shirt and collar	11·76	99·0	94·5	3·42	35·1	5·5	6·73	39·2	16·4
15. Clothing	18·47	90·3	92·0	19·49	17·4	9·8	35·34	28·8	25·1
16. Footwear	2·77	95·6	97·5	11·11	25·0	5·2	15·37	31·9	22·6
17. Timber, builders' wood	8·32	12·3	24·5	7·71	16·6	47·2	18·11	16·3	44·3
18. Furniture	2·89	9·8	46·5	6·71	2·7	9·6	12·41	8·6	18·2
19. Paper and board	5·05	36·2	83·1	15·33	16·2	41·1	29·58	18·8	45·7
20. Printing and publishing	6·31	58·5	—	17·76	11·7	17·3	37·26	9·1	19·1
21. Chemicals	9·30	6·2	32·5	26·04	7·1	29·9	69·94	27·6	29·8
22. Pottery, refractory goods	2·47	20·2	66·1	1·12	17·0	33·1	2·23	19·3	25·9
23. Glass/glassware	1·08	73·8	33·0	3·66	23·0	17·3	9·35	50·4	30·8
24. Cement and lime	2·04	0·8	24·5	4·97	22·7	2·3	11·33	5·2	7·2
25. Building materials	6·31	40·2	—	8·37	11·1	11·1	28·88	11·8	8·8
26. Metal products	7·46	51·0	38·3	27·42	18·3	25·2	59·84	19·6	25·5
27. Engineering/vehicles assembly	66·46	75·9	30·5	52·79	13·7	11·9	92·31	15·3	22·5
28. Electrical engineering	19·25	72·0	47·2	19·51	19·6	31·2	45·27	35·8	32·3
29. Miscellaneous	28·02	64·7	59·3	50·97	16·3	12·5	119·19	33·8	21·6
TOTAL	464·97	59·7	45·7	614·20	21·2	16·4	1245·13	28·3	19·6

Note: GO = Gross Output, X = Exports, M = Competing Imports.

Sources: Computed from *Input-Output Tables for Northern Ireland 1963*, Belfast: H.M.S.O. 1973, *Input-Output Tables for 1964*, Irish Stationery Office 1970, and various issues of the *Irish Statistical Bulletin*. Exports and competing imports for the Republic in 1964 are taken from McAleese and Martin (1973), Tables A2 and A5.

manufacturing industries: (*a*) exports as a percentage of gross output and (*b*) competing imports as a percentage of apparent consumption.[1]

The most striking feature of the table is the very pronounced difference between Northern Ireland's trade ratios and those of the Republic. The (weighted) average export ratio of Northern Ireland, 59·7 per cent in 1963, contrasts with the Republic's 21·2 per cent in 1964. The corresponding shares of imports in apparent consumption are 45·7 per cent for Northern Ireland as against 16·4 per cent for the Republic. This contrast is not the result of any freak aggregation bias. Nineteen out of the twenty-nine industries in Northern Ireland had export ratios greater than 50 per cent in 1963 compared with only two industries in the Republic in 1964. Similarly, in the case of import ratios, twenty-two industries in Northern Ireland had import shares greater than 30 per cent, as against the Republic's six industries.

Second, one notices the high level of intra-industry specialization in Northern Ireland relative to the Republic. High export and import ratios are found in many industries. Fruit and vegetable processing, drink and tobacco, confectionery, woollen and worsted, clothing, footwear, and leather are outstanding cases in point. In all these industries, Northern Ireland's export and import ratios both exceed 66 per cent. No fewer than nineteen industries in Northern Ireland have export and import ratios greater than 30 per cent while there is no such case in the Republic.

The corollary is that the manufacturing sector of neither Northern Ireland nor the Republic conforms to a pattern of specialization in which a set of industries with very high export ratios and negligible import ratios, on the one hand, contrasts with another clearly defined set of industries with high import and negligible export ratios, on the other.

A Spearman rank correlation test between export shares and import shares yielded coefficients which were not significantly different from zero.[2] However, this finding does not necessarily contradict the orthodox theory of inter-industry specialization. It is obviously conceivable that the free trade economy be more specialized in both intra-industry and inter-industry terms. That is, total manufacturing output (or employment) could be concentrated in a narrower band of industries in the free trade economy, and yet these industries could individually have high export and import ratios.

To test for inter-industry specialization, we use a measure of specializa-

---

[1] The actual figures and details of their sources, reliability, etc., are provided in McAleese (1976).

[2] The Spearman rank correlation coefficient (twenty-nine industries) was −0·111 and −0·225 for Northern Ireland (1963) and the Republic (1964) respectively. In a seventy-industry test for the Republic, the rank correlation coefficient was −0·014. None of these values were significantly different from zero.

tion analogous to P. Sargant Florence's (1948) coefficient of localization. The coefficient of specialization is defined as:

$$\tfrac{1}{2} \sum_i |Q_i - \mu|$$

where Q_i = the percentage share of the ith industry's output in total output

μ = 100 per cent divided by the number of industries.

The value of the coefficient lies between zero and 100 per cent. A highly specialized industrial structure will be reflected in a high value of the coefficient: and the more diversified the region's industrial structure, the lower the value of the coefficient. Thus specialization is defined by reference to a completely equal dispersal of industries throughout the manufacturing sector. This is not a wholly satisfactory procedure but it seems to be the best available.[1]

Specialization coefficients, computed in this manner, suggest very clearly that Northern Ireland's industry is more specialized than that of the Republic. Thus, as one would expect, there is more inter-industry specialization in the free trade economy than in the protected economy. On the basis of gross output data, Northern Ireland's coefficient emerges as 23 per cent higher than the Republic's (42·88 as compared with 34·86). If net output is taken instead of gross output, the contrast becomes even more marked, with the North's specialization coefficient rising to twice the level of the Republic's (45·55 as against 23·21 respectively).[2]

II. Industrial specialization and the move to free trade

Between 1964 and 1971, tariffs in the Republic were approximately halved and, under the terms of the 1966 Anglo-Irish Free Trade Area Agreement (AIFTA), provision was made for the complete removal of protective barriers on imports of U.K. origin by 1975. The 'expected' effects of this change in commercial policy would be to reduce the contrast between Northern Ireland and the Republic. Within industries one would expect an increase in import ratios due to the improved competitive position of foreign goods and an increase in export ratios as a result of a reduced 'bias against exports'. These effects would be achieved, at an individual firm level, by cutting back the range of products manufactured in each plant, by streamlining production, and by paying increased attention to

---

[1] Experimentation with different measures (e.g. using employment data instead of output, with less and more detailed aggregation) did not affect the Northern Ireland/Republic ranking.

[2] The reasons for this discrepancy are explained in McAleese (1976), where the limitations of the measure are dealt with in greater detail and where the results of alternative formulations are reported.

122   DO TARIFFS MATTER ?

export markets in order to maintain the volume of sales. Some inter-industry specialization would also be expected, as nonviable industries are forced into liquidation through loss of sales on the home market combined with inability to engage in exporting. It is worth while asking whether the observed effects are consistent with these theoretical expectations.

Post-1964 trade ratios have indeed changed in the expected direction. As Table I shows, the export ratio rose from 21·2 per cent in 1964 to 28·3 per cent in 1971 and the import ratio from 16·4 per cent to 19·6 per cent. The share of imports in consumption increased in twenty industries between 1964 and 1971, and export ratios rose significantly in all but four industries during this period.

While the degree of inter-industry specialization also rose in the expected direction, the increase is not as marked as in the case of the trade ratios. The specialization coefficient rose from 34·9 to 35·7 on the basis of gross output figures, and from 23·2 to 25·0 on the basis of net output figures. Thus the degree of specialization has increased during the period in both an inter-industry and intra-industry sense, but with a more pronounced emphasis on the latter.

Although these results conform with expectations, the increase in specialization cannot be attributed exclusively to tariff reductions. Other influences were at work favouring an increase in trade ratios. Thus, during the sixties, the growth of manufactured exports was encouraged by a generous system of export profits tax relief, capital grants to export-oriented enterprises and other export aids. It is impossible to disentangle the effect of these factors on the export ratio from that of the reduced bias against exports. Similarly, the trend rise in the imports ratio observed during the sixties owes something to the effects of rising living standards on the demand for variety, etc., as well as to tariff reductions. McAleese and Martin's (1973) study of the effects of the AIFTA tariff cuts, however, reveals a close correspondence between industries most affected by trade liberalization during the years 1966–70 and those registering the largest increase in import shares in Table I. The sixties marked a transition to outward-looking policies generally. The increase in trade ratios which occurred between 1964 and 1971 indicates the order of magnitude of the effects of this broad policy change, an important element of which was the removal of protection, rather than providing an exact quantification of the effects of the tariff reductions *per se*.

There remains the question of why intra-industry specialization effects dominated inter-industry effects. Without investigating this matter in detail, a number of hypotheses can be suggested to explain this. First, the process of inter-industry adjustment may take a much longer time than intra-industry adjustment, due to readier mobility of factors within industries than between industries. Second, one might argue, on 'infant industry' grounds, that many industries require protection in order to get them started but that, after a time and with suitable adjustment to their product range, they are well able to maintain viability in a free trade context. Third, the Republic's import concessions during the sixties applied mostly to imports from the U.K., whose relative factor prices and income levels are broadly comparable with its own. Had these concessions been offered on a multilateral basis, there might well have been greater inter-industry effects in certain sectors of Irish industry. Indeed, it is precisely the fear of high adjustment costs associated with reallocation of resources between industries which explains the cautious attitude of many governments, and not just the Republic's, to multilateral tariff reductions in general, and to trade concessions to LDCs in particular.

The distinction between intra-industry and inter-industry specialization is one of degree rather than kind. Obviously, what is intra-industry specialization at one level of aggregation can become inter-industry specialization at a more detailed level. Implicitly the assumption is being made that resource allocation within an 'industry' has different implications from resource allocation between 'industries'. In the present context, where the effect of transition from protection to free trade is being studied, we assume that the adjustment costs associated with, say, greater specialization within the 'clothing' industry are less than those involved in a shift of resources from clothing to food processing or any other industry. This is a restrictive assumption, since adjustment costs are ultimately related to the number and location of individual plant closures, but, given the limitations of data, it seems a reasonable and practicable assumption to work with.

III. Share of intra-industry trade

The empirical results of this paper can be related to the concept of intra-industry trade which has received much attention in the literature in recent years. Grubel and Lloyd in a comprehensive study of this phenomenon define intra-industry trade as 'international trade in differentiated products which are close substitutes' (1975, p. 1). Various indices have been devised to measure intra-industry trade, notably by Verdoorn (1960), Michaely (1962), Kojima (1964), Balassa (1966), Grubel (1967), and Grubel and Lloyd (1971, 1975). These measures are all rather similar in broad design, but the Grubel–Lloyd measure is perhaps the most satisfactory. Their measure of intra-industry trade is

$$\frac{\sum_i [(x_i+m_i)-|x_i-m_i|]}{\sum (x_i+m_i)} \cdot 100.$$

124   DO TARIFFS MATTER ?

Intra-industry trade is thus measured as the amount of trade overlap, i.e. exports matched by imports in each industrial group, expressed as a percentage of total commodity trade. There is also an 'adjusted' Grubel–Lloyd index which attempts to take account of bias arising from large trade imbalances.[1]

Indices of intra-industry trade report on the share of intra-industry trade in total trade and not on the ratios of trade (exports and imports) to production or consumption. It is the latter which are really important for the present discussion. The question of what happens to the ratio of one type of trade (intra-industry vs. inter-industry) to another type of trade is subsidiary, though of some intrinsic interest.

Intra-industry trade indices were computed using the two forms of the Grubel–Lloyd index. We used two sets of trade data: imports and exports at a two-digit SITC level, and exports and competitive imports for the twenty-nine industries of Table I. The latter set creates an upward bias in the index of intra-industry trade because it ignores non-competitive imports which are all inter-industry trade, whereas the former creates problems of comparability in that data for only thirty SITC divisions were available for Northern Ireland as against forty-four for the Republic. As the detailed calculations are reported elsewhere (McAleese, 1976), attention can be confined here to two summary observations.

First, the proportion of intra-industry trade is about half in Northern Ireland, and between one-third and one-half in the Republic, depending on the particular index and set of import figures employed. The similarity in the proportion of intra-industry trade is interesting. Since there is no *a priori* reason why a free trade country should have a higher or lower proportion than a protected economy, this result is not counter-intuitive.

Second, the proportion of intra-industry trade has risen quite remarkably in the Republic during the period 1964 to 1971. The Grubel–Lloyd index for forty-four SITC divisions rose from 0·353 to 0·428 and the adjusted version from 0·462 to 0·532 during the period. Direct observation of the data shows that this was a period of increasing industrial specialization. Hence, Balassa's contention that change in the intra-industry trade indices over time 'permits us to draw inferences regarding the effects of tariff reductions on (intra-industry) specialization' (1967, p. 90) is consistent with the evidence of this paper. The factors responsible for this increase in intra-industry trade, in turn, are presumably the same as those which brought about the increase in intra-industry specialization.

This last point raises the more general question as to whether the index of intra-industry trade is a decreasing function of protection. Our figures

[1] It does this by subtracting $|\Sigma x_i - \Sigma m_i|$ from the denominator.

DERMOT McALEESE   125

suggest that it is. One could argue that the index responds to both the extent of protection and the size of the protected country's economy.

Consider a small country with two sectors, a manufacturing sector and a primary goods sector. A decision is made to protect the manufacturing sector. While the effect of this policy on the ratio $|x-m|/(x+m)$ for manufactured goods is ambiguous, the weight attached to this fraction will fall because the proportion of manufactured goods trade in total trade declines. As the country approaches complete self-sufficiency in manufactures the weight approaches zero. This means that the value of $|x-m|/(x+m)$ for primary goods becomes predominant. Given that a small country has a limited natural range of resources at its command, we can expect intra-industry trade values to be very small in primary commodities. This last hypothesis certainly conforms with Irish experience. The intra-industry trade index for SITC sections 0–4, which can be taken as approximately the primary goods sector, amounts to only 0·339 (0·377 adjusted) in the Republic at a 2-digit SITC level. Hence, for such a country, the level of intra-industry trade is inversely related to the degree of protection of the manufacturing sector.

The argument can be pursued further by allowing the size of the economy to vary. The proportion of intra-industry trade in the primary goods sector will almost certainly be increased as the country's resources (human and non-human) become larger. If we subdivided the manufacturing sector into goods which are easily replaced by domestic production (e.g. clothing) and goods such as capital equipment which can be replaced only at high cost (because of economies of scale), an additional reason is presented for expecting a positive correlation between economy size and the level of intra-industry trade. The range of commodities protected by the small economy will tend to be concentrated in the former group; the latter group could, therefore, be considered in the same way as primary goods. The larger the size of the market, the greater the range of commodities which can be protected without incurring excessive costs due to loss of economies of scale.

One could, therefore, argue that the level of intra-industry trade is a decreasing function of protection and an increasing function of market size. But this hypothesis is proposed tentatively, keeping in mind the inadequacies and limitations of the intra-industry trade index. For one thing, none of these indices is a flawless measure of trade in 'differentiated goods which require similar input combinations'—the type of trade which is most interesting to proponents of the theory of intra-industry trade. Grubel and Lloyd (1975) admit that, at any given level of aggregation, a significant amount of intra-industry trade may consist of trade in differentiated products which require quite different factor proportions (e.g. metal

126   DO TARIFFS MATTER?

furniture and wood furniture) and which consequently may be explained
in terms of the standard Heckscher–Ohlin model.[1] Finally, and most
important, it is clear that all measures of intra-industry trade are sensitive
to the level of aggregation used.

IV. Summary of results

A comparison is made between two economies which are very similar,
except for the degree of protection. The question we asked is: what difference does protection make to the protected economy's industrial structure?
Do tariffs matter?

The results may be summarized briefly as follows.

Trade ratios in total and for most individual industries were significantly
higher in Northern Ireland than in the Republic in the mid-sixties. Inter-
industry specialization was also much higher in Northern Ireland.

Trade ratios in total and for most individual industries have risen in the
Republic following the reduction in protection during the period 1964–71.

Inter-industry specialization also increased in the Republic during this
period, but to a much smaller extent.

The share of intra-industry trade in total trade was somewhat higher in
Northern Ireland than in the Republic in the mid-sixties, but this proportion has risen significantly in the Republic in the period 1964–71.

These results are clearly consistent with the hypothesis that tariffs do
matter. They support the widely held view that the effects of protection on
inter-industry specialization, and its attendant implications for factor
mobility and income distribution, appear only in the long run, if they
appear at all. In the short run, changes in intra-industry specialization
are more to be expected.

Trinity College, Dublin

                             REFERENCES

1. BALASSA, BELA, 'Tariff reductions and trade in manufactures among industrial
   countries', *American Economic Review*, June 1966.
2. —— *Trade Liberalisation among Industrial Countries*, McGraw–Hill, 1967.
3. FINGER, J. M., 'Trade overlap and intra-industry trade', *Economic Inquiry*,
   December 1975.
4. FLORENCE, P. SARGANT, *Investment, Location and Size of Plant*, Cambridge
   University Press, 1948.
5. GRUBEL, H. G., 'Intra-industry specialisation and the pattern of trade',
   Canadian Journal of Economics and Political Science, Aug. 1967.

[1] This point is stressed by Finger (1975) and is clearly conceded in Chapter 6 of Grubel
and Lloyd (1975).

DERMOT McALEESE   127

6. GRUBEL, H. G., and LLOYD, P. J., 'The empirical measurement of intra-industry trade', *Economic Record*, Dec. 1971.

7. —— —— *Intra-Industry Trade: The Theory and Measurement of International Trade in Differentiated Products*, Macmillan, 1975.

8. HUFBAUER, G. C., and CHILAS, J. G., 'Specialisation by industrial countries: extent and consequences', in Herbert Giersch (ed.), *The International Division of Labour: Problems and Perspectives*, J. C. B. Mohr, Tübingen, 1974.

9. *Input–Output Tables for 1964*, Dublin, Government Publications Office (Prl. 985), 1970.

10. *Input–Output Tables for Northern Ireland 1963*, Belfast, H.M.S.O., 1973.

11. KOJIMA, K., 'The pattern of international trade among advanced countries', *Hitotsubashi Journal of Economics*, June 1964.

12. MCALEESE, DERMOT, *Effective Tariffs and the Structure of Industrial Protection in Ireland*, Dublin: The Economic and Social Research Institute, paper No. 62, 1971.

13. —— and MARTIN, JOHN, *Irish Manufactured Imports from the U.K. in the Sixties: The Effects of AIFTA*, Dublin: The Economic and Social Research Institute, paper No. 70, 1973.

14. —— 'Industrial specialisation and trade in two small economies: Northern Ireland and the Republic', *Economic and Social Review*, Jan. 1976.

15. MICHAELY, M., 'Multilateral balancing in international trade', *American Economic Review*, Sept. 1962.

16. VERDOORN, P. J., 'The intra-bloc trade of Benelux', in E. A. G. Robinson (ed.), *Economic Consequences of the Size of Nations*, Macmillan, 1960.

[12]

Journal of the Statistical and Social Inquiry Society of Ireland, Vol. XXIV, Part II, 1979/80, pp. 69–98

AN ANALYSIS OF THE GROWTH OF THE PUBLIC SECTOR IN IRELAND, 1953-77*

JOHN W. O'HAGAN

(Read before the Society, 6 March, 1980)

The purpose of this paper is to conduct an inquiry into the growth of public sector share (i.e. public sector expenditure expressed as a percentage of GNP) in Ireland for the period 1953-77.[1] This is done under a number of headings. First, the trends in the share of overall public sector expenditure and public sector expenditure by economic and functional category are examined in detail. Second, the trends in revenue are outlined and discussed. Third, the hypothesis that trends in "real" public sector share may have differed markedly from those for nominal public sector share is examined. Finally, the hypothesis that changes in the "visibility" of the tax system, coupled with changes in decision-making procedures, were important determinants of public sector share is assessed. The paper, therefore, examines trends in expenditure and revenue in detail and assesses the validity of what are considered in the literature to be the main hypotheses relating to the growth of public sector share arising from both a "producer" and "financial perspective".[2]

It may be worth emphasising at this stage that the paper is not, for a number of reasons, concerned with the desirability or otherwise of the trends, past or future, in public sector share. It should also be noted, perhaps, that there is a variety of other explanations for the growth in public sector share not looked at in this paper, mainly for reasons of space, and that therefore, it is not being suggested that the hypotheses posited here are the only or, indeed, the most important explanations.

1. OVERALL EXPENDITURE TRENDS

1.1 Definitional and Statistical Problems

There are advantages and disadvantages in any definition of the public sector and the one chosen will ultimately depend on the purpose of the analysis. Public expenditure as discussed in this paper, however, broadly corresponds to the total of the various types of expenditure or transfers made by general government.[3] As such it is intended to be as consistent as possible with the definitions in the internationally agreed system of national accounts used by the Statistical Office of the European Communities (Eurostat), where general government refers to the various authorities and departments of central, local and provincial or state governments which do not produce goods and services for sale in the market. It is worth pointing out that this definition of general government expenditure includes expenditure covered by those social security arrangements and by any private non-profit bodies which are imposed, controlled or mainly financed by public authorities, even though not a formal part of government. Given this definition of public sector or general government expenditure, the main exclusion is the expenditure of those government-owned enterprises or public corporations which primarily sell the goods and services they produce in the market place. As a result, the figures for public sector expenditure given here do not typically correspond to the expenditure covered by government budgets.

---

*This paper is based on Chapter 5 of the author's Ph.D. thesis. See O'Hagan (1979a). The author would like to thank Dermot McAleese and two anonymous referees for some very helpful comments on an earlier draft of this paper.

A major problem with the budget definition of public expenditure is that in some countries government budgets may include capital raising by, or on behalf of, various public corporations, with the consequence that the total of public expenditure can be affected by decisions to exclude or not to exclude particular public corporations from the budget sector. This, of course, may be considered by some to be an advantage of the budget approach. However, the view taken here is that what is of most interest is to identify separately that expenditure which will sooner or later have to be covered by taxation. In so far as current taxation does not fully cover total public expenditure, then, of course, it is assumed that future taxation will be sufficient to service the loans necessary to finance the present public deficit. In effect, then, public sector expenditure as defined here is that expenditure whose allocation is decided by non-market criteria, so that the benefits cannot be directly attributed to those who eventually pay. This definition of the public sector clearly includes not only the purchase of goods and services but also transfers and subsidies.

No matter what output measure is used as denominator in the public sector share measure, transfers will not constitute part of it and thus the inclusion of transfers in the numerator of the quotient is considered "false" by some.[4] However, transfers are financed by taxes and expenditures on transfers are determined by political decisions about allocative as well as distributional objectives, decisions which are of equal importance to those relating to other aspects of public sector expenditure. Thus the inclusion of transfer payments for the purposes of this study appears warranted, although this would not be the case for those studies examining the "contribution" of the public sector to national income. The output measure used in this paper is GNP at current market prices, although the use of either GDP or GNP at current factor cost would not appreciably alter the observed trend in public sector share. Since government purchases are made at market prices, the national income aggregate selected should, it could be claimed, be at market prices rather than at factor cost simply for reasons of consistency, although GNP at factor cost has, it must be noted, other advantages. To express government expenditure at constant prices raises almost insuperable problems. The major difficulty is the lack of market valuations for the goods and services provided by a government. This question, however, will be returned to later in the paper. As net factor incomes from abroad constitutes part of the income base for tax purposes it appears that the use of national product may be more appropriate than domestic product.[5]

1.2 Total Public Sector Expenditure

The main source for consolidated statistics on the public sector in Ireland is the Central Statistics Office's *National Income and Expenditure Series*. Column A of Table 1 outlines the ratio of public sector expenditure, as defined in this series, to GNP at current market prices for the period 1953-1977 inclusive. However, this definition of public sector expenditure does not coincide with the one being used here for a number of reasons. First, it includes expenditure on "loans and share capital" and this expenditure one would not in the normal course of events expect to be financed by taxation. Second, it includes the relatively large item "miscellaneous current receipts" and excludes the item "estimated public authorities depreciation (excluding depreciation of government trading enterprises)". Last, it includes expenditure on "redemption of securities and loan repayments", an item which is excluded from most definitions of the public sector. The reasoning behind this is that, apart from servicing costs, the expenditure associated with borrowing is already accounted for in the year in which the borrowing took place. Column B represents a measure of public sector share which excludes all of the above items and this is the measure of public sector share to be used throughout this paper. As may be seen, it differs substantially from Column A. In particular, as one would expect, the relative size of the public sector is greatly reduced in all years, with a drop of 9.3 percentage points in 1975 being the most dramatic illustration of this. Finally, Column C outlines the share of net public sector expenditure on goods and services plus public sector expenditure on gross physical capital formation as a per cent of GNP at current market prices. These are

Table 1: *Different Measures of Public Sector Percentage Share, 1953-1977*[1]

Year[2]	A	B	C
1953	33.2	29.6	16.7
1954	34.0	29.7	16.7
1955	32.8	29.6	16.4
1956	35.6	30.9	16.9
1957	32.7	29.3	15.1
1958	31.3	28.1	14.9
1959	31.4	27.4	14.7
1960	33.0	28.3	14.9
1961	33.7	29.8	15.1
1962	33.6	29.7	15.6
1963	34.3	30.8	16.1
1964	35.8	32.1	17.1
1965	37.0	33.5	17.6
1966	37.2	34.1	17.3
1967	38.8	35.5	17.3
1968	40.4	36.7	17.1
1969	41.7	37.2	17.7
1970	42.7	39.1	18.7
1971	43.5	40.2	19.6
1972	42.3	39.1	19.6
1973	44.7	39.5	20.6
1974	51.0	43.9	23.1
1975	57.6	48.3	24.8
1976	55.6	48.2	23.8
1977	56.0	47.1	23.0

Sources: National Income and Expenditure, various issues.

A = Total public sector expenditure (as defined in the Irish national accounts) divided by GNP at current market prices.

B = Total public sector expenditure less loans and share capital, less redemption of securities and loan repayments, less miscellaneous current receipts of public authorities, plus estimated public authorities depreciation (excluding depreciation of government trading enterprises), divided by GNP at current market prices.

C = Net public sector expenditure on goods and services plus gross physical capital formation divided by GNP at current market prices (i.e., less transfer payments and subsidies).

[1] The data are not strictly comparable for the whole period. In particular the figures for 1960-77 were compiled on a somewhat different basis to the 1953-59 data, although the difference in the totals to emerge using both methods is rather insignificant. See *National Income and Expenditure 1976*, pp 4-5, for details. A more serious difficulty is that the major revision in 1972 of the concept of GNP was not applied by the CSO to the pre-1960 GNP figures. An approximate reclassification was used here, giving GNP at current market prices for the years 1953 to 1959 (figures using pre-1972 GNP measure in brackets) as £509.8m (£524.5m), £513.2m (£527.9m), £535.6m (£550.7m), £543.5m (£558.8m), £564.7m (£580.8m), £584.7m (£600.9m), £622.4m (£638.8m). The revision basically was to subtract from the pre-1972 classification data on GNP "emigrants' remittances etc." and the "pensions and allowances" component of both private and government international transfers.

[2] 1953-1973 refer to the financial years 1953/54 to 1973/74 respectively.

71

the only components of public sector expenditure, in fact, which "contribute" to GNP and, as mentioned before, are considered by many economists as the only valid items of expenditure to be used in a measure of public sector share. The difference between A and/or B and C is quite dramatic, with 1975 again a clear example of this: in that year the public sector share using A was 57.6 per cent and only 24.8 per cent when C is used.

What is of most interest, however, is whether A, B and C display similar trends or not. With the exception of the 1973 to 1975 period, the trends in A and B are very similar. In those years short-term loans to the EEC Intervention Agency greatly increased the loans component of A, leading to a rather startling, but "artificial", increase in the public sector share when this measure is used. At this stage, then, it may be worth outlining the main trends in public sector share when B is used: (i) relative stability between 1953 and 1963, with a level of 29 to 31 per cent being maintained in eight years of the eleven-year period – the 1958 to 1960 period witnessed a 1 to 2 percentage downward deviation from this pattern; (ii) a steady upward shift between 1963 and 1971, with the 1971 level being maintained in 1972 and 1973 – with the exception of 1951, the public sector share in 1964 was never before attained and the "plateau" level of the 1971-1973 period was approximately 10 percentage points above the previous "plateau" of the 1950s and early 1960s; (iii) a dramatic increase between 1973 and 1975, with the 1975 level being broadly maintained in 1976 and 1977 – the public sector share increased by 8.8 percentage points in this two-year period, i.e. by the same amount as in the whole of the 1963-1973 period.

The question now is whether the trends in the public sector share as measured by C differed markedly, if at all, from those observed for the public sector share as measured by B. As may be seen from Table 1, the public sector share, as measured by C, in the 1964-1968 period was broadly similar to that pertaining in the 1953-1956 period. It was thus not until after 1968 that new "highs" were reached. Moreover, there was a marked drop in the public sector share between 1956 and 1959, with the increase back to previous levels taking place between 1959 and 1964. These somewhat contrasting trends for the 1953 to 1968 period for public sector share as measured by B and C can be seen quite clearly in Table 1. However, between 1968 and 1974 the public sector share for C increased steadily, from 17.1 per cent in 1968 to 23.1 per cent in 1974, and this level was maintained in the following years. The increase of 34.5 per cent between 1968 and 1977, on the 1968 level of C, in fact, compares with an increase of 28.3 per cent when B is used.

1.3 Public Sector Share by Economic Category

To ascertain to which components of government expenditure the increased public sector share observed in the last section can be attributed, it is useful, and usual, to look at public sector share by economic and functional category. Table 2 looks at: I. net current expenditure by public authorities on goods and services (also simply referred to as public consumption); II. gross physical capital formation by public authorities; III. expenditure on subsidies by public authorities; IV. current transfers plus national debt interest paid by public authorities; and V. capital grants to enterprises, other capital transfer payments paid, and payments to the rest of the world – all divided by GNP at current market prices. These five components combined give B in Table 1. This constitutes the economic classification of public sector share.

Public sector share as measured by C is the sum of Columns I and II in Table 2. As may be seen, the "dip" observed for 1958-1959 when using C is nearly fully due to the drop in the gross physical capital formation share in that period. Indeed, the latter shows a very distinct pattern over the 24-year period: between 1953 and 1956 it lay between 4.3 and 4.6 per cent; from 1957 to 1963 it varied between 2.8 and 3.7 per cent; from 1964 to 1973 it stayed within the 4.0 to 4.9 range, and only in the 1974-1975 period did it exceed previous levels, falling back again in 1976 and 1977. On the other hand, the net current expenditure on goods and services portion remained remarkably stable between 1953 and 1969, ranging only between 11.9 and 12.4 per cent from 1953 to 1963 and only between 13.1 and 13.3 per cent from 1964 to 1969. The upward shift of 1 percentage points or so between the two periods occurred between 1963 and 1964. Between 1969 and 1977, however, the share of net current expenditure on goods and services in GNP increased by 4.9 percentage points above previous levels, accounting therefore for the vast bulk of the observed increase of 5.3 percentage points in C in this period, and nearly half of the observed increase in B.

Table 2: *Public Sector Percentage Share by Economic Category, 1953-77*

Year	I	II	III	IV	V
1953	12.1	4.6	2.9	7.9	2.0
1954	12.3	4.4	3.3	8.2	1.5
1955	12.1	4.3	3.4	8.4	1.5
1956	12.6	4.3	3.4	8.9	1.7
1957	12.0	3.1	2.9	9.4	1.5
1958	12.0	2.9	2.6	9.1	1.4
1959	11.9	2.8	2.7	8.8	0.9
1960	12.2	2.8	3.2	9.1	1.1
1961	12.1	3.1	4.2	9.3	1.2
1962	12.2	3.3	3.6	9.2	1.3
1963	12.4	3.7	3.5	9.5	1.7
1964	13.1	4.1	3.6	9.7	1.7
1965	13.3	4.3	3.9	10.1	2.0
1966	13.3	4.0	4.1	10.9	1.8
1967	13.1	4.2	4.6	11.3	2.3
1968	13.1	4.1	4.6	11.6	3.4
1969	13.3	4.4	4.7	12.2	2.6
1970	14.4	4.3	4.8	13.0	2.5
1971	15.0	4.5	4.6	13.2	2.9
1972	15.2	4.5	4.2	12.9	2.3
1973	15.6	4.9	3.1	14.0	1.9
1974	17.0	6.1	3.3	15.5	2.0
1975	18.6	6.2	3.7	17.9	2.0
1976	18.8	5.0	3.6	18.6	2.1
1977	18.2	4.8	3.7	18.3	2.1

Sources: same as for Table 1.

I   =   Net current expenditure by public authorities on goods and services divided by GNP at current market prices.
II =   Gross physical capital formation by public authorities divided by GNP at current market prices.
III =   Expenditure on subsidies by public authorities divided by GNP at current market prices.
IV =   Current transfer payments plus national debt interest paid by public authorities divided by GNP at current market prices.
V   =   Capital grants to enterprises, other capital transfer payments and payments to the rest of the world by public authorities divided by GNP at current market prices.

Turning now to the other components of B, namely columns III-V in Table 2, it can be seen that the subsidies share in GNP has not shown any significant trend over the 24-year period. In fact, between 1974 and 1977 it was little higher than in the years 1953 to 1956. However, between these two periods it showed considerable variation, falling from 3.4 per cent in 1956 to 2.6 per cent in 1958, rising again to 4.8 per cent in 1970 and falling back to 3.1 per cent in 1973. A broadly similar conclusion applies to the capital transfers etc. share. Its level in 1977 was nearly the same as that pertaining in 1953, although it did vary considerably in the intervening years. It reached a low of 0.9 per cent in 1959 and a high of 3.4 per cent in 1968.[6] This leaves as the remaining component current transfer payments (including national debt interest). The share of this item of public expenditure in GNP has risen in nineteen of the twenty-four years covered and over the period as a whole its level has increased by approximately 10 percentage points. This accounts for nearly 60 per cent of the total increase in the public sector share as measured by B. Clearly, then, the growth in the share of current transfers in GNP has been the most important factor in the growth of the public sector share in Ireland. As may be seen, the main period of growth in this item has been the years of 1962 to 1976, with particularly rapid growth in the 1972 to 1976 period.

Table 3 provides a useful summary of the foregoing. The growth in total public sector share since 1961-63 is cearly highlighted, as indeed is the prominent role of current transfers in this growth. It may also be seen that of the 6.3 percentage points increase in the share of goods and services in GNP between 1953-55 and 1975-77, 5.3 of these occurred between 1967-69 and 1975-77.

Table 3: *The Average Percentage Share of Total Public Sector Expenditure, and Some of its Components, in GNP*

Period	Total Public Sector[1]	Goods and Services	Current Transfers	Capital Formation
1953-55	29.6	12.2	8.2	4.4
1961-63	30.1	12.2	9.3	3.4
1967-69	36.5	13.2	11.7	4.2
1971-73	39.4	15.3	13.4	4.6
1975-77	47.9	18.5	18.3	5.3
Changes, 1953-55/ 1975/77	18.3	6.3	10.1	0.9

Sources: based on data in Tables 1 and 2.

[1] As measured by B in Table 1.

1.4 Public Sector Share by Functional Category

(i) Transfers. Table 4 outlines the trends in the shares of current transfers and their main sub-components in terms of function for the period of most rapid growth in current transfers, namely 1963-77. Of the 8.8 percentage points increase in the share of total current transfers between 1963 and 1977, 2.7 (i.e. 31 per cent of the total) of these were accounted for by interest on the public debt, most of this increase coming between 1973 and 1977. Although data for the other sub-categories only exist up to 1975, it would appear that the GNP share of current transfers for "social security and welfare" purposes, which rose by 4.5 percentage points between 1963 and 1975, was in absolute terms the single most important source for the increased total transfers share. Expenditure on current transfers for educational purposes increased from 0.8 to 2.2 per cent of GNP between 1963 and 1975. Some of this increase of 1.4 percentage points may have been due to a reclassification, from 1970, of some items of expenditure, formerly under consumption, as current transfers. Indeed, the categorisation generally of expenditure on education into current transfers and goods and services is somewhat arbitrary and has to be viewed in this light. Finally, the categories of health and "other" rose by 0.4 and 0.5 percentage points respectively between 1963 and 1975.

The greatly increased expenditure on national debt interest is inextricably wound up with the methods used for financing public expenditure and will be returned to in a later section. However, the "social security and welfare" category warrants some closer scrutiny at this stage and Table 5 is intended for this purpose. As may be seen, unemployment relief and pensions accounted for 2.7 of the 4.5 percentage points increase in the "social security and welfare" transfers share between 1963 and 1975. If pay-related benefit and invalidity pensions are included, then in fact, they account for 3.1 percentage points of the increase. Thus unemployment relief and pensions are the main source of the increase in the "social security and welfare" current transfers share between 1963 and 1975.

Table 4: *The Percentage Share of Current Transfers by Function in GNP, 1963-77*

Year	National Debt Interest	Soc. Sec. and Welf.	Health	Education	'Other'[1]	Total
1977	5.7	n.a.	n.a.	n.a.	n.a.	18.3
1976	5.4	n.a.	n.a.	n.a.	n.a.	18.6
1975	4.6	10.2	0.4	2.2	0.5	17.9
1974	3.9	8.8	0.3	2.1	0.4	15.5
1973	3.7	7.8	0.3	1.9	0.3	14.0
1972	3.7	6.9	0.2	1.9	0.2	12.9
1971	3.8	7.3	–	1.8	0.3	13.2
1970[2]	4.0	7.1	–	1.7	0.2	13.0
1969	3.9	6.5	–	1.5	0.3	12.3
1968	3.7	6.2	–	1.3	0.4	11.6
1967	3.7	6.2	–	1.1	0.3	11.3
1966	3.5	6.2	–	1.1	0.1	10.9
1965	3.2	5.8	–	1.0	0.1	10.1
1964	3.0	5.6	–	1.0	0.1	9.7
1963	3.0	5.7	–	0.8	0.0	9.5

Sources: National Income and Expenditure, various issues.

[1]Derived by subtracting from the total the sum of the other components.
[2]The data for health and education were revised back to this year. Items of expenditure which formerly appeared as transfers under health were treated as expenditure on current goods and services. This meant that, using the new concepts, there were no current transfers under health prior to 1972. In that year "payments for medical goods supplied to households by pharmacists" commenced. Some items of expenditure on current goods and services for education were also now treated as current transfer payments. This made a difference of 0.1 percentage points to the share shown here for education in 1970.

A useful framework for analysing further the increases in the "social security and welfare" share has been suggested by the OECD.[7] Symbolically, if SST = social security and welfare transfers, GNP = gross national product, B = number of beneficiaries, I = size of population relevant to the programme, and N = total population, then,

$$\frac{SST}{GNP} = \left(\frac{SST}{B}\right) \times \left(\frac{B}{T}\right) \times \left(\frac{I}{N}\right) \times \left(\frac{I}{GNP/N}\right)$$

i.e. the share of social security transfers in GNP is identically equal to the product of four variables:

(i)   payments per beneficiary;

(ii) beneficiaries per "relevant" population;

(iii) "relevant" population as a ratio of the total population;

(iv) the reciprocal of GNP *per capita*.

The product of (i) multiplied by (iv) can be looked on as one variable, referred to as the "transfer ratio". (ii) is referred to as the "elgibility ratio" and (iii) the "demographic ratio". Using this approach then, the changes, for example, in the shares of unemployment relief and pensions observed in Table 5 can be decomposed into these three items.

Table 5: *The Percentage Share of Unemployment Relief and Pensions in GNP, 1963-77*

Year	Unemployment Relief[1]	Pensions[2]
1977	1.9	4.0
1976	2.1	4.1
1975	2.0	4.1
1974	1.4	3.7
1973	1.2	3.4
1972	1.2	3.0
1971	1.2	3.1
1970	1.2	3.0
1969	1.0	2.8
1968	1.0	2.8
1967	0.9	2.8
1966	0.8	2.9
1965	0.7	2.7
1964	0.6	2.6
1963	0.7	2.7

Sources: National Income and Expenditure, various issues.

[1] Unemployment assistance and unemployment benefit. The addition of pay-related benefit leads to figures of 2.2 (1977), 2.4 (1976), 2.2 (1975), and 1.5 (1974). Some of this pay-related benefit may not be for unemployment purposes though.

[2] Old age n.c. pensions, widows' and orphans' n.c. pensions, retirement pensions, old-age (contributory) pensions and widows' (contributory) pensions. The addition of invalidity pensions riases the figures for 1970-77 by 0.1 to 0.2 percentage points. However, data on invalidity pensions for 1963-69 are not given.

This would clearly give a much more complete profile of the changes undergone. Such a detailed analysis, however, is outside the scope of this paper, and only some speculative suggestions, based on the OECD findings are suggested at this stage.

Looking first at the share of pensions, it is unlikely that demographic changes played much part in the rise here, as the proportion aged 65 or more has remained nearly constant for two decades. Thus the increased share of pensions in GNP must be due to either increased eligibility and/or increased benefits relative to *per capita* GNP. Between 1961 and 1968 in Ireland, the period covered by the OECD study, there was in fact, little change in the ratio of pensions to GNP and thus we can derive little insight into the relative weights of the "elgibility ratio" and the "transfer ratio" from looking at their data for Ireland. However, we can ascertain in which respect Ireland had the most "catching up" to do in 1969, assuming, of course, that the OECD data were compiled on a strictly comparable basis. In that year the share of the population aged 65 and over in Ireland was 0.111, exactly equal to the average for the 17 countries surveyed. As mentioned already, this demographic ratio has since remained approximately constant in Ireland, in contrast to other countries, where it has increased. The eligibility ratio, i.e. pensioners as a proportion of the total number aged 65 or more, was 0.487 against an average of 1.003.[8] The transfer ratio, i.e. the ratio of pensions to GNP *per capita*, was 0.366, compared to a 17-country average of 0.360. Thus clearly the factor contributing most to Ireland's relatively low pension ratio in the 1960s was the low eligibility ratio.

Turning now to unemployment relief, a somewhat different picture emerges. The demographic ratio here, i.e. the unemployed as a per cent of the total population, can be usefully broken down into the product of the participation rate, i.e. the ratio of the labour force to the total population, and the unemployment rate, i.e. the ratio of the unemployed to the labour force. During the 1960s and 1970s in Ireland the participation rate has fallen, but this has been more than compensated for by the increase in the unemployment rate.[9] Thus changes in the demographic ratio were important in explaining the changes in the unemployment benefits share observed in Table 5. Likewise eligibility changes and transfer ratio changes were important. Between 1960 and 1970 the OECD study showed eligibility changes, demographic changes and transfer ratio changes in descending order of importance in contributing to changes in the share of unemployment relief to GDP. However, in 1970 in Ireland the transfer ratio was somewhat below average, and increases in it probably contributed relatively more in the 1970s. Besides, the eligibility ratio in 1970 was above unity and thus little change in this ratio was possible since then. Over the 1963-77 period as a whole then, demographic changes probably contributed most to the increased share of unemployment relief in GNP, with eligibility changes and transfer ratio changes contributing approximately in equal proportions to the remainder.

For the purposes of analysis it may be better to examine total current expenditure on education and health, since the distinction between expenditure on current goods and services and expenditure on current transfers in these areas reflects institutional diversities rather than underlying differences in public policy towards these areas. Before doing this, however, we turn to an examination of public sector expenditure on current goods and services by function.

(ii) *Current Expenditure on Goods and Services.* Table 6 presents details of the shares of public sector gross current expenditure on goods and services by main function. As may be seen, the major sectors for growth, in absolute terms, were "other general government services", education and health. Between 1963 and 1975 the last mentioned accounted for 3.0 of the 7.1 percentage points increase in the total. The other sub-categories listed showed fairly similar absolute percentage points increases. The important thing is that for every category shown there was a marked upward shift between 1967 and 1975, reflecting a pressure on public sector share that was general in nature. This lends substantial support to the view that an analysis of the determinants of overall public sector

Table 6: *The Percentage Share of Public Sector Current Expenditure on Goods and Services by Function in GNP, 1963-75*

Year	Defence	Other Gen. Govt.	Education	Health	Agriculture	'Other'[1]	Total[2]
1975	1.8	3.7	3.1	5.8	2.0	3.9	20.3
1974	1.6	3.4	2.7	5.4	1.5	3.7	18.3
1973	1.5	3.1	2.6	4.8	1.2	3.2	16.4
1972	1.5	2.9	2.6	4.5	1.2	3.3	16.0
1971	1.4	2.8	2.6	4.5	1.3	3.4	16.0
1970	1.3	2.7[3]	2.6[3]	4.3	1.2	3.2	15.3
1969	1.2	2.6	2.5	3.9[4]	1.2	2.7	14.1
1968	1.2	2.6	2.6	3.5[4]	1.2	2.8	13.9
1967	1.3	2.7	2.5	3.3[5]	1.2	3.0	14.0[5]
1963	1.3	2.7	2.3	2.8[5]	1.2	2.9	13.2[5]

Sources: National Income and Expenditure, various issues.

[1] Includes social security and welfare; housing; other community and social services; mining, manufacturing and construction; transport and communication; other economic services.
[2] Gross current expenditure on goods and services total. Net expenditure by function is not provided.
[3] The data for other general government services and education were reclassified back to 1970 and thus are not directly comparable with pre-1970 data. However, for 1970, the difference between the pre- and post-1970 classifications led to only a 0.1 percentage points discrepancy.
[4] The data for these years includes what was then listed as current transfers payments to make them comparable with post-1970 data. See *National Income and Expenditure 1973* for details.
[5] Not directly comparable with post-1968 figures.

share is warranted, as clearly there are forces in operation in the aggregate which a study of isolated sub-components of public sector expenditure might fail to detect.

A more detailed analysis of current expenditure on education and health may, however, be of some use at this stage. As mentioned above, it would appear to be more meaningful to look at these two areas of expenditure using data on both transfers and consumption, and this is presented in Table 7. As may be seen, expenditure on health increased by 3.4 percentage points between 1963 and 1975 and expenditure on education by 2.2 percentage points. This means that between 1963 and 1975 total current expenditure on health and education and expenditure on current transfers for "social security and welfare" combined accounted for 10.1 of the 15.5 percentage points increase in the share of public sector current expenditure in GNP between these years. This indeed, is a very high proportion of the total.[10]

The increased shares of education and health in GNP has been examined in a similar fashion to that for social security and welfare. As before, the expenditure share in output was sub-divided into three ratios, called for short the "demographic ratio", the "enrolment ratio" and the "cost ratio".[11] Ireland was not one of the countries surveyed by the OECD, but the general picture to emerge from their survey of 15 countries was as follows. First, between the early 1960s and early 1970s the largest increase, in percentage terms, was in higher education. Second, of the increase in the share of GDP of education expenditure, none could be attributed to changes in the demographic ratio. In fact, the increase could be entirely attributed to two factors whose weights are roughly equal – the increase in the enrolment ratio (especially at the higher level) and the rise in the cost ratio. The rise in the cost ratio was attributed to an increase in the relative prices of education, with "real" inputs remaining stable or falling sharply. This issue will be returned to in a later section. It is likely that the experience in Ireland mirrors that described above. Certainly the demographic ratio changed little over the 1963-75 period and thus enrolment changes and cost changes are likely to have been the main contributing factors to the increased share of education in GDP observed in Table 7. An examination of this, however, would involve a separate paper and will not be discussed any further here.[12]

Table 7: *The Percentage Share of Public Sector Current Expenditure (Including Transfers) on Education and Health in GNP, 1963-75*

Year	Education[1]	Health[1]
1975	5.3	6.2
1974	4.8	5.7
1973	4.5	5.1
1972	4.4	4.7
1971	4.4	4.5
1970	4.3	4.3
1969	4.0	3.9
1968	3.9	3.6
1967	3.6	3.3
1963	3.1	2.8

Sources: National Income and Expenditure, various issues.

[1] See footnotes to Tables 4 and 6.

Health expenditure has also been analysed in a similar manner to social security and education expenditure.[13] The share of health in GDP, however, was expressed in terms of four factors: (i) the proportion of total health expenditure covered by public expenditure, called the "transfer ratio";[14] (ii) the number of health units consumed per person potentially covered by the public health system, referred to as the "use ratio"; (iii) the number of covered persons as a proportion of the total population (indicating the ratio of the potential – not the actual – number of beneficiaries of the public schemes to the total population, called the "coverage" or "eligibility" ratio); (iv) the unit cost of health care in terms of GNP *per capita*, referred to as the "cost ratio". The results for the eight OECD countries surveyed over the period 1962 to 1974 were as follows. First, the growth of the health expenditure share during this time was 1.52 percentage points: changes in the "transfer ratio", the "eligibility ratio" and the "cost ratio" each accounted for approximately one third of one percentage point of the increase, with a rise of 0.54 percentage points in the "use ratio" accounting for the remainder. Third, the increase in the "cost ratio" to a large extent reflects an increase in the relative price of hospital care, with in fact, an apparent negative change in real inputs into hospital care. However, the difficulty of establishing proper price indices for hospital care must be noted at this stage and will be discussed in a later section.[15]

To what extent the experience in Ireland reflects that in the countries surveyed by the OECD is, of course, the important question that needs answering. Certainly entitlement, as measured by the combined effects of the eligibility and transfer ratios in the above identities, in Ireland has greatly increased in the last fifteen years or so.[16] It is also nearly certainly the case that the cost ratio increased substantially, and probably largely due to an increase in relative prices. This again would form a useful topic for further research.

(iii) Capital Formation. The last component of public sector expenditure to be examined by functional category is gross fixed capital formation. As noted above, it was only in the 1970s that the share of gross fixed capital formation in GNP increased significantly above previous levels and this is the period that is examined in Table 8. An average for 1963 and 1964 is also included for completeness. As may be seen, in absolute terms, housing has undergone the largest increase, from an average of 0.7 in 1963/64 to 1.8 per cent of GNP in 1975. There have also been substantial increases in the categories "other general government services" and "other community and social services". This reflects once again the fact that the upward pressure on public sector share has not been specific to one or two particular sub-categories, but has been widespread in its impact. It is of interest to note though that education, housing and other community and social services accounted for 1.6 of the 2.3 percentage points increase in the share of public sector gross fixed capital formation between 1963/64 and 1975. This mirrors the experience with public current expenditure, where the so-called "social welfare" areas also predominated in influencing the increase in public sector share.

Table 8: *The Percentage Share of Gross Fixed Capital Formation by Function in GNP, 1963/64-1975*

Year	Other General Govt.	Educ.	Housing	Other Comm. & Social Services	Transp. and Commun.	'Other'[1]	Total
1975	0.5	0.6	1.8	0.8	2.0	0.5	6.2
1974	0.6	0.6	1.7	0.7	1.8	0.7	6.1
1973	0.4	0.6	1.3	0.6	1.6	0.4	4.9
1972	0.3	0.4	1.3	0.5	1.5	0.5	4.5
1971	0.3	0.4	1.3	0.5	1.5	0.5	4.5
1970	0.4	0.5	1.0	0.4	1.6	0.4	4.3
Av. 1963/1964	0.2	0.5	0.7	0.4	1.8	0.3	3.9

Sources: *National Income and Expenditure*, various issues.

[1] Includes social security and welfare; agriculture forestry and fishing; mining, manufacturing and construction; other economic services.

2. OVERALL REVENUE TRENDS

Before examining in detail some of the reasons for the trends observed above, it may prove fruitful to first closely analyse how the increased expenditure share was financed. Changes in the method of financing government expenditure may themselves in fact be important determinants of public sector share and this issue is discussed later in the paper. Besides, a study of revenue trends is in itself of some interest, regardless of the relationship between revenue and expenditure shares.

Table 9 outlines the trends in the shares of each of the broad sub-categories of public sector receipts in GNP over the period 1953 to 1977. The picture that emerges here is quite clear. *First*, the share of taxes on income and wealth (including social security contributions) has increased by approximately 10.0 percentage points. Between 1953 and 1960 it showed no clear trend, and fluctuated little. However, between 1960 and 1973 it increased by 6.2 percentage points, and between 1973 and 1977 by a further 3.9 percentage points. Thus between 1960 and 1977 this form of taxation has increased its share of GNP by more than 260 per cent, an exceptional rise by any standards. *Second*, the share of taxes on expenditure (including rates) in GNP increased by only around 2.0 percentage points over the period. Between 1953 and 1965 their share fluctuated between 14.9 and 16.8 per cent, increased from 16.4 per cent in 1965 to 19.1 per cent in 1970

Table 9: *The Main Components of Public Sector Receipts as a Per Cent of GNP*

Year	Taxes on Income and Wealth (incl. Soc. Sec.)	Taxes on Expenditure (incl. Rates)	Other[1]	Borrowing[2]
1953	5.9	15.4	3.0	5.3
1954	6.2	15.5	3.1	4.9
1955	6.2	15.5	3.2	4.8
1956	6.1	16.8	2.9	5.1
1957	6.0	16.8	3.1	3.4
1958	5.8	16.7	3.1	2.5
1959	5.4	16.6	3.1	2.3
1960	6.3	15.6	3.1	3.3
1961	7.1	15.7	2.9	4.1
1962	7.4	14.9	3.0	4.4
1963	8.0	15.4	2.9	4.5
1964	8.3	16.1	2.8	4.9
1965	8.7	16.4	3.0	5.4
1966	9.5	17.7	3.2	3.7
1967	9.9	17.8	3.4	4.4
1968	10.2	17.8	3.5	5.2
1969	10.2	18.7	3.3	5.0
1970	11.4	19.1	3.3	5.3
1971	12.5	19.0	3.5	5.2
1972	11.9	18.4	3.6	5.2
1973	12.5	18.1	3.1	5.8
1974	13.5	17.6	3.5	9.3
1975	14.7	16.7	3.1	13.8
1976	16.3	18.5	3.3	10.1
1977	16.4	17.5	3.6	9.6

Sources: National Income and Expenditure, various issues.

[1] Includes net trading and investment income, current transfers from the rest of the world, taxes on capital, capital transfers from the rest of the world, and 'other capital receipts'.
[2] Defined as the difference between column B, Table 1 and the sum of columns 1-3 above. This is closely in line with OECD and Eurostat practice.

and decreased to 17.5 per cent in 1977. *Third*, the share of "other receipts" (which include taxes on capital, transfers from the rest of the world, net trading and investment income and other capital receipts) has been remarkably stable between 1953 and 1977, ranging only from 2.8 to 3.6 per cent of GNP. *Finally*, the share of borrowing, which is defined for the purposes of this study as the residual of public sector expenditure (as defined already) not covered by the three sources of receipts looked at above divided by GNP rose by around 5.0 percentage points between the beginning and end years of the period. As one might expect, this was the most volatile component of public sector receipts. Between 1953 and 1959 its share of GNP dropped from 5.3 to 2.3 per cent, rising again to 5.4 per cent in 1965 and remaining at approximately this level until 1972. Between 1973 and 1975 it showed an extraordinary rise of 8.0 percentage points, falling again by 4.2 percentage points between 1975 and 1977.

Relating these trends in the shares of receipts in GNP to the earlier discussion on expenditure shares the following points may be noted. *First*, it would appear that the expansion of the public sector share that occurred between 1963 and 1971 was primarily financed by increased revenue from taxes on income and wealth (including social security contributions), the remainder being accounted for by increased revenue from taxes on expenditure (including rates). *Second*, the dramatic increase in public sector share between 1973 and 1977 was financed by increased revenue from taxes on income and wealth (including social security contributions) and borrowing. These findings will be discussed later in the paper when the issue of taxable capacity and revenue constraints are considered as determinants of public sector share. However, to aid this discussion a more detailed analysis of taxation receipts is provided below.

Income tax and social security contributions constitute the vast bulk of taxes on income and wealth: in 1977 they accounted for 14.6 percentage points of the 16.4 per cent share of taxes on income and wealth in GNP. The trend in the share of both income tax and social security contributions in GNP is outlined in Table 10 for the years 1953 to 1977. Up to 1972 the trend in both was quite similar: relative stability between 1953 and 1961 and a rapid increase between 1962 and 1971. Between 1972 and 1976 the share of income tax in GNP continued to increase rapidly, from 7.7 per cent in 1972 to 10.2 per cent in 1976. However, the share for social security contributions rose even more dramatically, from 2.8 per cent in 1972 to 4.8 per cent in 1976. Thus, over the period as a whole the share of social security contributions in GNP rose by 3.8 percentage points, that is nearly five-fold on its base level. The share of income tax, however, accounted for a larger absolute increase, rising by 5.4 percentage points between 1953 and 1977.

Although, as noted earlier, the share of taxes on expenditure (including rates) did not increase markedly between 1953 and 1977, there were remarkable fluctuations in the shares of some individual taxes on expenditure. This can be seen clearly in Table 10. The share of customs duties fell from a high of 8.3 per cent of GNP in 1956 and 1957 to 4.5 per cent in 1975 and 0.2 per cent in 1976. The latter, however, may have been largely due to a change in tax classification. On the other hand, value added tax which accounted for 5.0 per cent of GNP in 1977 did not exist in 1953. In fact, its predecessors, turnover tax and wholesale tax were only introduced in 1963/64 and 1966/67 respectively, with value added tax being introduced in 1972/73. The share of excise duties showed little variation between 1953 and 1959, rose steadily until 1969, declined between 1969 and 1974, and rose dramatically in 1976, largely due to the reclassification of taxes mentioned above. Finally, the share of rates in GNP was fairly stable throughout the period, declining somewhat between 1972 and 1977.

3. "REAL" PUBLIC SECTOR SHARE

Up to this point the discussion has been in terms of the share of nominal public sector in nominal GNP. However, movements in nominal public sector share arise from changes in real public sector share and changes in relative prices (as between the public and private sector). It is, of course, perfectly possible then that changes in nominal public sector share arise solely from movements in relative prices. The explanation for observed trends in public sector share would then centre around a quite different topic – the reasons for differential price movements. This section attempts to ascertain the extent of the impact of relative price movements on nominal public sector share in Ireland.

Table 10: *The Percentage Share of Various Taxes in GNP, 1953 to 1977*

Year	Income Tax (incl. Sur-Tax)	Social Insurance Contributions	Rates	Excise Duties	Customs Duties	Value[1] Added Tax
1953	4.4	1.0	3.2	3.4	7.2	–
1954	4.6	1.0	3.4	3.3	7.2	–
1955	4.6	1.0	3.4	3.2	7.2	–
1956	4.4	1.1	3.7	3.2	8.3	–
1957	4.4	1.1	3.6	3.1	8.3	–
1958	4.3	1.0	3.6	3.0	8.2	–
1959	3.9	1.0	3.5	3.9	7.3	–
1960	4.2	1.1	3.5	4.7	6.3	–
1961	4.5	1.5	3.4	4.8	6.4	–
1962	4.8	1.5	3.1	4.6	6.2	–
1963	4.9	1.6	3.1	4.6	6.2	0.5
1964	5.2	1.6	2.9	4.7	6.1	1.5
1965	5.6	1.7	3.1	5.0	5.9	1.4
1966	6.2	1.9	3.2	5.3	6.6	1.7
1967	6.2	2.1	3.1	5.5	6.2	2.1
1968	6.3	2.3	3.1	5.7	6.0	2.2
1969	6.4	2.3	3.0	6.0	6.0	2.8
1970	7.1	2.5	3.1	5.5	5.6	4.0
1971	8.1	2.8	3.3	5.2	5.4	4.3
1972	7.7	2.8	3.2	4.6	5.1	4.4
1973	8.2	3.0	2.7	4.3	5.0	5.1
1974	8.5	3.7	2.7	4.0	4.8	5.1
1975	9.0	4.5	2.4	4.3	4.5	4.8
1976	10.2	4.8	2.5	9.2^2	0.3^2	5.6
1977	9.8	4.8	2.1	8.3	0.2	6.0

Sources: National Income and Expenditure, various issues.

[1]Turnover tax was introduced in 1963/64 and wholesale tax in 1966/67. Both of these were replaced by value added tax in 1972/73.
[2]The sudden rise in the share of excise duties and the dramatic fall in the share of customs duties in 1976 may be largely due to a reclassification of these items in this year.

Whilst a reasonably consistent and meaningful real GNP series is available from the CSO's *National Income and Expenditure Series*, this is not the case for real public sector expenditure. Only data for real net expenditure by public authorities on current goods and services are provided, and even here there are serious reservations. Net expenditure by public authorities on current goods and services is deflated in two parts. (i) Employee remuneration is expressed at constant prices by applying an index of employment to the base year remuneration. Where reliable employment data are not available the implied index of rates of remuneration is used to deflate current values. (ii) Other expenditure is deflated partly by the consumer price index and partly by the wholesale price index. Now the method described above of deflating employee remuneration, which is by far the largest component of net expenditure by public authorities on current goods and services, assumes no productivity gain amongst public employees, an assumption which might be considered rather extreme. There is indeed limited scope for improved productivity in the provision of publicly provided goods and services, but the widespread application nowadays of modern technology in some government departments must clearly raise doubts about the assumption of a zero productivity increase. The alternative of including an imputed productivity gain, as is done in Belgium and Germany, to account for higher efficiency of public employees is, of course, equally arbitrary, but at least in conjunction with a zero productivity gain assumption would outline a more acceptable range of possibilities for the growth in real net public expenditure on current goods and services. The main consideration arising out of this discussion when we come to examine Table 11 is that the growth in the share of real net public expenditure on current goods and services in real GNP is, if anything, likely to be understated.

Table 11: *Real Public Sector Percentage Share by Economic Category, and in Total, 1953-77*

Year	I	II	III	IV	V	VI	VII
1953	15.6	4.2	2.9	7.5	1.9	32.0	19.8
1954	15.8	4.1	3.1	7.6	1.4	32.0	19.9
1955	15.3	4.0	3.1	7.8	1.4	31.6	19.3
1956	15.6	3.9	3.2	8.2	1.6	32.5	19.5
1957	15.1	2.8	2.7	8.6	1.3	30.5	17.9
1958	15.2	2.7	2.5	8.5	1.4	30.2	17.9
1959	14.9	2.7	2.6	8.4	0.9	29.5	17.6
1960	14.5	2.6	3.0	8.6	1.1	29.8	17.1
1961	14.3	2.8	4.0	8.9	1.1	31.1	17.1
1962	14.2	3.1	3.5	8.8	1.2	30.8	17.3
1963	14.1	3.5	3.3	9.3	1.6	31.8	17.6
1964	13.9	3.9	3.5	9.5	1.6	32.4	17.8
1965	14.1	4.2	3.7	9.8	1.9	33.7	18.3
1966	14.1	4.1	4.1	11.0	1.9	35.2	18.2
1967	14.1	4.1	4.6	11.1	2.3	36.2	18.2
1968	13.7	4.1	4.5	11.4	3.3	37.0	17.8
1969	13.8	4.4	4.7	12.0	2.6	37.5	18.2
1970	14.4	4.3	4.8	13.0	2.5	39.0	18.7
1971	15.2	4.5	4.7	13.4	2.9	40.7	19.7
1972	15.3	4.6	4.4	13.6	2.4	40.3	19.9
1973	15.8	5.3	3.3	15.1	2.0	41.5	21.1
1974	16.3	5.6	3.0	14.2	1.9	41.0	21.9
1975	16.9	5.8	3.7	17.9	1.8	46.1	22.7
1976	17.8	4.7	3.7	19.0	2.0	47.2	22.5
1977	17.2	4.3	3.7	18.8	1.9	45.9	21.5

Sources: *National Income and Expenditure*, various issues.

I   Net current expenditure by public authorities on goods and services at constant (1970) prices divided by expenditure on GNP at constant (1970) market prices.

II   Gross physical capital formation by public authorities at constant (1970) prices (i.e. divided by the implicit deflator in *National Income and Expenditure* of total gross domestic capital formation) divided by GNP at constant (1970) market prices.

III   Expenditure on subsidies by public authorities at constant (1970) prices (i.e. divided by the implicit deflator in *National Income and Expenditure* of personal expenditure on consumer goods and services) divided by GNP at constant (1970) market prices.

IV   Current transfer payments plus national debt interest paid by public authorities at constant (1970) prices (see III above) divided by GNP at constant (1970) market prices.

V   Capital grants to enterprises, other capital transfer payments, and payments to the rest of the world by public authorities at constant (1970) prices (see II above) divided by GNP at constant (1970) market prices.

VI   The sum of columns I to V.

VII   The sum of columns I and II.

The remaining sub-components of public sector expenditure, as outlined in Table 2, also had to be deflated and here the methods used were as follows. Subsidies and current transfers were converted into constant price series by dividing by the implied deflator for personal expenditure on consumers' goods and services in various issues of *National Income and Expenditure*. In the absence of more information on how subsidies and transfers are spent by recipients, this appears a reasonable method to use. Gross fixed capital formation and capital grants to enterprises, etc. were expressed in constant price terms by use of the implicit deflator for total gross domestic fixed capital formation in various issues of *National Income and Expenditure*.

The net result of the adjustments outlined above is to be seen by comparing the trends to emerge in Table 11 to those already looked at in Tables 1 and 2. Comparing column VI, Table 11 and column B, Table 1, what emerges is the close similarity between public sector share when expressed in nominal and real terms. Apart from a few minor exceptions, the trends in real public sector share are very close to those outlined earlier for nominal public sector share: relative stability between 1953 and 1963, with a level of 29.5 to 31.8 being maintained in eight years of the eleven-year period; a steady upward shift between 1963 and 1973; and a dramatic increase between 1973 and 1975, with the 1975 level being maintained in 1976 and 1977. It would thus appear that in the Irish context there is little substance to the argument that differential movements in relative prices was a major factor explaining movements in public sector share in the aggregate. This removes one of the more substantive *a priori* explanations for movements in nominal public sector share.

The reasons for the above rather surprising finding are seen more clearly when total public sector share is examined by economic category. The expectation of a marked difference emerging between real and nominal public sector share rested crucially on the assumption of a large and growing productivity differential between the public and private sector. However, only columns I and II of Table 2 are affected by this factor, and in 1977 these two accounted for less than half of total public sector share. Moreover, the method of deflation used here for gross physical capital formation does not, in fact, allow for differential productivity gains. Thus only for column I would the effect of a differential productivity growth be expected to emerge and here, given the assumption of a zero productivity growth in the public provision of current goods and services, it is inevitable that a large difference does in fact appear. This can be seen by comparing column I of Tables 2 and 11. The main difference of note is that the real share of net current public expenditure on goods and services did not exceed the levels pertaining in the mid-fifties until 1974, as against 1964 for nominal public sector share. Moreover, over the period as a whole the real share increased by only 1.6 percentage points, as against a figure of 6.1 percentage points for the nominal share.

As against this the real share of transfers in GNP increased by 11.3 percentage points compared to 10.4 percentage points for the nominal share. Thus, if anything, the role of transfers is even considerably more pronounced when real shares are used: between 1953 and 1977 the share of transfers accounted for 11.3 of the 13.9 percentage points increase in total public sector share. The situation with respect to the remaining components of public sector is largely unaltered whether real or nominal shares are used.

Finally, it may be of interest to examine total real public sector share using the more restricted definition of the public sector mentioned earlier. This, as pointed out, would mean using only the sum of columns I and II in Table 11, and the results of this summation appear in column VII. As may be seen, using this measure, the real public sector share showed no growth between 1953-1955 and 1971-73. Since then there has been a marked upward shift, reflecting once again the displacement that took place in public sector share between 1973 and 1976 regardless of what measure is used. Nonetheless, the growth in real public sector share, when using column VII, was only 1.7 percentage points over the whole period, 1953-77. However, as mentioned already, this could be partly due to a large understatement in the share of the real public consumption component.

4. RESOURCE CONSTRAINTS AND PLANNING AS EXPLANATORY FACTORS

The total of public expenditures is clearly constrained by the need to raise correspond- ing revenues. Thus changes to both sides of the government's sources and uses of funds account are decided together – "that is, the desirability of additional expenditures is balanced against the anticipated costs of raising the necessary revenue, and in practice these costs may act as a more or less effective constraint."[17] The real difficulty, how- ever, is to establish the precise nature of the constraint. It can be hypothesised that people's willingness to pay taxes will largely reflect the benefits they foresee from the associated public expenditure. However, this connection between taxation and expen- diture is by no means clearly established for most people. Specifically, it is argued that the system and specific circumstances of revenue collection in any country can be impor- tant factors in establishing the broadly perceived relationship between expenditure and revenue for many people. The basis for this argument, perhaps, needs some comment at this stage. Drawing on the Downsian model, it can be asserted that each political party in a democracy pursues whatever policies it believes will gain the necessary votes to win elections. In relation to finances this would mean maximising the visible benefits from expenditure and minimising the visible costs of taxation. Now if the cost of the increased taxation/revenue needed to finance the observed increase in public sector share were not clearly visible and/or if the visible costs were now more clearly identified with visible benefits, then in the short to medium term these factors could prove to be powerful determinants of the increase in public sector share. In fact their impact could persist into the long-term due to the concept of organisational pressure. The argument is that even if people eventually become aware of the costs of past growth in the public sector share, there is by that stage a built-in reluctance to cut taxes. The reasoning is that such cuts, to the extent that they lead to a reduction in the level of services provided, pose a direct threat to jobs in the public sector. It is therefore not surprising that teachers, doctors and others employed directly or indirectly by government have, at least in the UK, tradition- ally taken the lead in objecting to reductions in public sector expenditure. These public employees, although accounting for only a minority of the labour force, are usually highly educated and articulate and have a strong vested interest in maintaining, if not further increasing, the public sector share. Thus "organisational" pressure may mean that movements in public sector share tend to be in one direction only.

A further extension of the above arguments is that, even if the costs of the increased public sector share were visible, during the period of growth there was a "basic asym- metry in the universe of politically articulated demands in favour of higher public expen- diture."[18] The argument is Downsian in nature, but reverses Downes' original assumption, and it asserts that the organisational machinery for translating a desire to reduce/or not increase taxes, into a political demand may not have existed in Ireland between 1953 and 1977. There may not have been any organised group dedicated to the single aim of cutting taxes – because the opposition to higher taxes is so diffuse and thereby difficult to express concretely. On the other hand the number of pressure groups that existed to translate wants for higher spending into well-articulated political demands proliferated during this time, leading to the basic asymmetry mentioned by Klein. Moreover, not until recently – emigration apart – was it known of taxpayers, as taxpayers, to "exit" the political system, whereas some organised groups for increased expenditure have fre- quently done so in the past, by withholding their co-operation from the government. In fact, this is one of the ways in which the introduction of economic planning in Ireland may have contributed to the increased public sector share.

Successful indicative planning, as is well known, depends on the co-operation of organised groups and of government departments. This, it could be argued, was partly responsible for the emergence of new organised pressure groups, as there was now not only a formal channel for the articulation of their views, but one which they were now actively encouraged to use. Moreover, to secure the co-operation of the groups involved the government may have felt compelled to spend more than they would have without the planning process. Another factor, perhaps of much more significance, is that the publication of the plans gave an increased public visibility to the relative position of each government department in future spending. Now both within the civil service, and outside, there is pressure on ministers, and indeed civil servants, to demonstrate their effectiveness in terms of maintaining, or increasing, their department's share of total public sector expenditure. The introduction of planning, therefore, it could be claimed, formalised, and more important, gave more publicity to the institutional framework for competition between ministers, thereby putting increased pressure on the Minister for Finance to increase the total in order to avoid conflict with a particular department.

These are, indeed, perverse and unintended side effects of economic planning, for as FitzGerald writes: "Quite apart from the role of planning in improving the quality and effectiveness of public policies, it may also have another narrower role in relation to the control of the rapid growth of public expenditure."[19] Nonetheless, the possibility that these "perverse" effects of planning existed is strong and there is evidence to support this in the Irish case. Irish planning has varied, of course, in both sophistication and comprehensiveness, and during the period of most rapid growth in public sector share there was no formal plan. Nonetheless, the consultative planning procedures initiated in the 1960s persisted throughout the seventies and planning in an informal sense continued.

The main evidence for the arguments above arises from the fact that when the level of output for the economy projected in the plans was not realised, the level of public sector expenditure was not in fact correspondingly scaled down. If governments acted to correct for the wrongly predicted growth rate by cutting the planned expansion rate of public expenditure to take account of the failure to reach the hoped for growth of national output target, then, by virtue of the above arguments, they would run the unacceptable political risk of incurring the wrath of the pressure groups and government departments involved. In both the Second and Third Programmes in Ireland, which corresponded with periods of growth in public sector share, the actual rise in GNP fell short of that planned. Besides, these were the only sophisticated plans actually published in the period under review and, as such, they provide a basis, albeit crude, for examining the hypothesis above.

Looking first at public capital programmes, it was the case that for the actual Second Programme period (1963/64 to 1967/68) capital spending was forecast to rise slightly faster than GNP and slightly slower for the period of the Third Programme (1969-72). However, both programmes were marked by significant over-achievement in the growth rate of capital spending and, as mentioned, an under-achievement in GNP growth. Capital projections, however, were regarded by the planners as very tentative and, thus, this part of the exercise might in some ways be only of statistical significance. Looking at current expenditure it can be seen that in aggregate terms current expenditure between 1963/64 and 1967/68 was rising at the rates envisaged in the Second Programme, although disaggregation shows that there had been reallocation of resources between current consumption and current transfers.[20] The official *Review of Progress* states that this reallocation was the outcome of current resource constraints and a change of policy,[21] although FitzGerald seems to suggest it was more mistaken classification of expenditures in the original programme.[22] In either case the fact that the GNP only increased by an annual average rate of 3.3 per cent in the four-year period 1964 to 1967, as against a projected increase of 4.3 per cent, meant, *ceteris paribus*, that the current expenditure share would show a greater increase than had been envisaged.

During the period of the Third Programme the estimated annual growth rate of GNP was 3.3 per cent, as against a projected figure of 3.8 per cent. However, the annual growth of public sector current expenditure not only matched the target increase of 5.8 per cent, but greatly exceeded it, rising by an annual rate of 7.3 per cent. Thus, the growth of the current public sector share between 1968/69 and 1972/73 was considerably faster than planned. The transfer payments component increased by an annual rate of 11.3 per cent (planned rate 6.9 per cent), and net expenditures on current goods and services by 6.5 per cent (planned 3.7 per cent).[23]

Paradoxically, then, the advent of comprehensive planning in Ireland coincided with not only a rising imbalance between economic growth and public expenditure growth, and thereby a major shift in the balance between the private and public sector, but with an imbalance part of which was not envisaged or planned for, a trend which planning was designed to control if not prevent. While there were certainly other factors at work during this time, the argument above that the introduction of planning itself may have in part contributed to the growth in the public sector share cannot be rejected on the basis of the evidence available.

The argument of the last few pages, to recap, is essentially suggesting that a basic asymmetry in politically articulated demands emerged in the 1960s in Ireland. The introduction of planning, it is argued, leads to new desires for increased public expenditure and, more importantly, to the organisational machinery for translating both new and old desires for increased expenditures into political demands. This occurred, however, without the introduction of any corresponding mechanism for translating voters' reactions to the increased taxation, that would be necessary to meet these desires for increased expenditure, into a political demand. Thus, even assuming that the costs of the rising public sector share were clearly visible, dissatisfaction with these rising costs could not be concretely articulated or acted upon. However, as mentioned at the beginning of this section, the costs of the increased expenditure may not have been visible to a large section of the electorate, at least in the short to medium term. This could arise from a subtle change in the system of taxation or in the circumstances under which the taxation system operates. Was this the case in Ireland during the period of growth in the public sector share? This is the question dealt with in the remainder of this paper.

Personal income tax, as was seen in Table 10, has been the dominant source of new revenue for the expansion of the public sector in Ireland for the period under review. The argument about lack of visibility here is that with rapid increases in money incomes, due to increased real incomes and/or inflation, an increasing proportion of people's income automatically accrues, *ceteris paribus*, to the government in the form of income tax. This, in the absence of action to adjust tax allowances and bands, leads to an automatic increase in the effective rate of taxation, an increase that to the vast majority of the electorate would initially be almost "invisible". Now while a decline in this form of tax illusion is nearly inevitable in the medium to long term, as evidenced by various recent events and developments,[24] for reasons mentioned earlier there is not likely to be a reduction in public sector share once the costs of previous rises in public sector share have been realised.

The potential for "fiscal drag" as it is called, has undoubtedly existed in Ireland, with very rapid increases in money incomes taking place, especially between 1968 and 1977. That "fiscal drag" has actually occurred is evidenced by the fact that the level of tax-free allowances has fallen sharply relative to earnings.[25] In 1976 the tax-free allowance of a single person as a percentage of average male industrial earnings was 18.1, as against 43.3 per cent in 1965. The equivalent figures for a married person were 29.0 and 73.1, and for a married person with four children 54.3 and 162.2 per cent respectively. As mentioned before, greater public awareness of fiscal drag is now in evidence.[26] However, the main impact of the fiscal reform to reflect this new awareness has been to keep the share of income taxes in GNP stable, rather than to decrease it.[27] This confirms the point above: the impact of the phenomenon of fiscal drag on public sector share tends to be permanent.

The other main source of current revenue which increased its share of GNP, as was seen in Table 10, was social security contributions. These were clearly visible, but what could be argued is that it was not evident to many workers that social security contributions for them are a "hidden" form of income tax. One of the reasons why the implementation of new social security taxes met with little resistance was that most workers may have believed that the benefits were highly individual, and thereby clearly visible. This belief was nurtured by the use of the term "social insurance contributions", although it is well known by now that the social security schemes in existence in Ireland are not in any sense operated on a strict actuarial basis.[28]

The final source of increased revenue share was borrowing, especially for the 1972 to 1976 period as was seen earlier. This form of revenue raising, at least temporarily, completely avoids the problem of raising visible taxes to meet the increased public sector share. In this case borrowing has to be seen as an appropriation of future taxation, both to service and repay the debt.[29] It could be argued that future generations should pay, and be prepared to pay, taxation for benefits received from capital equipment installed today. Even assuming though that additional public borrowing is used to finance investment producing services, the well known fundamental difficulty of ascertaining society's future preferences remains. Much more seriously, a large portion of the increased borrowing share was used to finance current expenditure.[30] Thus the government has been able to clearly increase visible benefits between 1972 and 1976, whereas the costs will not become visible until later years. It could be strongly argued that most of the electorate were not, at least at the time, aware of the subtleties involved in this method of financing the increased public sector share, or else that they have not yet had to consider the costs. However, given what has been repeatedly argued above, public sector share may be flexible upwards only. Thus, when the costs of increased public sector share between 1972 and 1976 eventually become evident to the electorate, it may be too late to do anything without serious social conflict. This indeed, is the case that has been argued repeatedly, for example, by NESC.[31]

The explanation of the growth in public sector share in terms of the raising of resource constraints to levels which, at least temporarily, were not visible to the majority of the electorate has considerable plausibility then in the Irish case. Taken in conjunction with the suggested "perverse" effects of indicative planning outlined above, then a rather strong case could be made for including the combined effect of these factors as an important determinant of the growth in public sector share in Ireland between 1963 and 1977.

5. CONCLUSION

This paper firstly examined the trends in public sector share in Ireland and it was shown that the percentage share of public sector expenditure in GNP rose from 30.8 to 47.1 between 1963 and 1977. The sub-components, by economic and functional classification, were examined in detail and the importance of expenditure on current transfers, and to a lesser extent that on public consumption, in the growth of the public sector were highlighted. The dominant position of income tax, social security contributions and borrowing as sources of revenue for this growth was also given considerable emphasis. Although final data for 1978 and 1979 are not yet available, it may be of interest to note at this stage that provisional estimates indicate that the public sector share rose to 47.6 per cent in 1978 and to 49.3 per cent in 1979.[32] Most of this increase of 2.2 percentage points on the 1977 level has been on public consumption expenditure, implying a somewhat greater importance for this item in the period 1963-79 than indicated here for the period 1963-77. The dominant source of revenue for the increase in public sector share in 1978 and 1979 has been borrowing, with income tax and social security taxes maintaining their 1977 shares. Thus the main impact on the revenue side from the extension of the period of this study to include 1978 and 1979 would simply be a relatively greater emphasis being placed on the role of borrowing.

The second concern of the paper was to proffer some explanations for the observed growth in public sector share. The most plausible of the explanations looked at, it was suggested, concerned the fact that the costs of the increased expenditure, at least in the short-term, were not fully visible and/or understood. Events in 1978 and 1979 would, if anything, add further support to this hypothesis.

A rather unsettling implication of this argument is that a portion of the increased public sector share took place without the approval, so to speak, of the majority of the electorate. This, of course, jolts the widely held assertion that, in a democracy, decisions relating to public expenditure and taxation reflect the expressed wishes of the community and that, thereby, the community "gets what it wants". However, only in the long run has this been held to be generally true. It is also the case that the community may, with the value of hindsight, have no regrets about what it got, i.e. the inspection effect may have been operational. To put too much emphasis though on the resource constraints argument would, perhaps, be misleading. Undoubtedly much of the increased public sector share in Ireland has resulted from reasonably well-informed democratic decision-making. In these situations the costs of new demands for public expenditure were clearly understood and agreed upon.

FOOTNOTES

1. O'Donoghue and Tait (1968) covered similar ground for the period 1953-64. Kennedy (1975), NESC (1976b) and OECD (1978) also looked at aspects of this topic.
2. These, however, are dealt with at length in O'Hagan (1979a and 1979b).
3. This and the next few paragraphs draw heavily on OECD (1978), p. 11.
4. See Ohlsson (1961).
5. For a discussion of these issues, see Marris (1954/55), Gupta (1967 and 1968) and Brown and Jackson (1978).
6. Much of this variation was due to variation in the item "payments to the rest of the world". These are payments under the Bretton Woods Agreement Acts, 1957 and 1969, and International Development Association Act, 1960, and European Communities Act, 1972.
7. See OECD (1976b). Expenditure on income maintenance accounts for the vast majority of expenditure on "social security and welfare" transfers.
8. An average of 1.003 is possible given that in many countries people qualify for a pension before they are aged 65 years.
9. See NESC (1977), Appendix B.1, for details.
10. For the OECD as a whole the increased share of GDP accounted for by these three functions accounted for over half of the 8.8 percentage points increase in the share of total public expenditure in GDP between the mid-1960s and the mid-1970s. See OECD (1978).
11. See OECD (1976a) for details.
12. See NESC (1976a and 1977) for some useful information on these matters, however. First, between 1961-62 and 1973-74 current expenditure on third level education increased from 7 to 13 per cent of total public sector current expenditure on education (NESC (1976), p. 10); second, the number of full-time pupils and students at all levels increased from 22.4 to 26.4 per cent of total population between 1963-64 and 1973-74 (NESC (1977), p. 74); third, while expenditure per enrolled student at current prices for secondary schools increased more than four-fold between 1961-62 and 1973-74, real expenditure per pupil on teachers' salaries actually declined (NESC (1976)). These pieces of information would tend to confirm the remarks in the text.
13. See OECD (1977).
14. This factor was not included in the OECD study because of lack of data.
15. The number of medical card holders increased from 29.7 to 37.2 per cent of the population between 1966 and 1975. See NESC (1976c), Table 4.8.
16. For a discussion on the limitations of each of the ratios, see OECD (1977).
17. OECD (1978), p. 39.
18. Klein (1976), p. 422. This paper contains an excellent discussion of the topics looked at in this section.
19. FitzGerald (1968), p. 204.
20. Between 1963/64 and 1967/68 total net current expenditure of public authorities increased by an annual average of 5.8 per cent, as against a projected rate of 5.9 per cent. However, the actual and projected figures for public consumption were 2.7 and 6.6 per cent, and 7.1 and 3.6 per cent for transfers (excluding national debt interest). See, *Second Programme for Economic Expansion: Review of Progress, 1964-67* (Pr. 9949) (1968). Dublin: Stationery Office. Table 34.
21. *Ibid*.
22. See FitzGerald (1968).
23. See, *Review of 1972 and Outlook for 1973* (Prl. 3090) (1973). Dublin: Stationery Office. Table H.
24. There is evidence to suggest that wage demands are increasingly formulated after allowing for the consequent increase in taxation. Major tax protests outside the parliamentary process have also taken place in recent years.
25. See Dowling (1977), Table 2.1.
26. NESC (1976b) clearly may have helped in this regard.
27. See OECD (1978).
28. See O'Hagan (1977).
29. The next few sentences draw heavily on OECD (1978), pp 61-62.
30. See Chapters 4 and 5 in O'Hagan (1978).
31. See, for example, NESC (1976b).
32. See Commission of the European Communities (1979) for details.

REFERENCES

BRISTOW, J.A. and TAIT, A.A., 1968. *Economic Policy in Ireland*. Dublin: Institute of Public Administration.

BROWN, C.V. and JACKSON, P.M., 1978. *Public Sector Economics*. Oxford: Martin Robinson.

CAMERON, D.R., 1978. "The Expansion of the Public Economy: A Comparative Analysis". *American Political Science Review*, vol. 72 (4).

COMMISSION OF THE EUROPEAN COMMUNITIES, 1979. *Annual Economic Review 1979/80*. Brussels: Commission of the European Communities.

DOWLING, B.R., 1977. *Integrated Approaches to Personal Income Taxes and Transfers*. Dublin: (National Economic and Social Council, Report no. 37), Stationery Office.

FITZGERALD, G., 1968. *Planning in Ireland*. Dublin: Institute of Public Administration.

GIBSON, N.J. and SPENCER, J.E. (eds.), 1977. *Economic Activity in Ireland*. Dublin: Gill and Macmillan.

GUPTA, S.P., 1967. "Public Expenditure and Economic Growth: A Time-Series Analysis". *Public Finance*, vol. 22 (4).

———, 1968. "Public Expenditure and Economic Development: A Cross-Section Analysis". *Finanzarchiv*, vol. 26.

KENNEDY, F., 1975. *Public Social Expenditure in Ireland*. Dublin: Economic and Social Research Institute Broadsheet no. 11.

KLEIN, R., 1976. "The Politics of Public Expenditure: American Theory and British Practice". *British Journal of Political Science*, vol. 6.

MARRIS, R., 1954/55. "A Note on Measuring the Share of the Public Sector". *Review of Economic Studies*, vol. 22.

NATIONAL ECONOMIC AND SOCIAL COUNCIL (NESC), 1976a. *Educational Expenditure in Ireland* (no. 12). Dublin: Stationery Office.

———, 1976b. *Report on Public Expenditure* (no. 21). Dublin: Stationery Office.

———, 1976c. *Towards a Social Report* (no. 25). Dublin: Stationery Office.

———, 1977. *Population and Employment Projections 1986: A Reassessment* (no. 35). Dublin: Stationery Office.

O'DONOGHUE, M. and TAIT, A.A., 1968. "The Growth of Public Revenue and Expenditure in Ireland", in Bristow, J.A. and Tait, A.A. (eds.) (1968).

O'HAGAN, J.W., 1977. "Social Security", in Gibson, N.J. and Spencer, J.E. (eds.) (1977).

———, (ed.,) 1978. *The Economy of Ireland: Policy and Performance* (Second Edition). Dublin: Irish Management Institute.

———, 1979a. *The Growth in Public Sector Share, Theory and Practice: A Case Study of Ireland, 1926-76*. Ph.D. thesis: University of Dublin.

———, 1979b. "The Growth of Public Sector Share in Ireland: Demonstration Effects, Displacement Effects and Wagner's 'Law'". Submitted to journal.

OHLSSON, I., 1961. *On National Accounting*. Stockholm. References in Gupta, S. (1968).

OECD, 1976a. *Public Expenditure on Education*. Paris: OECD.

———, 1976b. *Public Expenditure on Income Maintenance Programmes*. Paris: OECD.

———, 1977. *Public Expenditure on Health*. Paris: OECD.

———, 1978. *Public Expenditure Trends*. Paris: OECD.

DISCUSSION

Finola Kennedy: Mr. Chairman, ladies and gentlemen, Dr. O'Hagan will understand if I preface my proposal of thanks to him by expressing my great personal regret at the absence tonight, through illness, of the President of the Society, Dr. Brendan Menton. The paper this evening would have been of particular interest to Dr. Menton. I know that you will all join with me in wishing him a swift and sure recovery.

It is a privilege for me to offer Dr. O'Hagan the thanks of the Society for his paper. It is a paper which displays considerable industry and scholarship. It is a paper which I very much enjoyed.

There are many points on which I would like to comment but I will limit myself to just a few of these, one relates to the expenditure side; the others to the revenue side.

On the expenditure side I was struck by the fact that Dr. O'Hagan confirmed the overriding importance of current expenditure on education, health, social security and welfare in the rise of the current public sector share. Between 1963 and 1975 these three combined accounted for 10.1 of the 15.5 percentage points increase in the share of public sector current expenditure. This corresponds with the OECD data for other countries. It also coincides with the findings of Musgrave's classic study of a number of countries over a longer time-period of about 80 years. It may be of some interest that Dr. O'Hagan's findings differ from those of Musgrave on the question of the relative importance of purchases and transfers. Dr. O'Hagan lays very great stress on the importance of the role of transfers: "Clearly, then, the growth in the share of the current transfers in GNP has been the most important factor in the growth of the public sector share in Ireland. As may be seen, the main period of growth in this item has been the years of 1962-1976, with particularly rapid growth in the 1972-76 period".

I was most interested in this finding, partly because of some calculations which I did several years ago for the period 1947-1967. These showed that whereas in 1947 purchases accounted for 51.3 per cent and transfers 48.7 per cent of total expenditure of public authorities, by 1967 the picture was reversed. In 1967, purchases accounted for 47.6 per cent and transfers 52.4 per cent. (My coverage was somewhat different to Dr. O'Hagan's). However, Musgrave's study, which covered a much longer time-series, showed no discernible difference between purchases and transfers for the countries studied. For this reason it will be particularly interesting to see whether the big upward shift in the share of transfers, noted by Dr. O'Hagan, particularly in the years 1972-1976, is a matter of short-run timing or long-run trend. As Dr. O'Hagan points out near the end of his paper, in the years 1978 and 1979, there has been a sharp growth in the share of purchases of 2.2 percentage points, I thought it would be worthwhile to look a little more closely at the critical years 1972-76 to see if there were any special factors at work.

One item which occurs to me that might have a bearing on the question was the huge jump in the numbers receiving unemployment assistance and benefit. The pay-related scheme was introduced in April 1974 and in just one year the combined number of those receiving unemployment benefit/assistance jumped from 67,422 in 1974 to 98,394 in 1975. G.E.J. Llewellyn in his *NESC* study stresses the growth of unemployment payments at this time not only in Ireland, but throughout the OECD, and suggests that this must be distinguished from the secular trend.

Also at this time there was an important change with regard to eligibility for old age pensions. Apart from relaxation of the means test for the old age assistance pension, the qualifying age for receipt of old age pensions (insurance and assistance), which had been 70 for many years, was reduced to 69 in July 1973, to 68 in July 1974, to 67 in April 1975 and subsequently to 66 in October 1977. In the four years 1972-76 the total number of recipients of old age pensions (insurance and assistance) rose by 27,000 from 157,500 to 184,500. A detailed study of individual services at this time might throw up other items, such as these.

Turning to the growth of revenue, there are a number of hypotheses concerning the relationship between the growth of revenue and expenditure with which you are all familiar. Peacock and Wiseman have argued that expenditures grow because revenues grow rather than the other way about. Every so often the financing of a war leads to a widening of the tax system, which is maintained after the war. Musgrave has challenged the latter point, suggesting that there is a long run upward trend, even regardless of war. Professors Tait and O'Donoghue argued that the main constraint on the growth of government expenditure in Ireland has been the rate at which funds could be raised through borrowing. However, borrowed funds must be serviced, and in general such servicing is financed from taxation. In the longer run the Tait-O'Donoghue borrowing constraint boils down to the growth of tax revenue. In this context and in view of Musgrave's comments on long-term trend as distinct from short-run "displacement", it is interesting that the startling "artificial" rise which Dr. O'Hagan notes according to measure A in Table 1 between 1973 and 1975 does not appear to have been reversed subsequently. The 1977 share remained 11.3 per cent points above the 1973 share (7.6 per cent points according to the "B" measure).

Concerning the specific question of the contribution of different forms of taxes to revenue growth, Dr. O'Hagan lays stress on the importance of income tax, especially from

1963 onwards. I was a bit surprised that Dr. O'Hagan did not stress the importance of VAT in the text of his paper. Table 10 shows that the percentage share of income tax in GNP grew by 4.9 percentage points between 1963 and 1977, while the share of VAT and its predecessors jumped by 5.5 percentage points. In the *NESC* study to which I referred earlier, Llewellyn points out the growth in the importance of income tax, but he also attaches much importance to the growth in VAT. At the present time, when there is considerable clamour concerning the burden of PAYE, I think that it is important that we do not overlook the very high levels of indirect taxation in force. Relative to her EEC partners, Ireland is very heavily dependent on indirect taxation to finance public sector expenditure.

While modern tax structure development has been characterised by a shift from indirect to direct taxation, this is only one phase in a much longer development. As Hinrichs has shown, tax structure development began with direct rather than indirect taxation. The relative importance of different taxes varies at different stages of economic development. Writing in *The National Tax Journal* in 1964, Alan Tait listed as first of the principal problems of Irish public finance "a high proportion of revenue collected by indirect taxes." The growth in the importance of income tax must be seen in this context.

I would like to formally propose the vote of thanks to Dr. O'Hagan and to suggest to you that he deserves the best thanks of the Society for his most valuable paper.

Noel Whelan: I have pleasure in seconding the vote of thanks to Dr. O'Hagan on the presentation of an excellent paper. His paper is very timely. It focuses attention on a current problem which affects not just Ireland, but almost all countries. It sparks off much thought because the topic of increasing public expenditure, its cause and effect, is a deep and complicated one. It affects all of us either as taxpayers or as recipients of public services.

Dr. O'Hagan's paper has shown us clearly that the trend in the share of public sector expenditure in GNP in Ireland has been inexorably upwards since the 1950s with a noticeable acceleration in the 1970s.

Let us remember, however, that, rightly or wrongly, this is an international phenomenon – not just an Irish one. A similar broad trend is evident in, for example, other EEC and OECD countries. In the EEC, total general government expenditure has risen from about 33 per cent of Community GDP in 1960 to nearly 47 per cent in 1979. Commission estimates put the share of public expenditure in GDP for Ireland in 1979 to 49.3 per cent, which is lower than The Netherlands (58.3 per cent), Luxembourg (54.4 per cent) and Belgium (52 per cent), but higher than Denmark (47.7 per cent), Germany and France (46.4 per cent), Italy (46.3 per cent) and the UK (42.8 per cent).

Underlying public expenditure trends such as those highlighted in Dr. O'Hagan's paper is the more general issue of the increasing range of government responsibilities. Public administrations have historically been responsible for the provision of goods and services where the mechanisms of the free market are not interested or are considered not to produce the desired results. These responsibilities tend to grow and expand nowadays as a result of many influences, not least of which is the increasing concern with the distribution of income and resources in support of social groups, such as the elderly and unemployed or unemployable, which lack economic bargaining power. This implies that an increasing range of social demands must be met through the political/governmental system rather than through the private economic system.

For whatever reason, the responsibilities of government, almost world wide, have been increasing both in range and depth. This is leading to rapid growth in the scale, complexity and costs of public administration and, most importantly, in the need for public administrators to have a wide variety of expertise and skills. Given finite resources there is thus an increasing need for public administrators to operate more effectively and efficiently and with greater productivity. Matters such as optimal resource allocation; cost-effective programme choice; efficient productive and cost-effective public sector operations, are all of paramount importance and will be increasingly so.

Dr. O'Hagan has covered a very wide area. There is much one could raise in connection with the paper. So, I'll be selective. I want to react to the paper on three fronts:

(1) to the explanations put forward in the paper for the observed growth in public sector share; These are:
   – the fact that the costs of the increased expenditure, at least in the short term, were not fully visible and/or understood;
   – the role which indicative planning may have played as a cause of expenditure growth.

(2) to the implication, referred to in the paper, that a portion of the increased public share took place without the approval of the majority of the electorate and Dr. O'Hagan's reference to the fact that this jolts the widely held assertion that, in a democracy, decisions relating to public expenditure and taxation reflect the expressed wishes of the community and that, thereby, the community "gets what it wants".

(3) to some aspects of the methodology used in the paper.

Explanations put forward in the paper for the observed growth in public sector share: Dr. O'Hagan regards the combined effect of indicative planning over the years and the fact that the main costs of public expenditure (i.e., personal income tax, social security contributions, and borrowing) may not have been "visible" to the public as an important determinant of the growth in public sector share in Ireland between 1963 and 1977.

In effect, indicative planning up to 1977 is regarded in the paper as being partly responsible for public sector growth. Yet, in the conclusion indicative planning is dropped and the fact that the costs of the increased expenditure were not very visible is regarded as the most plausible of the explanations.

I agree with the conclusion and I agree in particular with Dr. O'Hagan that an analysis of the determinant of overall public sector share is warranted. I am not so sure however about the thrust of argument in the paper relating to indicative planning and its effects on public expenditure. Indicative planning does not necessarily bring about inbuilt pressure for increased expenditure. On the contrary, indicative planning can and ought to be a constraining rather than an expansionary influence on expenditure in so far as it facilitates decision making and resource allocation as between Departments and enables Ministers to assess their own departmental priorities in the framework of an overall objective. Dr. O'Hagan makes a number of points about indicative planning in his paper and I want to comment on them as follows:

   – organised groups and government departments will exist, whether or not indicative planning is practised. Indeed they are a vital ingredient in the process of government. Nowadays, government can only take place effectively on the basis of broad socio-economic consensus existing between the main interest groups in society and government. It is doubtful that indicative planning itself is responsible for new organised pressure groups which increase public expenditure. Indicative planning does not give an increased public visibility to the relative position of each government department in future spending such as would lead to greater demands for expenditure than if it did not exist; the pressures upon ministers and departments for expenditure are there anyway in abundance! Indeed, indicative planning can be a very potent force for imposing rational choice on competing and conflicting claims for public expenditure.

   – the contention that planning gives more publicity to the institutional framework for competition between ministers, thereby putting increased pressure on the Minister for Finance to increase the total in order to avoid conflict with a particular department does not really accord with the reality of modern collective government responsibility. Such responsibility operates continually in an environment where demand for services exceeds supply and where trade-offs are necessary and unavoidable.

- the pressures for growth in public expenditure are present in all western democracies. There is no readily observable relationship between the presence of different types and degrees of indicative planning and public sector growth.

- indicative planning did not have a high visibility in the mid 1970s and yet the trend-increase in the public sector growth continued.

Some public management considerations relevant to increasing public expenditure. The explanation (for growth in public sector share) that costs of increased expenditure ... were not fully visible and/or understood has led Dr. O'Hagan to conclude that:

"A rather unsettling implication of this argument is that a portion of the increased public sector share took place without the approval, so to speak, of the majority of the electorate. This, of course, jolts the widely held assertion that, in democracy, decisions relating to public expenditure and taxation reflect the expressed wishes of the community and that, thereby, the community 'gets what it wants'."

Dr. O'Hagan has raised here a fundamentally important issue. It affects all democratic governments and is an important dimension of any discussions on the growth of the public sector or on increasing public sector share of GNP. It is, simply, how and to what extent can governments ensure nowadays that when deciding on the level and composition of public expenditure they are reflecting the real wishes of society. There are many problem areas here relating to:

- government and public administration in the face of increasing complexity;

- the marriage of long-term goals for societal development with short-term electoral expediency;

- communication between government and the electorate in circumstances where government policies are many-faceted and complex and their effects are to be reaped mainly in the medium to long-term.

These issues are of critical importance to public policy formulation and to the management of public sector expenditure programmes.

The essence of the situation lies in the fact that the ability of governments to perform well, and indeed to survive, will depend partly on their ability to fulfil the demands which society makes upon them and partly on their ability to influence these demands. This requires of governments an ability to formulate in advance and anticipate policies relevant to the demands of society and also an ability to adapt their policies to take account of changes in these demands. It also requires of governments an ability to deliver these policies, in programme form, to society. A government which is served by a public administration with a weak and cumbersome policy formulating and implementing capacity cannot expect to meet this requirement satisfactorily. Furthermore, society and community requirements of government and the relationship of government to society are constantly changing; these changes give rise to some general trends which also call for adaptation in public administrations. I wish to refer here to two trends which have implications for both the growth in public sector share of GNP and how it is managed:

(i) *The increasing complexity of society and, in turn, of government operations*: Nowadays, policies formulated under the aegis of governments do not automatically fall within the confines of any one sector. There is a need to take account of interactions between sectors which have in earlier times been self-contained and thus dealt with separately by the government; also, there is a need in various cases to introduce new sectors or dimensions which did not exist previously (perhaps to reflect the changing values of society or its higher sensitivity as a result of increasing levels of education). This leads to a situation where the policy formulating process under governments is becoming increasingly more complex and where it is necessary, very often, to trace or project the consequences of various policies in areas other than those at which they are primarily aimed or from which they have arisen.

In addition, there is the growing experience amongst governments of inter-national interdependence. Many policy areas, such as monetary, economic and trade systems, communications, environmental pollution and maritime explora-tion, require international solutions. National policies and public expenditure programmes have increasingly to be developed within the context of international commitments and norms.

(ii) *Diminishing understanding by the electorate of the full implications of govern-ment policies.* Hand-in-hand with the increasing complexity of policy issues which have to be dealt with by modern governments, there is the decreasing ability of the average elector to grasp and understand fully these complexities. Consequently, much of what is being developed by governments in the name of various elec-torates is being allowed happen through an act of faith by many electors. This leads to a diminution of that aspect of democratic systems which holds that the electorate should be able to evaluate a government through its awareness and appraisal of the results of that government's actions *while it is in power.* For instance, important results from a policy decision in areas such as environmental and educational policies may come about many years after that decision has been taken, thus leaving the elector with little chance of making his views known to the group which took the decision. There are two broad implications for public service adaptation here: first, to ensure that the machinery of government is equipped to ensure full consideration of both the short-term and longer-term consequences of various policies, particularly when the political system is inclined to press for short-term solutions which correspond with a particular electoral cycle; second, to ensure that the capacity of the public administration can articulate adequately the various implications, both short-term and long-term, of complex policy issues so that these can be communicated effectively to the electorate by the politicians.

To recap the matter raised by Dr. O'Hagan (in his paper) on electoral perceptions of public expenditure is very important — not least for public sector change in areas such as: struc-tures, institutions and expertise for policy formulation; institutions and systems for com-munication and dialogue between government and the community; institutional systems, procedures and practices leading to effective, productive and efficient administration.

(iii) *In relation to: Methodology used in the paper*: I have one general observation. *Column B of Table 1* is taken as "the measure of public sector share to be used throughout the paper". This is a useful indicator of the "total influence" of Government. But, for subsequent evaluation, it probably is desirable to distinguish between public sector claims over *real* resources and the distribution which occurs through the public sector. The public sector claims over real resources can be measured by the sum of net public sector expenditure on goods and services plus gross physical capital formation of the public authorities (measured in column C of Table 1). The re-distribution through the public sector can be measured by public authorities' transfer payments as a proportion of personal income. The disability of column B as a measure of public sector share is that it groups to-gether claims on real resources with transfer payments. The underlying economic effects of these two broad components of expenditure are quite different. Hence, column B should be interpreted in terms of the *trends* which it shows, rather than in terms of the significance of any particular percentage share.

Mr. President, I have great pleasure in seconding the vote of thanks to Dr. O'Hagan.

John Blackwell: I would like to be associated with the vote of thanks to John O'Hagan for his invaluable and meticulously compiled paper.

In Section 4, Dr. O'Hagan examines some possible explanations for the increase in the public sector share, and refers to the costs of raising the revenue to finance public expenditure. But this can be a rather confusing use of the term costs. It turns out that resource costs are not being referred to. Rather, these costs seem to consist of the income distribution effects of the taxation which is needed to finance government expenditure. Now, this raises a number of pertinent questions, which are not addressed in Section 4. There are, in a fully employed economy, resource costs associated with an increase in public sector claims on real GNP. The "costs" of the transfer payments of public authorities is another matter. There *may* be resource costs if the required taxation leads to reductions in output, either directly or via wage bargaining. With regard to the direct effects on output – this has been the subject of much more mythology than hard evidence – indeed there is hardly any evidence that any significant reductions in output occur. One may indeed hypothesise that "peoples' willingness to pay taxes will largely reflect the benefits they foresee from the associated public expenditure" (Section 4). But the tax and transfer system is probably the most efficient re-distributor which we have, and it will never be possible to ensure – even for groups of taxpayers – an equation between benefits received and taxes paid.

In the years 1974 and 1975, the public sector share rose under the influence of discretionary fiscal policy. A ratchet effect seems to have occurred since then, which indicates the difficulty of using counter-cyclical policy with current government expenditure. The effects of automatic stabilisers in increasing expenditure on transfer payments during the years 1974 and 1975 would have to be allowed for. In general, there could need to be an allowance for the effects of automatic stabilisers, when examining the change in the public sector share over time.

Dr. O'Hagan tentatively explains the increase in the public sector share in terms of increasing resource constraints and the effects of indicative planning. For reasons given above, the use of "resource constraints" in this context is ambiguous. One has some doubts about the postulated effects of indicative planning, since the displacement effect occurred in a short period in the mid-1970s when indicative planning was invisible. There is likely to have been, in the 1970s, a general desire to move towards the level of social welfare provision in the UK – but this laudable aim can hardly be laid at the door of indicative planning.

Dr. O'Hagan's paper shows that there was a steady increase in the share of public sector claims over real resources (measured in col. C of Table 1) between 1968 and 1973, then a big increase in the two-year period from 1973 to 1975, followed by a decline in the period to 1977. The sharp increase in 1974-1975 inclusive mirrors an equally sharp increase which occurred in column B of Table 1. The fact that this displacement was concentrated in these two years is not given sufficient emphasis in Dr. O'Hagan's paper. Between 1964 and 1977, the proportion of public consumption plus public investment to GNP (i.e. column C) increased by 5.9 percentage points; in the two year period 1974-1975 the increase was 4.2 percentage points. By comparison, using measure B, between 1964 and 1977 the share of public sector expenditure rose by 15.0 percentage points, and 8.8 percentage points of this occurred in 1974-1975 inclusive.

One question arises regarding the measure of public sector claims on real resources which is inherent in column C of Table 1 – whether public authority grants to enterprises, and grants to local authorities should not be added to give a more widely defined public investment series. This would be a public investment series which would include the leverage effects of public authority grants. To take some of the biggest categories, these capital grants include farm modernisation grants, and grants by the IDA, and it is likely that the grants are quickly reflected in gross physical capital formation of the private sector.

With regard to the income re-distribution which occurs through the public sector, rather than calculate public authority transfer payments as a proportion of GNP, it may be more pertinent to calculate the share of personal income. This is because this re-distribution in a sense, results in a certain proportion of private consumption being financed by transfer payments. An indication of the impact of this re-distribution may be had from the personal income and personal expenditure table in the national accounts. In 1970, national debt interest plus transfer income (including net transfers from the rest of the world), amounted to 17.5 per cent of personal income; the proportion in 1973 was 17.6 per cent. There was a big increase in the proportion between 1973, and 1975 when the share was 20.1 per cent; there was a slight decline to 20.8 per cent in 1977. Dr. O'Hagan says that the main period of growth in the share of current transfers in GNP has been 1962-1976 "with particularly rapid growth in the 1972 to 1975 period": but it is worth pointing out that the sub-period 1974-1975 inclusive saw a sharp increase of 3.9 percentage points, compared with 5.7 percentage points in the period 1973-1976 inclusive.

In Section 4 Dr. O'Hagan makes the interesting point that not until recently was it known of taxpayers, as taxpayers, to "exit" the political system. In the United States, where local taxes are used to fund many local authority services, there has been some migration as a result of tax resistance. This option is not available in Ireland due to the lack of tax-gathering power which has been devolved to local authorities.

S. Cromien: Dr. O'Hagan is to be congratulated on his excellent paper. I am sure that it will be used – or depending on your point of view misused – by my colleagues in the Department of Finance when they are examining trends of public expenditure. The paper raises very relevant questions, particularly in Part 4. As Dr. O'Hagan explains in the introduction, it was not possible, mainly for reasons of space, to go into these topics in detail. Although understandable, this is a pity because there is so much that might usefully be said about them, particularly at present when the tax burden associated with high public expenditure has generated great interest and controversy.

There seems to be a dilemma in modern democratic societies. A voracious appetite for increased public expenditure appears to co-exist with a growing – and in recent years very obvious – reluctance on the part of the community to pay higher taxes for this expenditure. The paper draws attention to the pressure for increased expenditure which comes from public employees. Although such pressure may at times exist, the demand for an expansion of public services appears to be much more diffused through the economy. Anyone associated with government is aware of the widespread calls for government assistance continually being voiced.

The paper makes an interesting point about the role of economic planning in encouraging public expenditure. I wonder if this has been really significant. Dr. Whelan has commented on this. Besides the points which he has mentioned there is the further one that expansion of public expenditure is as much a feature of countries such as the United States and Germany where there has been no economic planning in our sense.

A very important exercise in communications is obviously needed to get clearly into the minds of all of us the equation: "increase in current public expenditure = increase in taxation". The difficulty is that we all are tempted to think of an equation which says: "increase in current expenditure which I desire = increase in tax to be paid by someone else".

I agree with Dr. O'Hagan when he expresses doubts about the assumption made in the Irish national accounts of a zero productivity increase for the public sector. It seems quite unreasonable to continue to maintain this convention, or fiction, given the steady improvement in productivity which must result from computerisation in the public service and the introduction of other modern techniques.

I join with the other speakers again in complimenting Dr. O'Hagan on his stimulating paper.

Gabriel Noonan: I would like to be associated with other speakers who have commended Dr. O'Hagan's paper. It is a valuable contribution to the continuing debate on public expenditure and its role in the creation and sharing of national resources. I have been involved with the planning of the public finances for some years but, nevertheless, I found that the paper clarified and made more precise one's perception of the evolution of the present pattern of public expenditures.

I would like to endorse the point which other speakers have made that more work requires to be done on the determinants of various public expenditures, including transfers; I see the availability of resources more as a limiting constraint on increasing public expenditures than as a determinant of those expenditures. The driving forces which underlie pressure to increase public expenditures up to the limits of resource availabilities and even beyond need to be studied more closely and understood if effective action is to be taken to contain them.

I would also like to support Dr. Whelan's arguments that planning, of itself, has not been the cause of a significant increase in sectoral lobbying. Such lobbying has long been a feature of American politics despite the fact that the emphasis there on planning has been less than in Ireland. Instead, I think that expenditure outturns will tend to exceed planned expenditures wherever there is a close association between the control and planning functions, as there has been in the Department of Finance. Such an association leads to acceptance by planners of expenditure projections which are less than realistic but meet the spartan requirements of their colleagues responsible for expenditure control. Expenditure over-runs are inevitable if the projections themselves are not realistic in relation to Departments' economic and social objectives.

In concluding, I would like to suggest that one lesson which could be drawn from Dr. O'Hagan's paper is the need to make more visible the opportunity costs of public sector decisions, whether these costs be by way of other programmes foregone, operated at reduced levels or of taxation increased and private expenditure thereby foregone. Improved information on the full costs of public expenditure decisions – in addition to estimates of how much cash is involved – could contribute to more rigorous and balanced judgements about the worth of at least some public sector activities.

P. O'Huiginn: I join the other speakers in thanking and congratulating Dr. O'Hagan. His paper is extremely valuable and timely. I thought he might have referred to the inflationary effects of the growth of public expenditure and its financing. As the most open economy in the OECD area and dependent for growth on the ability to trade competitively, inflation is our greatest single economic problem, particularly with our EMS exchange restraints. Because of the greater openness of our economy – imports represent nearly 70 per cent of our GNP as compared with only 25 per cent in the case of the Federal Republic of Germany – we import inflation from others to a relatively high degree. It has been estimated at nearly 40 per cent of the total in 1976. Increased public expenditure and taxation, particularly indirect taxation, increases further this basic inflation trend. We obtain a much higher proportion of our taxation revenue from indirect – and inflationary – taxation than the Community or OECD averages – 53 per cent in 1979 as against 25 per cent in 1977 for both the Community and OECD. This is a factor of our limited direct taxation base. But in the end it goes back to the size and cost of the public sector. Our concern with their growth is not unique, it is a general concern throughout the OECD area. A conclusion in a recent OECD study was that we may be forced to think in the future of the Welfare Society rather than the Welfare State in an effort to find less bureaucratic and costly ways of administering social services.

[13]

Excerpt from Art Cosgrove (ed.), *Marriage in Ireland*, 132–50.

MARRIAGE IN IRELAND IN THE TWENTIETH CENTURY[1]

Brendan M. Walsh

A profoundly adverse effect on the psychology of the people must be produced where so many do not marry at all, or else postpone marriage to ages higher than are customary elsewhere or are desirable and natural. There is something gravely wrong in a community where there is such widespread frustration of a natural expectation, and, in our considered view, the low marriage rate is one of our two great population problems — the other being emigration ... Commission on Emigration and other Population Problems 1948-1954, *REPORTS*, (Majority Report, para. 164).

Ireland's peculiar marriage patterns symbolized the despondency that gripped the country in the middle of the twentieth century.[2] An abnormal reluctance to marry was seen as both cause and consequence of the economic and social stagnation that seemed to settle on the country even during periods, such as the 1950s, when the rest of Europe was growing vigorously. So prevalent was the lack of enthusiasm for marriage and sexual activity in general that Ireland at mid-century may well provide an example of what Malthus called 'a decay of the passion between the sexes', a phenomenon that he thought was rare in view of the evidence that 'this natural propensity exists in undiminished vigour' throughout the world.[3] It is important to emphasise this apparent lack of libido to younger generations of Irish students, just as it was necessary to explain it to foreigners in the past, lest they be misled by standards alien to the Ireland of the 1950s to assume that the low marriage rate merely reflected a widespread preference for extra-marital activity of various degrees of exoticness!

A low-level equilibrium was established in Irish marriage patterns around the turn of the century. There was little change in the marriage rates of the generations born between 1896 and 1910. They displayed the greatest reluctance to marry of any Irish generation and indeed of any national cohort for which reliable and comparable marriage patterns can be established. A summary of this pattern is presented in Charts 1 and 2, which are based on the data in successive censuses of population.[4]

Various statistics can be used to summarise the pictures displayed in these two charts. The most striking is the proportion of each generation of men and women who never marry. The level of 'definitive celibacy', to use the French phrase, was 30 per cent for Irish men, and 25 per cent for Irish women born about the turn of this century. The comparable figures for 'normal' European countries such as France and Britain was just under 10 per cent for men and somewhat higher for women. But this single statistic understates the weakness of the Irish marriage pattern, because even those who married did so at an age that was advanced by comparison with countries where much higher proportions eventually married. The average age at (first) marriage of Irish grooms of these generations was about 33 years, and of brides about 29 years, compared with about 27 years for both sexes in France and Britain. Another way of summarising marriage patterns is to calculate the age by which a majority of a generation has married. A majority of Irish males born about the turn of the century was still single at age 35, of women at age 31. The corresponding ages in other western European countries were five to ten years younger.

It should not be thought that comparing Ireland with a country such as France exaggerates the exceptional situation in this country. As shown by Hajnal,[5] the marriage pattern in northern Europe as a whole during the nineteenth and early twentieth centuries was unusual by comparison with that recorded in other times or regions. Ireland was the extreme example of a pattern of restraint in regard to marriage that emerged in western Europe after the reformation and reached its greatest intensity at the end of the nineteenth century in Ireland. The 'normal' pattern outside western

134   **MARRIAGE IN IRELAND**

CHART 1   *Proportion of Generation Single at Successive Ages, Females*

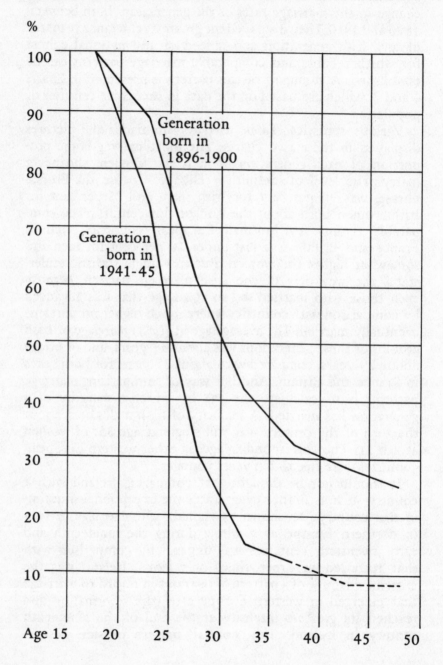

CHART 2 *Proportion of Generation Single at Successive Ages, Males*

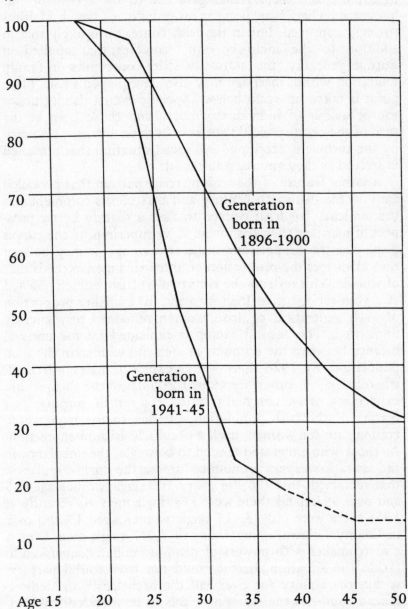

Europe and in western Europe at earlier times was the marriage of virtually all the population within a few years of reaching sexual maturity. It is beyond the scope of the present chapter to explore the factors that gave rise to the spread of this 'preventive check' on population growth, of which Malthus strongly approved, but in the Irish context it is likely that in addition to the socio-economic variables that applied in Europe generally, the unusually strict constraints on family limitation within marriage may also have played a role. (This point is taken up again below.) Specific events also influence the behaviour of individual cohorts, and those born at the turn of the century would not have been encouraged to marry by the turbulent economic and social situation that prevailed in Ireland as they entered adulthood.

Another feature of the Irish marriage pattern that prevailed early in the twentieth century and that merits comment was the tendency for Irish women to have a slightly better prospect of marriage than Irish men. If we superimpose the curves displaying the proportions single at each age, it may be seen that at all ages the proportion of unmarried men exceeds that of women. This reflects the facts that (i) Irish women married at a younger age than Irish men and (ii) a smaller proportion of each generation of Irish women remained permanently unmarried. The second factor is explained by the unusual balance between the numbers of men and women in the Irish population. By 1926 there was an excess of males in Ireland, whereas in all other developed countries the higher life expectancy of women had resulted in a female surplus. This feature of the Irish population was due to the higher emigration rate for women, itself a peculiarly Irish phenomenon. As those who emigrated tended to be single, the imbalance in the sex ratio was very pronounced among the single population that remained. In 1926, for every 100 single women aged 15 and over in Ireland there were 123 single men. As recently as 1961 there were only 3,415 single women aged 15 and over in County Leitrim, compared with 7,027 single men. Even if a matchmaker with powers of compulsion had been asked to tackle the situation, he/she could not have found partners within the county for over half the bachelors![6] In Mediterranean countries the situation tends to be reversed: the out-migration of men to work in industry has led to a considerable surplus of women in the villages and rural areas.

A relatively large gap between the ages of brides and grooms was also a feature of Irish marriages. Details of this phenomenon were first collected in the census of 1946. Almost half (47 per cent) of all grooms were at least five years older than their brides, and among those living in rural areas this reached 54 per cent. In rural marriages over one in nine of grooms were 15 years or more older than their brides. As is to be expected, the older the groom, the greater the average gap in age between him and his bride. Thus, to some extent, the unusual disparity in age at marriage was due to the pattern of late marriages, although it was not an inevitable consequence. The Commission on Emigration described this phenomenon and noted that a combination of late marriages and a large age-disparity between husbands and wives led to a relatively large number of widows and orphans in the community (Majority Report, para. 160).

Significant differences in marriage patterns existed between different population groups. In general, the characteristic Irish marriage pattern was most pronounced in the poorer rural communities. The urban population displayed a better marriage pattern, but there were interesting differentials between socio-economic groups. The professional and managerial groups (and more prosperous farmers) tended to have the lowest level of 'definitive celibacy', but they married relatively late. Manual workers, on the other hand, tended to marry early, but relatively high proportions in these groups remained unmarried. These differentials are associated with the educational and career paths of people in these groups.

The effect of religious affiliation on marriage patterns has been the subject of some controversy. The Commission on Emigration commented in the following terms on this issue:

> There is a fairly widespread belief that our poor marriage background is partly attributable to the fact that, since the great majority of the people of Ireland are catholics, marriage is to them an indissoluble contract and family limitation by contraception is against the moral law. It is said that the indissolubility of marriage and . . . the

fear of large families deter many from marriage altogether and others until a relatively advanced age. No
convincing evidence has been put before us in support
of this view (Majority Report, para. 166).

However, a detailed examination of catholic/protestant differentials in marriage, north and south of the Irish border,
and of marriage and fertility patterns by social class in the
Republic, supports the hypothesis that the prospect of a large
family acted to deter marriage.[7]

A consideration that should be raised before leaving this
review of Irish marriage patterns at their nadir is that all of
the data so far relate to the Irish *remaining in Ireland*. For
the generations born at the end of the nineteenth century,
the loss due to emigration was very substantial. Out of 100
males recorded in the 0-14 age group in 1901, only 42 were
still alive in Ireland 50 years later. About half the cohort had
emigrated from the country. In presenting material from the
Irish censuses for the cohort as it ages, we are looking at a
sub-group that may not be a random sample of the original
cohort. It is, however, interesting to note that Americans of
Irish descent ranked highest in 1950 of all ethnic groups in
their propensity to marry late or never to marry. Thus the
attitudes and values prevailing in Ireland at the turn of the
century seem to have been carried over to the United States.[8]

The low marriage rate that I have illustrated with reference
to the generation born about the turn of the century lasted
for several decades. Change was hardly perceptible until the
generation born in the immediate post-independence years
reached marrying age. With the maturing of the generation
born during and after the second world war, the pace of
change accelerated dramatically. The depressed economic
conditions of the 1950s did not check the upward trend. As
the Commission on Emigration was drafting its *Reports*, the
results of the 1951 census of population revealed a significant
rise in the proportions married in the young adult age groups.

It is simplest to compare the exceptionally low marriage
pattern displayed by the generation of 1900 with the pattern
now almost completed by those born forty years later. Some
extrapolation is required as these people had only reached

age 40 at the time of the census of 1981. Charts 1 and 2 illustrate how radically marriage patterns have altered since the beginning of the century. Half the females born in the 1940s had been married by their 25th birthday, about 6 years earlier than was the case for the generation of 1900. Half the males born in the late 1940s had been married by their 27th birthday, about 9 years earlier than the generation of 1900. The proportions unmarried may eventually fall as low as 8 per cent for women and 13 per cent for men of this generation. However, this change does no more than bring Irish marriage patterns into line with those that prevailed in France among women born over a century ago.

It may be seen that the change in marriage patterns has more profoundly affected men than women. This is clearest with respect to age at marriage. The median age at first marriage declined from 25 years 10 months for the brides of 1957 (the first year for which this statistic was collected) to 23 years and 4 months in 1974, a fall of two and a half years over a 17 year interval. But the male age at marriage fell by more than four years, from 29 years and 5 months in 1957 to 25 years and 4 months in 1974. There has been little change in the median age at marriage in the years since 1974.

As a consequence of the more rapid fall in the age of grooms than of brides, the disparity in age at marriage between brides and grooms has fallen sharply. This is shown in Table 1. There is now a much greater tendency for marriages to occur to men and women of roughly the same age than was the case, especially in rural areas, in the past. In 1946 54 per cent of rural grooms married women that were at least five years younger than them compared with only 20 per cent in 1981. In over three quarters of all marriages registered in 1981 the bride and groom were within four years of each other's age, compared with less than half of all, and only 41 per cent of rural, marriages in 1946.

Changing marriage patterns have been accompanied by changes in the nature of marriage. The most important change, and the only one that I shall attempt to document, lies in the number of children born to each marriage. As the marriage rate rose, fertility of marriage or average family size declined. While it would be unjustified to infer cause and

Table 1 Disparity in age at marriage in Ireland.

Percentage distribution of difference between the ages of brides and grooms, first marriages, 1946, 1957, 1979 and 1981

	Urban	1946* Rural	Total	1957	1979	1981
Groom younger than bride						
5 years or more	3.5	4.4	4.0	4.1	2.5	2.8
1 to 4 years	14.8	10.8	12.5	13.6	17.5	17.8
Groom and bride same age	8.6	5.6	6.9	8.2	13.1	12.9
Groom older than bride						
1 to 4 years	36.4	24.8	29.6	34.0	47.0	46.3
5 to 9 years	23.3	26.9	25.4	24.0	16.0	16.3
10 to 14 years	9.0	16.4	13.3	10.4	3.0	2.8
15 years or more	4.4	11.1	8.3	5.6	1.0	1.0
Total	100.0	100.0	100.0	100.0	100.0	100.0

*All marriages.
Sources: Census of population, 1946 and *Annual reports on vital statistics.*

effect, this development is in keeping with the hypothesis, discussed above, that high fertility of marriage acted in the past as a deterrent to marriage.

The fall in the fertility of marriage is shown in Table 2 by comparing the number of births per 1,000 married women in the child-bearing age groups for the years 1961, 1966, 1979 and 1982. The fertility rate was relatively stable over the period 1961-66, but declined rapidly between 1966 and 1979. It may be seen that the decline in fertility has been more pronounced among older married women. The trend in the fertility of marriage over the period 1961-81 is summarised in Chart 3, which shows that the fall over these two decades amounted to 38 per cent.[9] Had the fertility rates of the 1950s been maintained as the number of young married couples increased, well over 100,000 legitimate births would

Table 2 Legitimate births per 1,000 married women

Age	1961	1966	1979	1982	1982 as % of 1961
15-19	612	639	541	455	74
20-24	478	484	344	296	62
25-29	392	370	276	253	65
30-34	299	281	197	183	61
35-39	202	186	108	104	51
40-44	77	71	35	29	38
45-49	6	6	3	3	50

Sources: Annual report on vital statistics and National Economic and Social Council, *A review of the implications of recent demographic changes*, April 1984.

CHART 3 *Index of Fertility of Marriage, 1961-81 (based on Census years and interpolation*

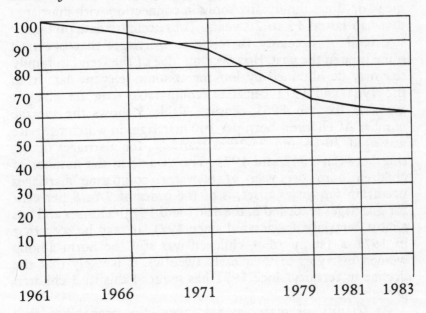

1961   1966   1971   1979   1981   1983

have been recorded annually by the early 1980s, compared with roughly 70,000 in the peak year, 1980. Thus, if there had been no decline in fertility as the marriage rate increased, Ireland would now have a birth rate of over 30 per thousand, more typical of a less developed Asian or African, than of a northern European, country. Since 1980 there has been a pronounced fall in the number of births recorded. The combination of continuing reductions in fertility and the apparent reversal of the upward trend in marriages may mean that 1980 was the year when the total number of births reached its maximum. By 1983 the number of births registered had fallen by over 7,000 or almost 10 per cent.

While it is natural to think in terms of 'average family size' when discussing the fertility of marriage, it is not easy to summarize the situation using this measure. The number of children born to a marriage depends on the age of the wife and (to a much lesser degree) of the husband at marriage, and on the duration of the marriage. One of the characteristics of Irish marriage until recently was the tendency for the period of child-bearing to be very protracted, so that one could speak of 'final family size' only in connection with marriages that had lasted 15 to 20 years. Thus accurate data on family size tend of necessity to relate to marriages that occurred some time in the past. However, an idea of the trend in family size may be obtained by looking at some relevant data from the 1961 and 1971 censuses (comparable data are not yet available for the 1981 census). Table 3 shows the average number of children born per 100 marriages in which the wife was aged 20-24 and 25-29 at marriage, for marriages occurring between 1942 and 1971. The decline in the number of children born *per year of marriage*, comparing marriages occurring ten years apart, is of the order of 7 or 8 per cent for marriages recorded in the 1961 and 1971 censuses and has almost certainly accelerated since 1971. It may be seen that in 1971 a family of 4 children was still the norm among women marrying in their early twenties. It is likely that the decline in fertility since 1971 has reduced this to 3 children per family.

As fertility of marriage has fallen, the probability that unmarried women would bear children in Ireland has risen.

Table 3 Average family size for marriages occurring between 1941 and 1971.

Number of children born per 100 marriages classified by age of wife at marriage and marriage duration, based on data in the 1961 and 1971 censuses of population.

Duration of marriage (years)	Date of marriage	Age of wife at marriage	
		20-24	25-29
0-4	1957-61	117	112
	1967-71	108	104
5-9	1952-56	303	281
	1962-66	282	275
10-14	1947-51	425	373
	1957-61	402	374
15-19	1942-46	499	410
	1952-56	488	414

Sources: Census of population of Ireland, 1961, Volume VIII, Table 4a and Census of population of Ireland, 1971, Volume X, Table 4a.

This is shown in Table 4. Depending on age, it is now two to three times more likely that an unmarried woman will have a child than was the case a quarter of a century ago.

The combination of declining fertility within marriage and increasing fertility among those who are not married has reduced the gap between the married and the unmarried population in the probability of child-bearing. Whereas in 1955 the probability that an unmarried woman of child-bearing age would have a child was at most 1.4 per cent of that of a married woman of the same age, by 1982 this had risen to over 6 per cent for women in their twenties and thirties (see Table 4). Throughout the first half of this century about 2 per cent of all births registered in Ireland were classified as illegitimate,[10] but by 1983 this proportion had risen to 6.8 per cent. At the same time there seems to have been a marked increase in the incidence of pre-nuptial conceptions. The evidence for this is indirect, being based on the

Table 4 Illegitimate births per 1,000 unmarried women

| Age | 1955 | 1979 | 1982 | Illegitimate rate as % of legitimate rate | |
				1955	1982
15-19	3	9	11	0.4	2.4
20-24	6	15	19	1.3	6.4
25-29	5	14	16	1.4	6.3
30-34	3	9	12	1.0	6.6
35-39	2	5	7	1.0	6.7
40-44	1	1.5	1	1.2	3.4

Source: Annual reports on vital statistics.

proportion of marriages[11] in a calendar year to which a birth is registered in the same year. This proportion rose from 7.0 per cent in 1961 to 15.5 per cent in 1979. If this is taken as a rough estimate of the number of pre-nuptial conceptions, then illegitimate births plus pre-nuptial conceptions amounted to almost 9 per cent of all births in 1979 compared with about 4 per cent in 1961. The lower level of emigration than in earlier years may imply that a higher proportion of extra-marital conceptions result in births in Ireland now than in the past, but the rise in 'illegitimate' births has continued long after the reversal of migration patterns in the early 1970s, suggesting that a continuing change in patterns of sexual behaviour is occurring.

The rise in marriage rates has been recorded across a wide range of socio-economic groups. A detailed examination of the data for 1961 and 1971 for males shows that in all groups the proportions single were lower in 1971 than in 1961 (see Table 5). The rise in the marriage rate of the professional, salaried employee and other non-manual groups is particularly striking. Higher incomes and an increased proportion of working wives among members of this group are likely to have contributed to this trend. Whilst the proportions single at the younger ages among farmers and manual workers also declined, there was relatively little change in the proportions unmarried

Table 5 Proportions single by socio-economic group 1961 and 1971: males

Age:	20-24		25-29		30-34		35-39		40-44		45-54	
Socio-ec. group	1961	1971	1961	1971	1961	1971	1961	1971	1961	1971	1961	1971
Farmers	98.8	97.0	89.8	78.8	74.3	59.2	60.0	50.0	48.5	45.9	39.9	40.9
Ag. Labourers	94.9	87.4	75.8	61.2	59.8	53.2	51.2	50.5	46.6	50.8	43.1	47.1
Higher Professionals*	96.9	62.7	68.8	50.0	39.1	21.9	24.7	17.3	21.4	15.6	22.8	15.9
Lower Professionals	95.3	89.0	64.2	51.8	34.7	23.5	22.4	15.2	15.6	13.0	13.3	11.7
Employers & Managers	91.6	85.9	47.8	31.8	23.3	11.4	15.1	6.7	10.7	7.0	8.7	5.8
Salaried Employees	90.0	85.1	51.8	37.2	26.0	14.3	17.1	9.6	12.8	8.3	10.5	7.4
Intermediate Non-Manual	93.3	87.8	64.4	47.4	39.3	24.9	26.1	19.1	22.0	19.9	18.5	17.7
Other Non-Manual	86.9	76.3	52.3	38.5	34.2	23.1	23.3	19.9	19.7	18.8	17.1	16.0
Skilled Manual	88.2	79.5	51.3	37.0	31.7	19.4	22.8	16.4	18.7	15.7	16.5	14.5
Semi-skilled Manual	87.5	77.8	55.1	41.5	36.6	26.8	26.9	25.0	22.0	20.6	18.6	18.1
Unskilled Manual	88.1	78.4	60.0	49.6	43.7	39.2	33.6	35.3	29.9	32.6	24.8	27.7

*Excluding professed clergy.
Sources: Census of population of Ireland, 1961 and 1971, Volume V.

at older ages in these groups. Thus, despite the changes that have occurred during the post-war period, pronounced socio-economic differentials in marriage patterns persist. The fall in the proportion of the total population that is unmarried reflects not only the higher marriage rate in individual groups, but also the declining share in the total population of the groups where marriage rates are very low (agricultural and unskilled urban workers). There has been a very rapid increase in the numbers in the 'Lower Professional' and 'Salaried Employee' socio-economic groups, among whom marriage rates are high.[12]

The rise in marriage rates may be attributed primarily to rising real incomes and improved economic prospects in Ireland. This factor would have been particularly important for the generation entering the labour market during the 1960s. For this and subsequent generations increased availability of contraception, and a willingness to use it, may also have played a role in encouraging marriage by reducing the resultant family size. However, the availability of contraception may in the longer run reduce the propensity to marry, in some socio-economic groups at least, by making more accessible some of the benefits that were formerly available only within marriage.

The general impression is that new patterns of living have become important in recent years, but statistical evidence of this phenomenon is difficult to obtain. A new 'other' marital status category was introduced in the 1979 census of population. The explanatory note to the census form stated that

> The category "Other Status" relates only to persons who have obtained a divorce in another country.

Publicity immediately before the 1981 census urged all divorced persons, and not merely those divorced outside the state, to return themselves as 'other'. This may affect the comparability of the 1979 and 1981 returns. A total of 2,379 males and 5,245 females were returned in this category in 1979. In the 1981 census these numbers had increased to 4,900 and 9,000. The 1983 Labour Force Survey sought information on the actual, as distinct from the legal, marital status of the respondents. Those who had ever been married were asked to classify themselves into one of the following categories:

> Widowed.
> Married.
> Married but separated:
>> Deserted.
>> Marriage annulled.
>> Legally separated.
>> Other separated.
> Divorced in another country.

These categories would seem to be exhaustive, but following the publication of the results of the survey, complaints were voiced about the possibility that this form of question might have encouraged some couples to classify themselves as 'married' even though their original union had terminated. There were 8,300 males and 21,100 females returned in the combined separated groups (over half were 'separated' and about a quarter 'deserted'). This is about double the number recorded as 'divorced' in the 1981 census. The numbers separated amount to just under 2 per cent of the married population among women aged 25-34, and a smaller percentage in other age groups.

The returns of the 1979 census were analysed on an experimental basis by 'family units'. One category included in this tabulation is 'persons enumerated as husbands and wives or couples'. The total number of single persons returned in this category came to only 175 males and 191 females. This suggests that we are still a very long way from the situation in some European countries where 'consensual unions' have become a significant demographic category.[13]

The evidence for the late 1970s and early 1980s indicates that the marriage rate may now have peaked and begun to fall. The first indication of this came from the fall in the marriage rate per 1,000 'at risk' (that is, single and widowed women) during the 1970s.[14] The returns of the 1979 and 1981 censuses of population and the 1983 Labour Force

Survey revealed that there has been a significant *increase* in the proportions single in the age group 15-34 in recent years (Table 6). This marks the end of the decline in the proportions unmarried in these age groups that had been recorded at successive censuses between 1936 and 1971. It is difficult at this stage to distinguish the short-run, and possibly transitory, effects of the current recession from longer-term trends, especially in regard to marriage, where postponement is a readily available strategy in a period of economic difficulty.

It has taken a long time for Ireland to attain marriage patterns that are 'normal' by the standards that prevailed until the 1970s in Europe. These standards are changing now and it is difficult to anticipate what sort of marriage patterns will be considered normal a generation from now. On the evidence of the past, Ireland will be slower to change than its neighbours. A certain archaism will persist in our marriage patterns. At present, the most striking contrasts between Ireland and other European countries are the very small proportion of marriages that end in divorce, the apparently small numbers living in consensual unions, the low proportion of total births recorded to unmarried women, and, despite the sharp fall over the last two decades, the relatively large size of families. It is a safe prediction that change will continue and possibly accelerate in all these areas, bringing Irish patterns of behaviour more closely into line with those found elsewhere in western Europe. The long evolution of the nature of marriage in Ireland that has been the subject of this series of papers will continue.

Table 6 Recent trends in proportion of the population single.

Age	Males				Females			
	1971	1979	1981	1983	1971	1979	1981	1983
15-19	99.5	99.3	99.4	99.6	97.9	97.3	97.7	98.3
20-24	84.6	81.6	82.4	86.6	68.9	66.3	67.7	74.9
25-29	49.2	43.2	43.6	47.6	31.1	27.9	28.8	32.0
30-34	32.1	24.3	24.3	24.6	19.4	14.5	14.6	15.2

Sources: 1981 Census of population and 1983 Labour Force Survey.

Notes

1. My thanks are due to John Blackwell of the Resource Environmental Policy Centre, U.C.D. for helpful comments on an earlier draft, and to Donal Garvey of the Central Statistics Office for comments and for making statistical material available to me.
2. Throughout this chapter 'Ireland' refers to the Republic of Ireland.
3. See chapter iv of the *Essay on the principle of population* (1798).
4. See also Michèle Brahimi, 'Nuptialité et fécondité des mariages en Irlande' in *Population* 3 (1978), pp 663-703.
5. John Hajnal, 'European marriage patterns in perspective' in D.V. Glass and D.E.C. Eversley (ed), *Population in history* (London, 1965), pp 101-43.
6. The manner in which the male/female population within counties tended to improve the marriage prospects of the women is explored in Brendan M. Walsh, 'A study of Irish county marriage rates: 1961-66' in *Population Studies*, 24 (1970), pp 205-16.
7. See Brendan M. Walsh, *Some Irish population problems reconsidered*, Economic and Social Research Institute Papers, 42 (Dublin, 1968).
8. See D.M. Heer, 'The marital status of second-generation Americans' in *American Sociological Review*, 26 (1961), 233-41. Heer hypothesizes that 'the proportion never married varies directly with emphasis on attaining high status and inversely with permissiveness concerning birth control' (p. 239).
9. The index shown in this chart has been calculated by applying the 1961 age-specific fertility rates to the number of married women in each age group in 1966, 1971, 1979 and 1981. The hypothetical or expected number of legitimate births thus estimated was expressed as a percentage of the total actually recorded. This extends a similar chart in Brendan M. Walsh, 'Recent demographic changes in the Republic of Ireland' in *Population Trends* (H.M.S.O.), 21 (1980), pp 4-9.
10. At earlier dates the proportion was at most four per cent. See S.J. Connolly, 'Illegitimacy and pre-nuptial pregnancy in Ireland before 1864: the evidence of some catholic parish registers' in *Irish Economic and Social History*, 6 (1979), pp 5-23.
11. Excluding marriages with intended future residence outside the state.
12. The socio-economic groups are defined by the occupation of the respondent or, in the case of a woman, the respondent's husband. The group to which a woman is assigned is thus influenced by whether or not she is married. For this reason, this discussion of marriage patterns by socio-economic group is confined to the male population.
13. Alternatively, the willingness of respondents to reveal changes in their behaviour may lag further behind that of other countries.

14. This was noted in National Economic and Social Council, *Population and labour force projections by county and region, 1979-1999*, Paper no. 62, 1982.

[14]

Excerpt from Colin Holmes and Alan Booth (eds), *Economy and Society: European Industrialisation and its Social Consequences*, 58–83. This article has been abridged by the author.

4 Textiles and regional economic decline: Northern Ireland 1914–70[1]

Philip Ollerenshaw,
University of the West of England

In the long debate on the decline of the British economy, increasing attention has been given recently to a 'matrix of rigid institutional structures' in industrial relations, enterprise and market arrangements, education (especially technical and higher), finance and government–industry relations that evolved in the nineteenth century and persisted in many cases until the recent past. In contrast to the neo-classical view that atomistic market structures and competition offer the 'best guarantor of economic well-being', those who stress institutional rigidities hold that it was precisely those same structures that militated against widespread adoption of modern, mass produced methods and corporate managerial hierarchies.[2] Hitherto, research has concentrated, unsurprisingly, on the staple industries, and in textiles has been typified by a series of powerful surveys of the British cotton industry by William Lazonick. Lazonick suggests that institutional rigidities effectively prevented the emergence of corporate organization until the 1960s and inevitably produced chronic technological backwardness and long-term industrial decline.[3]

This essay focuses primarily on the decline of another textile industry, linen, which was mainly located on the north east of Ireland and which, 'until the outbreak of war in 1939, probably remained the closest of all British industries to the free competitive ideals of the nineteenth century.[4] The industry comprised firms involved mainly or exclusively in flax spinning, linen thread manufacture, weaving and finishing piece goods made wholly or mainly from linen, and the making up of household linen products. In the first section we examine the long term structural problems of the industry, and then proceed to consider some other aspects of its decline, including research and advertising and its relationship with government.

Industrial structure and regional problems

In some of his recent writing, Sidney Pollard has emphasized the role of the region in the industrialization of modern Europe and, with other scholars, has redirected our attention to the perpetual process of regional advance and decline. In his major work on this theme he concentrates explicitly on

Textiles and regional economic decline: Northern Ireland 1914-70   59

Table 4.1 Regional Unemployment in the United Kingdom 1939-54*

Region	1939 July	1946 July	1948 June	1950 June	1952 June	1954 June
London and S.E.	4.9	1.0	1.5	1.0	1.2	0.8
Eastern	4.8	1.0	1.0	0.9	1.1	0.9
Southern	2.9	1.0	1.5	1.1	1.2	0.8
South West	4.0	1.0	1.5	1.2	1.2	1.1
Midland	5.3	1.0	0.5	0.5	1.0	0.5
North Midland	6.4	1.0	0.5	0.5	1.1	0.5
E. and W. Riding of Yorks	8.0	1.5	1.0	0.9	2.3	0.8
North Western	10.9	3.0	2.0	1.5	4.9	1.3
Northern	12.3	5.0	3.0	2.6	2.3	2.0
Scotland	10.2	4.5	3.0	2.7	3.2	2.4
Wales	14.2	8.5	5.5	3.4	2.6	2.1
Great Britain (average)	7.5	2.5	2.0	1.4	2.1	1.1
Northern Ireland	20.2	8.8	6.5	5.5	10.6	6.3

*The figures are percentages of all insured workers aged 14 and over unemployed in industry and agriculture.
Source: Isles, K.S., Cuthbert, Norman, 1957, *An economic survey of Northern Ireland*, HMSO, Belfast, p. 18.

industrialization, and once a region became industrialized, it fades from view.[5] From the First World War, however, the manifold problems of traditional industrial regions loom large in the UK experience and nowhere was the intractable nature of 'the regional problem' demonstrated more forcefully than in Northern Ireland – a low wage region with a poor stock of natural resources and a highly specialized industrial base dominated in 1914 by linen and shipbuilding.

The partition of Ireland in 1920 cut twenty-six counties out of the UK and created Northern Ireland as a six county state, with its own regional government in Belfast. Over the next fifty years, Northern Ireland established its reputation as the most economically backward region within the UK. It had no monopoly of intractable economic problems, but most indicators confirm the province's position as the most disadvantaged part of a national economy that was itself in relative economic decline. For example, expressed as percentages of the UK average, net output per employee was 84.6 in 1968 and per capita income was 72 in 1972.[6] In the latter year, unemployment was three times the national average. Indeed, since 1936, unemployment in the province has been higher than in any other UK region,[7] and it failed to achieve full employment even in the favourable economic environment after 1945 (see Table 4.1).

Central to any account of the economic history of Northern Ireland is the contraction of its textile industry, and this survey is intended to provide a necessarily brief examination of this important aspect of deindustrialization down to about 1970. Within Northern Ireland textiles dominated the manufacturing sector and, as late as the mid-twentieth century, accounted for more than a third of manufacturing employment – a much greater proportion than even in north west England. Textiles also contributed more than a third of net manufacturing output in the province. From this it follows that the performance of the textile industries, which were dominated by linen until the 1950s, was a key influence on the economy of Northern Ireland generally and its manufacturing sector in particular.[8] Some general data on the industry's output, capacity and employment are provided in Table 4.2.

On the eve of the First World War, the north east of Ireland was the world's leading linen producing area, and had been so since at least 1870. Regional specialization, so characteristic of textile industries since the early industrial revolution, became more emphatic after 1860. In the linen industry, the small Yorkshire output centred on Barnsley declined further while in east-central Scotland, jute increasingly replaced linen, though in 1914 there was still a significant Scottish linen industry specializing mainly in coarse goods.[9] Ulster accounted for some three quarters of UK linen output and specialized in the medium and fine end of the market, a fact that helped to protect it from foreign competition before 1914.

The most serious challenge in the home market came from Belgium, which successfully undercut relatively coarse yarn prices in Ulster and led directly to Irish spinners moving to the higher ground of finer yarns. Even if foreign competition in linen did become more evident from the later nineteenth century, a far more serious threat came from other textiles, most notably cotton. A number of early twentieth century observers noted that, as a result of increasing competition, the European linen industry stagnated between 1870 and 1914 – or even contracted, 'a fact that seems to show that the volume of the world's linen trade has fallen absolutely'.[10]

The significance of this trend did not become fully apparent until after 1914. Until then, Ulster linen production benefited from the decline of the industry elsewhere in the UK, and took advantage of cheap foreign flax, tow and yarn to keep costs down. It was also assisted by the fact that wages were lower than in any other UK textile industry, even jute.[11] Clearly related to this was the extremely low rate of unionization and the low rate of labour productivity. In the British cotton industry, where almost half the labour force was unionized by 1910,[12] the strength of trade union organization is sometimes cited as an important reason why managers could not invest significantly in more capital intensive machinery, even had they wished, and so were forced to retain traditional labour intensive techniques.[13]

In linen, there was no similar constraint since it is doubtful whether unionization exceeded ten per cent by 1914, or even by 1920, and it remained at a low level until the 1940s.[14] Whereas organized labour in British cotton may have held the 'balance of power', in the linen industry sectional and sectarian conflicts, the lack of alternative employment for a largely female labour force, and an unsubtle blend of paternalism and repression,[15] all meant that employers in Ulster were typically in a stronger position than their Lancashire counterparts. On the issue of productivity it might be noted here that data from the 1907 Census of Production indicated that output per worker in flax, hemp and jute at £61 per annum was significantly lower than either the £70 in

Table 4.2 Output, Capacity and Employment in the Linen Industry of Northern Ireland, 1912-51

Year	Flax Yarn Production Tons	Linen Thread Production Tons	Linen and Union Cloth Production Millions Sq Yards	Spindles	Powerlooms	Employment Thousands
1912	31,017	2,440	211	926,000	34,000	76
1924	28,050	2,060	161	930,000	37,000	75
1930	20,050	1,550	116	866,000	31,000	56
1935	28,850	1,450	146	868,000	28,000	57
1951	22,200	2,360	99	775,000	22,000	56

Source: Black, William, 1957, 'Variations in employment in the linen industry', unpublished Ph.D. thesis, Queen's University of Belfast, pp. 232, 235.

the woollen or the £79 in the cotton industries. If the cost of labour was relatively low in Ulster linen, the cost of technology was relatively high and this too discouraged labour saving techniques. One estimate in 1913 suggested that a cotton mill with mule spindles could be completely equipped for about 27s 6d per spindle, and a mill with ring spindles for 32s 6d. A flax mill using flyer spinning would cost about £7 per spindle. Similarly, a cotton weaving shed making medium grade goods could be built and equipped for some £36 per loom whereas the medium grade linen weaving shed would cost £45.[16]

Apart from a few vertically integrated concerns, most firms specialized in a single process, though the degree of vertical specialization in 1914 was not as great as in British cotton.[17] There was only limited movement towards greater integration before the 1950s. Each section of the industry had its own representative bodies which dealt with a range of issues including, for example, the implementation of short term working during recession, or the level of wage rates. Clearly, with a high degree of specialization within the industry, there was considerable scope for friction between different firms whose interests did not coincide. In an effort to overcome this problem the Council of the Irish Linen Industry, comprising representatives from all the main sections, was established, though it tended to be dominated by the most powerful sections: the Flax Spinners', the Irish Powerloom Manufacturers' and the Linen Merchants' Associations.

In terms of its sources of raw material, linen was typical of UK textile industries in its heavy dependence on overseas supply. Irish flax acreage had declined on trend since the late 1860s, and the 1912 figure was only 28 per cent of that for 1870. More than 80 per cent of the raw material for Irish linen came from Russia and Belgium.[18] As long as there was peace in Europe, this dependence was not a problem, though the implications for the linen industry of large-scale conflict in north west Europe were indeed serious.

Another feature which made linen characteristic of UK textiles was its export dependence. Ulster specialized in medium and fine linens and found its customers in relatively affluent markets, especially the USA – in contrast to the market orientation of British cotton. As a contemporary noted in 1913: 'While British cotton manufacturers look East for their customers, selling most largely in India and China, flax manufacturers look to the West, for with the exception of a diminishing amount shipped to Europe, the linen exports go west, and the US alone takes half the total'.[19] Market conditions in the US were thus a key determinant of linen production in Northern Ireland and had been so since at least the 1830s. High quality, strength and durability had been the characteristics that had enabled linen to hold out against the repeated incursions of cotton products, but the danger was that changes in tastes or fashion might mean that those same qualities which had once been indispensible assets would turn into chronic liabilities.

It was the First World War, rather than the inter-war depression, that first brought home to linen manufacturers the precariousness of their position, and nowhere was this more obvious than in the supply of raw material. Given that medium and fine linen goods were essentially luxuries, it might be expected that they would have low priority as war materials, and at the start of the war this seemed to be the case. Three developments, however, transformed the military importance and competitive position of the linen industry. First, the capture of key flax growing and flax spinning areas and the ability of Germany to prevent other governments from exporting flax and yarn, had serious adverse consequences in Ireland.[20] The export of high quality Belgian flax effectively ceased from an early stage in the war and Russian flax, hitherto exported through the Baltic states, had to be directed through the inconvenient and ice-prone port of Archangel. Second, and of much longer term significance, was the disruption to Russian flax exports caused by the 1917 revolution. Imports of flax and tow into the UK held up remarkably well until the revolution, but collapse was rapid thereafter: 77,280 tons in 1917; 23,696 in 1918; and a mere 3,895 in 1919.[21]

This curtailment of the principal sources of raw material as a result of war and revolution would have been bad enough under normal demand conditions, but it was compounded by a third development which had a profound short-term impact – the massive increase in military demand for linen products. As a government report of 1918 noted:

> The military importance of such textile raw materials such as flax, wool and cotton is at first sight less obvious than that of such hardware materials as steel or timber. At the present stage of the war, however, it is impossible to avoid recognition of the importance of the raw material of aeroplane linen fabric, whilst the national need of the heavier classes of Flax Textile products is obvious on consideration of the inevitable Naval and Military demands for canvas covers, sail cloth, tent duck, machine gun belts etc; there is also the universal demand for linen sewing thread.[22]

The need to secure raw material supplies, curtail exports, stimulate domestic flax production, encourage substitutes, and meet tight government deadlines all led to increasing government control of the linen industry which culminated in the establishment of the Flax Control Board[23] in 1917. After that the industry was controlled 'from the flax field to the cloth store'.[24] In general the military orders, which included some 50,000 miles of aeroplane cloth, were delivered remarkably successfully.

An inevitable result of demand pressures and supply constraints, however, was rapid inflation – which created a more serious problem for linen than for any other textile industry in the UK.[25] Indeed the ratio of cotton to flax prices decreased markedly during the inter-war period and this must be seen as one of a number of factors which diminished the competitiveness of the linen industry in the long term.[26] To some extent, and with government encouragement, the raw material problem was offset by an almost threefold increase in Irish flax acreage between 1914 and 1918, but this was purely temporary. Shortage of flax was also partly overcome in the First World War, as in the Second, by the substitution of other fibres to make 'unions'. So widespread did this practice become that as early as 1915, a Belfast linen trade report pointed out that 'cotton is now a very big feature in the local trade, and enters into the composition of almost everything that is made here'.[27]

In the light of the above, it is clear that the First World War demonstrated the insecurity of the linen industry's position, and even the short post-war boom enjoyed by so much of British industry was far more muted in Ulster.

The raw material problem drove up prices to such an extent by 1918 that linens were 'only compatible with a millionaire's tastes.'[28] The difference in experience between Britain and Ulster is indicated by the fact that at the same time as the British economy reached a cyclical peak, in March 1920, the Flax Spinners' Association reduced the hours worked by its members' mills to 25 per week. In fact, short time working had been typical of most spinning mills ever since the cyclical downturn which began just before outbreak of war.[29]

Even before the armistice was signed, however, a small number of informed commentators had begun to identify the formidable range of problems that the linen industry would have to overcome if it was ever to regain anything like its former levels of activity. These problems included the uncertain supply and high price of flax, the high degree of vertical specialization and frequency of internecine disputes within the industry, the threat of cotton-based substitutes, the rising tide of protection in overseas markets, the lack of research and development and inadequate marketing policies.[30] In addition to these problems there was some evidence of fundamental ignorance on the part of businessmen of cost accounting techniques. This last weakness has been identified as a common problem in British business in the early twentieth century,[31] and seems to have been typical of the linen industry. According to one accountant speaking in Belfast in 1918, 'not five per cent of those engaged in manufacturing linen knew really with any exactitude the cost of producing their goods'.[32]

Historians have appreciated some of these problems but have stressed that solutions to them, certainly in the inter-war period, were not within the grasp of linen manufacturers since the world demand for linen was contracting.[33] To some extent this was undoubtedly true. At the end of the 1920s it was clear that changes in tastes and fashion had adversely affected the demand for linen:

> Entertaining is now largely done at hotels or clubs in preference to the home and this has resulted in a virtual abandonment of the tradition whereby a generous supply of linen was regarded as a necessity in every well furnished household. Moreover, the unsatisfactory treatment of linen by laundries and the expense of laundering are not without influence on the Purchaser.[34]

A more general point was made at the same time: 'the public today as a rule prefer to buy the cheaper article and renew it at an earlier date rather than expend a somewhat large sum in order to obtain an article of lasting worth.'[35] This trend had particularly serious effects on the use of linen damasks, bed linen, bedspreads, dress linens and shirting cloths.

It remains the case, however, that recent historiography has not given sufficient attention to the shortcomings of the industry itself, and has therefore been somewhat fatalistic in tone and tended to argue that the industry performed creditably in the face of uncontrollably adverse demand conditions. Although accepting that market conditions were far from promising, it will be suggested that certain steps could have been taken to improve the industry's performance, but that ultimately these steps were not taken or were taken too late to be of benefit.

One of the most important features of the linen industry in Northern Ireland

Table 4.3 Paid Up Capital in Private and Public Joint-Stock Companies, 1953 (£000s)

	Paid up capital in private cos.	% of total	Paid up capital in public cos.	% of total
United Kingdom	2,391,000	37	4,088,000	63
Northern Ireland	41,443	61	25,790	39
Linen industry (spinning and weaving)	5,682	66	2,882	34

Source: Black, 'Variations in employment in the linen industry', p. 20.

has been the resilience of the small or medium size private family firm. Indeed, as late as the 1950s the ratio of paid up capital in private to public companies in this industry was two to one. Private firms figured much more prominently in the economy of Northern Ireland than in the UK as a whole and their prominence was especially marked in the linen industry (see Table 4.3). In a region where there were few immediate or obvious alternative industries into which entrepreneurs or workers might transfer, where unemployment was chronic, and whose textile industry faced secular decline and a weak degree of unionization, the temptation to plod on regardless was one to which most firms succumbed. Also important is the fact that the industry really lacked any external influence which could force the pace of rationalization or amalgamation. But it should be emphasized here that no linen enterprise was sufficiently dominant to take the initiative in industrial reorganization,[36] and neither the banks nor the Northern Ireland government took it upon themselves to offer such a lead. Under these circumstances it was perhaps surprising that the question of rationalization found its way onto the agenda at all.

In the immediate aftermath of the First World War, however, there were several indications that firms in the linen industry did co-operate in order to promote price stability and financial liquidity in the face of severe economic fluctuations. The issue of prices did not become prominent until the sharp downturn of spring 1920, and the lengthy discussion of price fixing arrangements which continued over the next eighteen months reflected the difficulties facing single process firms in different sections of the industry whose interests were not the same.[37] Fixing minimum prices for yarn helped spinners, but might place weavers at a disadvantage by increasing their input costs. Similarly, fixing minimum yarn prices for firms in an open economy such as the UK might be a futile exercise if cheap foreign yarn was available to undercut the domestic product.

A minimum price yarn agreement between Scottish and Irish spinners was hammered out in 1920, and strenuous and briefly successful attempts were made to extend the scope of the agreement to include French and Belgian spinners.[38] Although the agreement held for a few months in late 1920, the European spinners, whose raw material supply position was much more favourable than for those working in the UK, flatly refused to continue it from January 1921.[39] As the need for minimum prices – or at least more price stability – intensified, so the ability of the industry to achieve that goal diminished.

Rather more success in furthering co-operation seems to have been achieved by the Irish Linen Society, established in 1920, which embraced various trade associations and organizations associated with research, flax supply, manufacturing and marketing, and was overseen by a central council. As far as individual firms were concerned, the advantage of the Irish Linen Society was that it did not threaten their independence but held out the prospect of a greater degree of intra-industry collaboration than ever before. According to the *Textile Recorder*:

> More good for the advancement of the linen trade as a whole has been effected [by the ILS] than was ever achieved during the last half century prior to its progress. It has meant that narrow inter-firm prejudices and rivalries have been totally abolished in favour of a broad progressive principle, based on co-operation and a whole hearted desire.[40]

Unfortunately this optimism was wholly unwarranted and the 'narrow inter-firm prejudices' continued for decades afterwards, but at least the industry now had a representative forum into which various sections had an input.

One of the most pressing problems facing linen firms from 1920 was the accumulation of unsold stocks, and, in an industry where the small and medium size firm was the norm, this was bound to affect liquidity sooner rather than later. In order to meet this particular difficulty, the Irish Linen Trade Corporation was formed in 1921 as a limited company, with an initial nominal capital of £500,000. Established with the 'goodwill and co-operation' of the banks in Northern Ireland, the LTC was essentially a warehousing operation which provided cash (at Bank Rate plus a small commission) to firms on the security of stocks deposited with the LTC and valued by its board of directors, who were leading figures in the industry. This initiative was thought to be largely responsible for the fact that there were very few failures in the industry following the downturn and severe depression of the early 1920s.[41] It is important to note, however, that both the ILS and the LTC left the structure of the industry intact, though as hopes of a full recovery faded a number of commentators began to argue the case for full blown rationalization.

There were two stimuli to the discussion of rationalization. First, there was the problem of excess capacity. Between 1921 and 1928, while spinning and weaving capacity declined only slightly, an average of 44 per cent of spindles and 43 per cent of looms were idle, and many more worked short time.[42] The second stimulus was the well publicized attempt, beginning in the late 1920s, to rationalize the British cotton industry – an attempt which was led by the Bank of England and other banks with an obvious interest in bolstering the stability of the banking sector in the face of the huge indebtedness of hard pressed cotton firms.[43] Between 1928 and 1930 the linen industry in Northern Ireland, under the auspices of its newly formed Remedies Committee, actively considered rationalization and called in expert advice in the person of Sir Gilbert Garnsey of the leading London-based firm of accountants, Price Waterhouse.

Garnsey produced a preliminary scheme for rationalization[44] but believed that it was inadvisable to proceed further unless firms indicated their willingness to entertain the idea. Those most closely involved with canvassing opinion on this question discovered the main difficulty was that 'firms who are in a fairly comfortable financial position, and successful in their daily business, would feel some diffidence in proposing to go into full amalgamation with firms not quite so successful'.[45] In the event, nothing came of the proposed rationalization scheme and so the best opportunity to effect radical structural change was lost. Moreover, if such a scheme foundered in the profound depression of 1930 its chances of success at a later date were, to say the least, remote.

In the later 1930s and 1940s proposals for greater inter-firm co-operation were normally limited to the promotion of price control, standardization of products, or the establishment of a central selling organization. Comparatively few argued the case for rationalization, and the recommendation of the 1944 Post-War Planning Working Party Report on this issue was vague and tepid. As one critic noted, 'although the Committee appear to be half convinced of the desirability of some reduction in the number of small independent firms, they appear content to wait upon some obscure process of natural evolution.'[46]

In fact, 'natural evolution' rather than government or bank-led reorganization remained the order of the day throughout the twentieth century history of the linen industry. From the 1920s onwards there was some increase in both horizontal and vertical integration, though neither process accelerated significantly until after the Second World War. Although in 1954 five composite firms (i.e. those that were both horizontally and vertically integrated) controlled some 30 per cent of the industry's capacity, single process firms remained the norm and 'rugged individualism was still a matter of pride'.[47]

Over the next decade, however, fundamental structural change did occur and one in three large firms disappeared (see Table 4.4). Horizontal integration, particularly in the spinning section, increased as firms sought to reap economies in both purchasing and handling, diversification of product lines and in order to use capital equipment more fully – an especially important consideration in an industry where short time working was so common. Similarly, vertical integration was motivated by the greater assurance of inputs, the abolition of intermediaries, the greater potential for efficient stock control, and the increased control over marketing strategy and distribution channels. The growth of composite firms, which in theory were in the best position to achieve maximum benefit from both types of integration, also typified the period. Integration was, of course, still no guarantee of survival as was demonstrated by the symbolically important closure in 1961 of the York Street Flax Spinning Company Ltd, one of the oldest, largest, most integrated and recently modernized firms in the industry. At industry level, perhaps one of the most enduring legacies of the single process firms which had dominated the industry for so long was that there was a clear shortage of managers to run the integrated concerns – very few knew how to 'think vertically'.[48]

Table 4.4 Large Plants in the linen complex of Northern Ireland, 1954 and 1963/4

Industry	Employment		Establishments	
	1954	1964	1954	1963
Spinning*	21,952	12,304	53	37
Weaving	15,360	8,045	74	43
Making up	8,144	6,747	67	55
Trade hemstitching	4,911	2,902	54	35
Textile finishing**	6,047	3,959	50	31
Total	56,414	33,957	298	201

NB   Data refer to establishments employing 25 or more persons
*   includes threadmaking
* *   includes textile printing

Source: Steed, G.P.F., 1971, 'Internal organization, firm integration and locational change: The Northern Ireland linen complex, 1954–1964', *Economic Geography*, 47: 373.

The profound structural changes in the later 1950s and the 1960s took place after the onset of much tougher competition in international textile markets, and failed to stem the decline of the linen industry. If the paucity of management skills to run vertically integrated concerns was a factor in slowing down the rate of structural change and perhaps impeding the success of those concerns, the belated nature of the effort to integrate at all seemed to point to management's 'inclination to adjust after the event'.[49]

Research and Advertising

The structural problems of the linen industry remained apparent until after the mid-twentieth century and, as we have suggested, managerial failings were also apparent. We now consider the industry's policies in two areas to which economic historians have recently paid increasing attention – research and advertising.

Several writers have pointed to the poor innovative record of British industry, emphasizing firms' reliance on government funded co-operative research associations and also focusing upon the frequently tenuous links between academic and applied industrial research. A major new initiative in the United Kingdom, during and after the First World War, was the establishment of Research Associations under the auspices of the Department of Scientific and Industrial Research. The initial budget to finance these projects amounted to £1m. The aim was to promote co-operative research at industry level to compensate for the perceived lack of research facilities in individual firms. It was originally envisaged that the government and the relevant industry would finance RAs jointly for an initial period of five years, after which the industry itself would take over funding. Despite the fact that tax benefits accrued to firms making contributions to RAs, the response to this government initiative was generally disappointing. In the event, subsidies had to be continued beyond the original five year period, since private funding proved inadequate in all but one of the twenty-four RAs.[50]

The Linen Industry Research Association (LIRA) was one of those set up under the scheme, but both the short and long term responses of the industry to it were weak. By 1927 it was estimated that firms representing between only one-quarter and one-third of the capital in the industry had joined the RA, compared with two-thirds and eighty-five per cent in the RAs which served the woollen/worsted and cotton industries respectively.[51]

Before the formation of LIRA in 1919, the efforts of the linen industry to engage in research were confined to a tiny number of atypical large firms – so much so that at the inaugural meeting of the Association, James Crawford (Managing Director of the York Street Flax Spinning Company) believed that 'the idea of research at all . . . marked an epoch in the history of the trade'. Linen manufacturers had been willing to rest on their reputations for far too long 'with little or no concern beyond their next balance sheet, without an idea of the wider vision of those who had gone before and without taking time to look ahead or to consider the questions which lay at the very basis of industry and commerce.'[52] Even on so basic a question as knowledge of the flax plant, they knew appallingly little. Crawford's reasoned plea for both pure and applied research, his emphasis on the need for patience in achieving results, and his optimism about the ultimate benefits seem not to have been generally shared within the industry. This might be explained by the fact that his firm was not only vertically integrated but also the largest in the industry, with far more resources to devote to research than the typical, small, single process enterprise.

A further possible indicator of the general lack of interest in scientific methods was the low membership of the Irish section of the Textile Institute, which stood at a mere 25 at the end of the First World War – a figure which seemed to confirm that 'the old methods . . . are still in vogue'.[53] Yet another sign of weakness was the apparent absence of research facilities for the linen industry at the Queen's University of Belfast. A series of lectures on the industry organized by the university's Faculty of Commerce towards the end of the war was described as a 'very momentous innovation',[54] but as far as research effort was concerned, unfavourable comparisons were made between Queen's and the University of Leeds. Despite the tiny size of the English linen industry, Leeds had a long-established research and experimentation capability within its Textile Department, including a flax farm at Selby. The Belfast area, notwithstanding its 90,000 linen workers, received 'no special university attention, but merely the continuance of the haphazard "what-was-good-enough-for-grandad-is-good-enough-for-us" policy'.[55] Similarly, while the importance of fabric design was acknowledged in the linen industry, there appear to have been few contacts between this industry and the municipal College of Art in Belfast.[56] This may well have contributed to a conservatism in design, and emphasized the fact that competitors gave more attention to 'the production of novelty goods and attractive designs at popular prices'.[57]

Once underway, the work of LIRA impressed even the most vocal of the

70   *Philip Ollerenshaw*

industry's critics. Led by Dr Vargas Eyre, a highly qualified and experienced research chemist, the Association set about improving flax yields and the consistency and resilience of linen dyeing and finishing.[58] Given the fundamental importance of this type of work, the Belfast Chamber of Commerce found itself at a loss to understand why so few firms actively supported its efforts, 'especially as the cost when distributed falls so lightly on the individual concern'.[59]

The problem of inadequate funding and organization of research was one which persisted into the later twentieth century. In the major report of 1928 into the causes of depression in the linen industry, lack of research is not mentioned. In contrast, in the Report of the Post-War Planning Working Party of 1944, it was suggested that LIRA take control of all flax and linen research, its organization be strengthened and its emphasis be switched more to the problems of flax production and processing in addition to the 'more strictly industrial problems' of linen manufacture on which it had previously concentrated. While this was a welcome recognition of the significance of research, the working party still envisaged that half of the projected £50,000 research expenditure would be provided by government.[60] After the Second World War LIRA diversified its activities in several directions, including the implications for the linen industry of the introduction of spun rayons into Northern Ireland, though it still felt its work was not sufficiently appreciated by its members.[61] Further extensions of its work came through efforts to improve technology and the formation, in 1965, of a Merchanting Research Sub-committee. As the industry contracted, the traditionally low rates of subscription to LIRA declined still further to the point where it was in danger of losing its eligibility for any government funding.[62] Indeed, looking at the half century from 1919 it must be doubted whether, in the absence of sustained government assistance, the linen industry would have been willing to undertake *any* significant research effort.

If research into flax cultivation and linen manufacture was belated and poorly financed, the advertising techniques of the industry were also wanting. Before 1914 there was no concerted initiative to advertise linen products, and this was attributed to Ulster manufacturers' 'possession of a virtual monopoly' especially in the high quality end of the market.[63] The loss of civilian markets during the First World War, together with intensified competition from cotton, encouraged a reappraisal of advertising policy and marketing policy in general.

An obvious difficulty facing the linen industry was the finance and co-ordination of an advertising strategy for dozens of small and medium size firms. A related problem also arose from the atomistic market structure of the industry, namely the multiplicity of product lines inevitably produced by large numbers of specialist firms. After the First World War, some of the most informed commentators pointed to the urgent need to cut down on the number of products offered by individual firms. As one such commentator put it in 1918: 'An inspection of the catalogues of even moderate size linen manufacturing concerns will show that each of them is attempting to make almost every class of linen. The aim, in each case, is to put on the market a complete range of cloths which shall comprise everything demanded by a linen consumer.[64]

The results of this were damaging, both to individual firms and to the industry as a whole. Lack of standardization meant that short runs of production were far too common and changes of setting to machinery too frequent, leading inevitably to idle capacity. In 1918, a year of very strong demand in the linen industry, it was estimated that some 25 per cent of machinery lay idle because of the 'evil of short runs', and this contributed significantly to the relatively poor productivity of linen workers compared to those in cotton.[65] Despite this, the prospects for persuading linen manufacturers of the benefits of standardization were not thought to be good, and indeed seem not to have made much headway ten years later.[66]

However, a decision to undertake a concerted advertising campaign was made in 1919 and can be viewed as one of the earliest signs that the industry in general had begun to appreciate its lack of effort in the past. Co-ordination of the new initiative was undertaken by the Irish Linen Society, and the main aim was to improve sales in the US market. An initial budget of £30,000, later increased to £90,000 over three years, was raised by requesting Society members to contribute subscriptions according to their annual turnover.[67] Another part of the sales drive, aimed particularly at distinguishing linen products from close substitutes, was the introduction in 1921 of the 'True Irish Linen' hallmark, which was designed to instil a 'true guild spirit of salesmanship and pride of products into all associated, whether spinner, weaver or merchant'.[68]

Welcome though such initiatives were, their utility was diminished by the unprecedented price instability of linen goods after 1918. Stable supplies of raw material and stable market conditions had meant that linen prices had been fairly predictable before 1914. After the war, this was no longer the case. Once the economic downturn began, from mid-1920, retail buyers simply ordered the absolute minimum – in the firm expectation that prices would fall lower still. Neither the advertising campaign nor the one third reduction in the prices of linen goods in New York succeeded in achieving much beyond 'limited purchasing by those who were really in need of certain articles'.[69]

A further obstacle for linen in the American market during the 1920s was the highly effective advertising campaign mounted by one of its most serious competitors – US-made, linen finish cotton damasks. According to the Belfast Chamber of Commerce, linen manufacturers and merchants were simply not effective enough in promoting their products and had no answer to the Americans, thus 'they are letting the case go by default, and they are losing business thereby'.[70] What contemporaries could not fail to notice was that the extreme buoyancy of the US economy in the years after 1921 was not reflected in a strong demand for linen. In 1928, for example, the US took 78 per cent less linen (by weight) from the UK than it had in 1912.[71]

Frequent criticisms of its advertising efforts at home and abroad, together with the possibilities offered by the apparently endless economic boom in the US, led to a belated decision by both Irish and Scottish linen manufacturers and merchants to mount a more intensive campaign. In the home market, by 1928 the Irish Linen Guild had organized the distribution of trademarked and standardized goods (table damasks, bed linen and face towelling) at uniform prices to 700 firms in 300 locations throughout Britain and Ireland.

72   *Philip Ollerenshaw*

Standardization of size, price and quality was welcomed by the major retail outlets such as Selfridges 'and others of the great London stores'.[72] In the US, a delegation from Irish and Scottish linen industries arrived to promote their products at the end of the 1920s, but their arrival coincided almost exactly with the collapse of the New York Stock Exchange on Wall Street in October 1929.[73] If linen exports to the US had been disappointing in the 1920s, their prospects after 1929 were far worse.

While in the United States, however, the delegation received confirmation of a number of respects in which the linen industry was considered to be old fashioned or inefficient. These included obsolescent styles and designs, the fact that there was still too little standardization of quality, unnecessary duplication of distribution effort and excessive internal competition between firms in the same industry.[74] None of these criticisms was new, but the failure to tackle them effectively meant that the linen industry consistently failed to take advantage of its most important and prosperous if increasingly tough market during the 1920s.

The clear message was that a co-ordinated marketing and distribution strategy was essential to revive demand. The need to rethink marketing strategy, and in particular to anticipate demand through market research, continued to be stressed into the 1950s. As a leading linen manufacturer put it in 1954, 'To me, one of the peculiar features of the Irish linen trade has always been its patient waiting for the customer to state his needs rather than a "commencing-upon-manufacturing" and aggressive sales policy based upon a study of the consumer markets and the catering for their potential demand in advance.'[75]

The role of government

The various problems confronting the linen industry from the 1920s onwards and the growing pressure for some kind of protection inevitably raises an important long term issue: the relationship of the new devolved government of Northern Ireland with the region's most important manufacturing industry. It is sometimes suggested that at Westminister in the earlier part of the twentieth century industrialists, compared with the City, 'were less well integrated into the policy making structure and could never manage to speak with one voice on major issues'.[76] The position of industrialists in the Northern Ireland government was, however, very different from that at Westminster.

During the Home Rule debate from the 1880s until the partition of Ireland in 1920, most of Ulster's industrial, commercial and agrarian élite was firmly in the Unionist camp, and the creation of a regional government enabled them to exercise a degree of political power that would have been almost inconceivable under any other circumstances. The first general election in 1921 produced forty unionist MPs and a dozen nationalists/republicans. Of the unionists, no fewer than ten were connected with the linen industry.[77] As far as the executive was concerned, the roll call of ministers 'read like an executive committee of Northern industry and commerce',[78] and they retained their business interests throughout their usually long spells in office. A classic example was J Milne

Textiles and regional economic decline: Northern Ireland 1914–70 73

Barbour, chairman and managing director of the Linen Thread Company, who also served as unpaid Minister of Commerce from 1925 to 1941, after which he became Minister of Finance.

Even if it would be perverse to suggest that the Northern Ireland government had an anti-industrial ethos, or that there were no conflicts between ministers, it can be claimed that in the long term the government showed itself unimaginative in economic policy and, perhaps predictably, keen to prop up the traditional textile industry of the province. To a large extent, of course, Northern ministers were no different from those at Westminster in their commitment to strictly limited state intervention in industrial affairs, and in this they clearly had the support of the Belfast Chamber of Commerce, the oldest and largest organization of businessmen in the province. In 1920, for example, the Chamber 'once more' and unanimously passed a resolution calling on Lloyd George to reduce public expenditure to balance the budget, to reduce the national debt, and for 'Government control of business [to] . . . be terminated as soon as possible'.[79] However, even had the Northern government wished to pursue an independent and positive economic policy, its scope for doing so was limited by the ultimate supremacy of the Westminster government. A further obstacle to decisive action was the fact that although the Minister of Commerce was in theory responsible for assisting industry and trade, virtually all other ministers had a 'finger in the pie', thus making inter-departmental confusion and conflict more likely.[80]

In the 1920s the Northern government did attempt to assist the linen industry in a rather negative way by lobbying for it to be included under the Safeguarding of Industries legislation.[81] This attempt, the result of increasing linen import penetration from European producers, was unsuccessful – much to the disappointment of the prime minister, Sir James Craig, who in 1926 confessed himself a firm believer in protection for home industry.[82] One possible area in which the government might have played a positive role was in the rationalization of the linen industry, but it was clear that no government-led initiative would be forthcoming. Craig, while deeming it desirable that the industry secure expert opinion on the feasibility of any rationalization scheme, also judged it preferable for industrialists to perceive and act on this need for themselves, rather than being forced into it by government.[83] At the same time, J. M. Andrews, Minister of Labour, took a strictly short term view of the impact of rationalization, and thought it unlikely to lower unemployment since it would necessarily involve the disappearance of some firms and the scrapping of excess capacity.[84] During the debate on rationalization in the late 1920s and early 1930s the Ministry of Commerce indicated that they 'would not take any part in negotiations'.[85]

In the 1930s, most policy actions which were considered to benefit the linen industry came not from the Northern but from the Westminster government, and none of them addressed the problems that continued to characterize the industry. The abandonment of the Gold Standard, together with the introduction of tariffs were seen as significant for the industry, with one leading commentator going so far as to say that their combined effect 'has been to save the Irish linen trade from very great peril'. Further optimism was engendered by concessions won at the Ottawa Conference in 1932, especially with regard to the Canadian market which took ten per cent of total UK linen exports. The UK clearly dominated the Dominion market for linen goods: in 1930 its share of total linen imports into Australia was estimated at 87 per cent, Canada 95 per cent, New Zealand 96 per cent and South Africa 78 per cent. Even so, contemporaries warned that neither simplification nor reduction of Dominion tariffs would guarantee that the linen industry would benefit unless manufacturers advertised their products 'more intensively in the Dominion trade and general press.'[87] Well into the 1930s, then, the old complaint about ineffective advertising was still being voiced.

The fourth area of government policy that was widely expected to be advantageous to the linen industry, perhaps more than to any other UK industry, was the Anglo-American Trade Agreement of 1938. The US remained the largest single export market for linen goods and this market was worth about as much as the combined exports of the UK cotton and woollen industries to the US. The significance of linen as a dollar earner, to the tune of around £1.5–2 million in the late 1930s, was not lost on contemporaries.[88] It is not surprising then that reductions ranging from ten to twenty per cent *ad valorem* on virtually all classes of linen goods were widely welcomed by the industry and by the Northern Ireland government, and seemed to offer some respite from decades of rising tariff barriers in this crucial market.[89] Any potential benefits, however, soon evaporated on the outbreak of war in the following year.

Although protection and the Ottawa agreement had inevitably increased the significance of the home and Dominion markets, the departure from Gold (at least in the short term) had increased export competitiveness[90] and the 1938 agreement offered some hope in the US market, the fundamental and long-appreciated problems of raw material supply and price instability were still acute. As an example, raw material prices in the linen industry rose by about 70 per cent during 1934, and at the same time the UK depended on foreign sources for some 95 per cent of its raw material.[91]

Given the overwhelming dependence on imported raw materials, it is no surprise that between 1939 and 1945, as in the First World War, disruption of flax supplies together with strong government demand quickly 'raised the price level of all grades to a point that must inevitably preclude the use of flax fibre in the production of any but essential government supplies'.[92] The raw material problem became acute after the German invasion of Belgium in 1940. UK textile industries were quickly brought under government control, though the economy of Northern Ireland generally was slow to mobilize, apparently because of the reluctance of its government to become integrated into the national structure of area boards under the Ministry of Supply.[93]

In the case of the linen industry, an important opportunity for introspection might have been afforded by the appointment of a Post-War Planning Committee whose unanimous report was presented in March 1944. Ten of the Committee's eleven members were directly involved in the linen industry and it would seem that in the interests of unanimity they took care to 'recommend nothing that would disturb any existing interest in the industry'. While not hesitating to ask for more government financial assistance, their argument, in the words of one impartial expert, was that 'the industrialists' pre-war sovereignty should not be challenged in any way'. All in all, the 1944 Report was 'a most disappointing document'.[94] Although it contained some positive proposals on the organization of flax buying and appreciated the need for co-ordinated research – supported, as ever, by considerable government finance – it seemed to assume that the industry was highly efficient and therefore played down or ignored the potential for structural change or modernization of machinery.

The 1944 Report signally failed to explore the extent to which the industry could use non-flax fibre, or extend production runs through standardization, or eliminate excess capacity. In short, there was little in the report to indicate that the industry intended to change direction in the post-war world. In any case, because the economic climate was generally buoyant in the six years after 1945, the need to change direction at all seemed much less pressing. Exports of linen goods from the UK increased by nine per cent between 1947 and 1951, and it was not until the severe slump of 1951–2 that the industry relapsed into its familiar pattern of unemployment, short-time working and depressed profit levels.[95]

Between 1939 and 1951, however, while the fortunes of the linen industry temporarily improved, the shortage of raw material forced manufacturers to experiment with the use of man-made fibres – though the initial opportunity for Ulster linen manufacturers to do this owed more to luck than to skill. In 1941 the government imposed a system for the allocation of rayon. This meant that the purchase of all rayon yarn was under government control, with the exception of yarn from staple more than three inches long when spun on woollen or linen machinery. This loophole, which was not closed until 1945, enabled rayon staple to establish itself quickly as a major new raw material in the textile industry of Northern Ireland. Moreover, the price of rayon was both lower and more stable than that of flax. If after 1918 linen had become more expensive relative to cotton, so after 1939 it became more expensive in relation to rayon.[96]

Before the end of the Second World War no rayon was actually spun in Northern Ireland, and the province received the bulk of its supplies from spinners in Yorkshire. After the war, with indispensable government assist-ance, the development of man-made fibre production became extremely important in Northern Ireland – and within twenty years its contribution to net manufacturing output in the province was double that of linen (see Table 4.5). If the loophole of 1941 had enabled Ulster's textile industry to substitute man-made fibres into their production process more easily than cotton manufactur-ers, the province was also fortunate in its ability to offer financial inducements to industry that were more wide-ranging and more generous than in Britain.[97] This relative generosity became a permanent feature from the later 1940s onwards, and by the early 1970s it was estimated that Northern Ireland was able to provide assistance to new projects to the extent of 62.9 per cent of capital costs, as against 50.6 per cent in Development Areas and 31.4 per cent in other British regions.[98]

This special position was largely due to the province's exclusion from the 1945 Distribution of Industry Act, the cornerstone of post-war British regional policy.[99] Even before the end of the war, however, discussions had taken place between Sir Basil Brooke, Prime Minister of Northern Ireland, and Courtaulds

76   *Philip Ollerenshaw*

Table 4.5 Net output of the textile industry as a percentage of total net manufacturing output in Northern Ireland 1949–75

Year	Textiles	Textiles other than linen	Linen
1949	31.5	2.9	28.6
1954	24.9	5.4	19.5
1958	18.7	4.7	14.0
1963	18.6	7.5	11.1
1968	20.5	13.6	6.9
1972	20.6	15.1	5.5
1975	16.6	11.3	5.3

Source: Reports on the Census of Production, Ministry/Department of Commerce (Belfast)

which centred on the possibility of securing a site for a staple fibre factory in the province.[100] Availability of labour and materials, argued Brooke, would enable work on a new site to begin immediately – even in wartime. Despite the fact that building costs were higher and the local market obviously much smaller than in Britain, the opportunity to start construction without delay was the clinching argument in favour of a Northern Ireland site for Courtaulds. In the event, the immediate start did not prove feasible, Northern Ireland therefore no longer seemed so attractive, and the claims of alternative sites increased in strength. The Courtaulds board, however, decided to keep its promise to Brooke and the company went on to build a plant at Carrickfergus which opened in July 1948.

Courtaulds' move into Northern Ireland brought prestige and employment, and it turned out to be the first of several instances of inward investment by British, European or American multinationals. Courtaulds opened a second plant in 1953, and within ten years others followed including Monsanto in 1958, Du Pont in 1960, and British Enkalon and ICI in 1963. The rising trend of inward investment in textiles was reflected in the ever more extensive financial assistance provided to industry by the Northern Ireland government. From a level of £600,000 in 1951–2, government direct assistance increased to £40 million by 1969–70 and totalled £230 million during the period 1945–70.[101]

In a region which found it impossible to achieve full employment, it might be expected that the arrival of such major companies as Courtaulds would have been universally welcomed. At first, however, there were several important voices within the linen industry and the Northern Ireland government which regarded new firms almost entirely as a threat. Criticism of the Industries Development Acts (1932, 1937 and 1945) centred mainly on the argument that they paid insufficient attention to the track record, current requirements and future prospects of firms in traditional industries which, it was claimed, were now losing labour to new firms.[102]

Moreover, many still considered it axiomatic that it was the traditional industries which 'in the testing time ahead would allow Northern Ireland to

avoid large scale unemployment by their ability to adapt and sell in competitive world markets.'[103] Accordingly, a series of financial packages beginning with the Re-equipment of Industry Act (1951) was designed to provide
traditional industry with every opportunity to modernize technology and
buildings. The need for modernization was indeed acute. By 1948, no new flax
mills had been built for over forty years, while in many mills the average age of
machinery in active operation was forty or fifty years. Any new machinery 'was
installed to suit existing housing with the result than in many instances
conditions extant today are far removed from those required to ensure
maximum output at minimum cost'.[104]

The demand for re-equipment grants was strong, and of 160 applicants for
assistance by 1954, about half came from the textile industries. Government
assistance enabled Ulster firms to re-equip with modern automatic looms for
weaving rayon to such an extent that by 1957 the region had the most modern
machinery of any UK textile region using rayon.[105] Many mills, however,
continued to operate obsolete plant and informed opinion pointed to other
problems which still needed to be addressed, not least cost accounting and
production planning.[106] Within the linen industry, less attention apparently
went into solving these problems than was devoted to airing complaints about
the allegedly punitive levels of taxation and the adverse impact this had on
private investment, and indeed significant concessions were made by the
government in response to these complaints during the 1950s.[107] Moreover
there were some who claimed that the scope for technical change in the linen
industry was small because of the difficulties inherent in processing the flax
fibre, and for this reason the industry was bound to retain its 'craft' character.
In the view of one linen manufacturer, government grants were too easily
available and rather than spending vast sums on re-equipment firms would be
well advised to pay more attention to training the labour force:

> Far too many Northern Ireland linen manufacturers still employ rule-of-thumb
> methods in determining matters, and supposed economies are too often more than
> discounted by the higher overheads which pile up when the older craft methods of
> manufacturing give way to so-called modern ones. In successful linen weaving, as in
> spinning, patience, dexterity, indeed inherited skill, can play a greater part than
> anything else in making for success . . . In the past there has been too much "leaving
> it to chance" to provide recruits who in many cases received only indifferent training,
> and as a result took too long in becoming proficient operatives . . .[108]

Although there was some truth in this, there was a danger that it would be
taken to extremes and used as an argument against technical change *per se*,
and there were some informed critics who took linen manufacturers to task for
their 'craft obsession'.[109]

Notwithstanding all the government aid and the buoyancy of the international economy, Northern Ireland still failed by a considerable margin to
achieve full employment during the period after 1945. The chronic difficulties
faced by the linen industry were reflected in its continuing decline as an
employer: 58,300 in 1949, 25,300 in 1968, and also in the emphatic collapse in
its contribution to net manufacturing output in the province (see Table 4.5).

78   *Philip Ollerenshaw*

As the decline accelerated two Queen's University economists, K. S. Isles and Norman Cuthbert, compiled *An Economic Survey of Northern Ireland*, commissioned in 1947 by the then Minister of Commerce, Sir Roland Nugent, and published ten years later. Apart from being arguably the finest survey of any UK region ever published, the report contains in places a penetrating critique of the province's industrial structure. Its authors analysed in great detail all the problems involved in sustaining innovation and expansion that stemmed from a predominance of small, family-run private firms in the linen industry – though they did note that in the 1930s such firms may have persevered when other types of enterprise would not.[110]

Though it was not part of their brief to recommend possible courses of action, the authors amply fulfilled their wish to provide data and numbers which would be beneficial in the formation of economic policy. Indeed, their criticisms of the structure of the province's traditional industries and government industrial policy, and their suggestion for a Development Corporation, were more soundly based and better argued than anywhere else. Perhaps for that reason, the reception to the *Economic Survey*, on the part of the very Ministry that had commissioned it, was distinctly cool. Lord Glentoran, Minister of Commerce at the time of the report's publication was particularly unimpressed with the argument for a Development Corporation since it 'showed a sorry lack of faith in the vitality of Ulster industry'.[111] That lack of faith was largely justified.

The history of government relations with the textile industries in Northern Ireland in the decades after 1921 is a mixture of 'negative' intervention, such as pressure for safeguarding or protection between the wars, combined with 'positive' financial assistance, which played a crucial role in sustaining both research and advertising effort throughout the period down to 1970. If both those efforts were lacking, the fault lay far more with the industry than with the government. After the Second World War government assistance played a more important role, not only in research and advertising, but also in the finance of modernization at firm level and in actively promoting inward investment. As far as the latter was concerned, the policy seemed to succeed until the early 1970s. The arrival of many large man made fibre and other manufacturers helped to divert attention from the decline in linen, but it also increased the province's dependence on corporations controlled from elsewhere. By 1975, 45 per cent of Northern Ireland's largest industrial enterprises, employing 500 or more workers, were controlled from Britain, 20 per cent from the United States, and ten per cent from other European Community countries.[112] The ability to attract inward investment began to decline sharply following the outbreak and continuance of political conflict in Northern Ireland after 1969. Moreover, the province was far more dependent on oil for energy than the rest of the UK and the oil price shocks after 1973 posed a major problem for the energy intensive man-made fibre industries. These factors, coupled with huge overvaluation of sterling between 1979 and 1983,[113] led to a dramatic collapse of the man-made fibre industries in Northern Ireland, with the closure of many plants including Courtaulds, ICI, British Enkalon and others, and massive redundancies at those plants that remained. This collapse, together with the longer term decline of linen and the province's other staple industry, shipbuilding, are crucial elements in one of the most acute cases of deindustrialization in Western Europe since the Second World War.

Conclusion

In this paper we have tried to highlight the problems encountered by a traditional industry in a peripheral region. If some of these problems stemmed from forces that were outside the industry's control, others did not. Some, but by no means all, of the latter were a direct consequence of the competitive nature of the industry and the predominance of small, family firms. We have noted weaknesses in research, advertising and marketing, cost accounting techniques, production planning, fabric design and, perhaps, an overemphasis on the 'craft' aspects of production at the expense of technology.

Furthermore, though the Northern Ireland government helped to compensate for the industry's lack of effort in some areas, it did nothing to promote structural change. It was also unmoved by independent criticism of the organization and strategy of the industry itself. The fact that from 1921 to 1972 Northern Ireland was governed by one party with little opposition, together with the fact that leaders of the linen industry actively supported and were integrated into the government, greatly reduced the scope for debate and the critics' chances of a sympathetic hearing.

From the evidence presented here, two conclusions might be drawn. First, the decline of the linen industry had many more causes than a contracting world market, and the shortcomings of the industry itself need to be emphasised far more than they have been hitherto. Second, while there is no doubt about the tenacity and strength of structural and institutional rigidities in the linen industry and the economy in which it operated, there is, as both Alford and Coleman have recently stressed, a need to recognize the limitations of explanations of industrial decline that rest on institutional or structural factors. In particular, such explanations play down or ignore the attitudes and commerical practices of businessmen.[114] Certainly our evidence points to the need to give very considerable weight to the latter in explaining the decline of the linen industry during the twentieth century. As one of the more reflective linen manufacturers put it in 1954: 'many of our industry's past troubles are the result of lack of courage, imagination and enterprise'.[115]

Notes

1 Financial assistance to undertake research for this paper was provided by the Economic and Social Research Council and the Pasold Research Fund, to whom I am most grateful. I would also like to thank Hilary Ollerenshaw for her comments on an earlier draft.
2 Elbaum, Bernard, and Lazonick, William (eds), 1986, *The decline of the British economy*, Oxford University Press, Oxford, ch. 1, esp. p. 2.
3 See in particular ibid., pp. 18–50 and Lazonick, 1983, 'Industrial organization and

80   *Philip Ollerenshaw*

technological change: the decline of the British cotton industry', *Business History Review*, 57(2); 195–236.

4 Beacham, A., 1945, 'The Ulster linen industry', *Economica*, 11(2): 205.

5 Pollard, Sidney, 1981, *Peaceful conquest: The industrialization of Europe 1750–1970*, Oxford University Press, Oxford, p. v.

6 Keeble, David, 1976, *Industrial location and planning in the United Kingdom*, Methuen, London, pp. 207, 218.

7 Murie, A. S. *et al.*, 1969, 'A survey of industrial movement in Northern Ireland between 1965 and 1969', *Economic and Social Review*, 4(2): 231.

8 Thomas, M. D., 1965, 'Economic geography of manufacturing industry in Northern Ireland', unpublished Ph.D. thesis, Queen's University of Belfast, pp. 15, 31, 40.

9 Durie, Alastair, 1979, *The Scottish linen industry in the eighteenth century*, John Donald, Edinburgh, p. 169.

10 *The Statist*, 4 August 1917: 194.

11 Clark, W. A. G., 1913, *Linen, jute and hemp industries in the United Kingdom*, Department of Commerce, Washington D.C., Special Agents series number 74, p. 61.

12 Clegg, H. A., Fox, A., Thompson, A. F., 1964, *A history of British trade unions since 1889, Volume I, 1889–1910*, Oxford University Press, Oxford, p. 468.

13 Lazonick, W., 1986, 'The cotton industry', in Elbaum and Lazonick (eds), *Decline of the British Economy*, pp. 24–28.

14 Black, William, 1957, 'Variations in employment in the linen industry', unpublished Ph.D. thesis, Queen's University of Belfast, p. 110.

15 Ibid.; Patterson, H., 1985, 'Industrial labour and the labour movement 1820 to 1914', in Kennedy, L., Ollerenshaw, P. (eds), *An economic history of Ulster 1820–1939*, Manchester University Press, Manchester, pp. 175–6.

16 Data on productivity and costs are taken from Clark, *Linen, jute and hemp industries*, pp. 9, 12.

17 Ibid., p. 21.

18 *Flax supply association report for 1919*, Belfast, 1920, p. 19.

19 Clark, *Linen, jute and hemp industries*, p. 19.

20 Notes on flax control, May 1918, P.R.O. MUN 4/6506. See also *The Statist*, 15 September 1917: 445–6.

21 *Flax supply association report for 1919*, p. 19; *Textile Recorder*, 15 May 1918: 31–2; *Textile Manufacturer*, 15 July 1918: 182; *The Statist*, 22 February 1919: 315.

22 Notes on flax control, para 1.

23 Government control ceased on 31 August 1920, but the Flax Control Board was revived early in the Second World War to meet similar problems.

24 *Textile Recorder*, 15 January 1918: 316.

25 On prices before and after the war see *The Statist*, 17 Febuary 1923: 43; Report of the committee appointed to investigate the principal causes of the depression in the linen industry, 1928, P.R.O.N.I. COM 27/1: 16–21, (hereafter cited as 1928 report on depression).

26 Black, 'Variations in employment in the linen industry': pp. 213–4.

27 *Textile Recorder*, 14 August 1915: 123.

28 Ibid., 15 May 1918: 31.

29 *Northern Whig*, 7 February 1914; flax spinners association minute book 1912–20, P.R.O.N.I. D.2088/29/4, *passim*. Short time working began on 2 March 1914.

30 See in particular *Textile Recorder*, 15 November 1917: 213; 15 January 1918: 315–6; 15 March 1918: 402; 15 May 1918: 3–4; 15 July 1918: 86–7.

31 Alford, B. W. E., 1986, 'Lost opportunities: British business and businessmen

during the first world war', in McKendrick, N., and Outhwaite, R. B., (eds), *Business life and public policy: essays in honour of D. C. Coleman*, Cambridge University Press, Cambridge, p. 220.

32 *Textile Recorder*, 15 November 1918: 249.

33 See for example Johnson, D. S., 1985, 'The Northern Ireland economy 1914-39', in Kennedy and Ollerenshaw, *An economic history of Ulster*, pp. 196-7.

34 1928 report on depression, p. 9.

35 Ibid.

36 Beacham, 'The Ulster linen industry': 205.

37 Flax spinners association minute book 1912-20, 18 June 1920.

38 Ibid., 16-18, 25 June 1920; ibid., 1920-34, 2, 30 July; 6 August 1920. Irish powerloom manufacturers' association minute book of the association and council, P.R.O.N.I. D.2088/30/3, 4 June; 9 July; 13 August; 19 October; 16 November 1920.

39 Flax spinners association minute book 1920-34, 7 January 1921.

40 *Textile Recorder*, 15 November 1920: 54.

41 Ibid., 15 February 1921: 70; 15 March 1921: 52.

42 1928 report on depression, pp. 1-2.

43 Bamberg, J. H., 1988, 'The rationalization of the British cotton industry in the inter-war years', *Textile History*, 19(1): 83-102.

44 Memorandum by Sir Gilbert Garnsey KBE dealing with a proposed scheme of amalgamation, 19 March 1929, P.R.O.N.I. COM 25/8. This memorandum estimates that in Northern Ireland there were 50 firms engaged in spinning, some 100 in weaving and over 130 in merchanting.

45 Flax spinners association minute book 1920-32, meeting of the spinning trade, 11 April 1930, evidence of H. R. Ross, a member of the Linen Industry (Remedies) Committee.

46 Beacham, A., 1945, 'Post-war planning in the Ulster linen industry', *Economic Journal*, 55(1): 119.

47 Steed, G. P. F., 1971, 'Internal organization, firm integration, and locational change: the Northern Ireland linen complex, 1954-64', *Economic Geography*, 47(3): 375. The following paragraph is based on this excellent study.

48 Ibid.: 376.

49 Steed, G. P. F., Thomas, Morgan D., 1971, 'Regional industrial change: Northern Ireland', *Annals of the Association of American Geographers*, 61: 348.

50 Mowery, David, C., 1986, 'Industrial research 1900-50', in Elbaum and Lazonick, *Decline of the British economy*, pp. 189-222, esp. 205-7.

51 Committee on Industry and Trade [Balfour Committee], 1927, *Factors in industrial and commercial efficiency*, pp. 308-23.

52 *Textile Recorder*, 15 October 1919: 208.

53 Ibid., 15 May 1918: 4.

54 Ibid., 15 December 1917: 253.

55 Ibid.

56 Ibid., 15 February 1919: 366; 15 August 1919: 146.

57 1928 report on depression, p. 15.

58 *Textile Recorder*, 15 January 1920: 363; 15 April 1920: 456. In the long term it did not prove possible to increase flax yields significantly. See Black, 'Variations in employment', p. 249.

59 *Belfast Chamber of Commerce Journal*, April 1923: 10.

60 *Textile Recorder*, June 1944: 28.

61 Ibid., February 1952: 96.

62 Ibid., March 1959: 52; May 1959: 34; May 1965: 34.

82   *Philip Ollerenshaw*

63   *The Statist*, 1 March 1919: 365.
64   *Textile Recorder*, 15 November 1918: 251.
65   Ibid. and 15 July 1926: 51–2.
66   1928 report on depression, p. 15.
67   *Textile Recorder*, 15 March 1919: 435.
68   Ibid., 15 September 1921: 58.
69   Ibid.: 67.
70   *Belfast Chamber of Commerce Journal*, I, April 1923: 10.
71   *The Statist*, 17 August 1929: 26.
72   *Textile Recorder*, 15 November 1928: 55–7; *The Statist*, 5 October 1929: 482.
73   *The Statist*, 7 December 1929: 986.
74   Ibid.
75   Larmor, Sir Graham, 1954–5, 'Mechanization and productivity in the Ulster linen
     industry', *Journal of the Statistical and Social Inquiry Society of Ireland*, 19(3):
     334.
76   Cain, Peter, Hopkins, A. G., 1987, 'Gentlemanly capitalism and British expansion
     overseas II: new imperialism, 1850–1945', *Economic History Review*, 40(1): 4–5.
77   *Textile Recorder*, 21 June 1921: 105.
78   Farrell, Michael, 1976, *Northern Ireland: The Orange state*, Pluto Press, London,
     cited in Buckland, *Factory of grievances*, p 12.
79   Belfast chamber of commerce letter book 1919–20, P.R.O.N.I. D.1857/1/BA/12,
     B.C.C. to the Rt. Hon. David Lloyd George, 28 March 1920.
80   Buckland, *Factory of grievances*, pp. 9–36, 105–29.
81   Irish power loom manufacturers' association minute book of the association and
     council, P.R.O.N.I. D.2088/30/4, 11 May 1928.
82   *Textile Recorder*, 15 January 1926: 10.
83   Buckland, *Factory of grievances*, p. 118.
84   Ibid.
85   Meeting of the spinning trade 11 April 1930, cited above, see note 45.
86   *Textile Recorder*, 15 January 1933: 27.
87   Ibid., and 15 November 1932: 21.
88   Beacham, 'The Ulster linen industry', p. 199.
89   *Textile Recorder*, 6 December 1938: 16.
90   Although depreciation of sterling was expected to boost exports, it did increase the
     price of imported flax and yarn.
91   *Textile Recorder*, 15 January 1935: 18.
92   Ibid., 6 June 1940: 26.
93   Bew, P., Gibbon, P., Patterson, H., 1979, *The state in Northern Ireland 1921–72:
     political forces and social classes*, Manchester University Press, Manchester, p.
     104.
94   Beacham, 'Post-war planning', 121.
95   Black, 'Variations in employment', pp. 47–9; *Textile Recorder*, June 1952: 122;
     August 1952: 96; October 1952: 118.
96   This account is based on Hague, D. C., 1957, *The economics of man-made fibres*,
     Macmillan, London, pp. 272–8.
97   The best account is McCrone, G., 1969, *Regional policy in Britain*, George Allen &
     Unwin, London: esp. pp. 139–42.
98   Murie *et al.*, 'Survey of industrial movement in Northern Ireland': 232.
99   See McCrone, *passim.*; Edwards, R. S., Townsend, H., *Business Enterprise*,
     Macmillan, London, pp. 424–31.
100 Coleman, D. C., 1980, *Courtaulds: an economic and social history; volume III,
     crisis and change, 1940–65*, Oxford University Press, Oxford, pp. 7, 42–3. The ease

of effluent disposal, not mentioned by Coleman, was also seen as a factor in Courtaulds' decision to go to Carrickfergus. Thomas, 'Economic geography of manufacturing industry': 39.

101 Ministry of Commerce, Belfast, 1970, Facts and figures about industrial development in Northern Ireland: 10.
102 Bew, Gibbon, Patterson, *The state in Northern Ireland*, p. 137.
103 Ibid.
104 *Textile Recorder*, July 1948: 45.
105 Hague, *Economics of man made fibres*, pp. 276–7.
106 *Textile Recorder*, January 1952: 106.
107 Bew, Gibbon, Patterson, *The state in Northern Ireland*, p. 141.
108 Larmor, 'Mechanization and productivity', p. 33.
109 Steed and Thomas, 'Regional industrial change', p. 349.
110 Isles, K. S., Cuthbert, N., 1957, *An economic survey of Northern Ireland*, HMSO, Belfast.
111 Bew, Gibbon, Patterson, *The state in Northern Ireland*, p. 144.
112 Keeble, *Industrial location and planning*, p. 237.
113 Kennedy, K., Giblin, T., McHugh, D., 1988, *The economic development of Ireland in the twentieth century*, Routledge, London, pp. 108–9.
114 Alford, 'Lost opportunities', pp. 225–6; Coleman, D. C., 1988, Review of Elbaum and Lazonick , *Decline of the British economy, Business History*, 30(1): pp. 130–1.
115 Larmor, 'Mechanization and productivity', p. 34.

Name Index